The
Good
Body

The
Good
Body

Asceticism
in
Contemporary
Culture

edited by

Mary G. Winkler

& Letha B. Cole

Yale
University
Press

New
Haven
&
London

Designed by Deborah Dutton
Set in Joanna type by
Keystone Typesetting, Inc.,
Orwigsburg, Pennsylvania.
Printed in the United States of America by
Vail-Ballou Press, Inc., Binghamton, N.Y.

Library of Congress Cataloging-in-Publication Data

The Good body : asceticism in contemporary culture
/ edited by Mary G. Winkler and Letha B. Cole.

p.   cm.

Based on papers presented at a conference held at the Institute for
the Medical Humanities at the University of Texas Medical Branch,
Galveston, Tex. in 1991.

Includes bibliographical references and index.

ISBN 0-300-05628-1 (alk. paper)

1. Body image—Social aspects—Congresses.   2. Control
(Psychology)—Congresses.   3. Eating disorders—
Congresses.   4. Asceticism—Congresses.   I. Winkler,
Mary G.   II. Cole, Letha B., 1951–

BF697.5.B63G66   1994

302.5—dc20   93-48225

CIP

A catalogue record for this book is
available from the British Library.

The paper in this book meets the
guidelines for permanence and durability
of the Committee on Production
Guidelines for Book Longevity of the
Council on Library Resources.

10 9 8 7 6 5 4 3 2 1

Contents

Part Three
Interpretive Narrative and
the "Good Body"

Part Four
Cultural Ideals and the "Good
Body"

Acknowledgments

Many people have contributed to the completion of this book. We thank all of them. First, we thank our contributors for their understanding of the difficulties inherent in speaking across disciplines. This interdisciplinary conversation has been especially rich and rewarding.

The conference from which this book grew was generously supported by the Jesse H. Jones Research Endowment Fund at the Institute for the Medical Humanities, The University of Texas Medical Branch in Galveston, Texas.

Finally, there are individuals who have given time, expertise, thought, and advice. We thank Dale L. Meyer and Nina C. Fox for their assistance in preparing the manuscript, and Thomas R. Cole and Eleanor H. Porter for offering their editorial expertise. Dorothy L. Karilanovic deserves particular recognition for help in organizing the conference and preparing the manuscript.

Introduction

Letha B. Cole

Most writers in the fields of psychology and medicine—even those who focus primarily on the physical manifestations and consequences of eating disorders—acknowledge that cultural context plays a role in the etiology of these illnesses. Yet the medical literature has not explored the etiologic factor of culture seriously.

To understand eating disorders we must look beyond the behavioral sciences into those disciplines that consider cultural practices relating to the body. In so doing we must suspend our assumptions about the potential range of "normal" behavior. What appears to be normal in response to one set of circumstances may be viewed as quite pathological in another.

A reader whose interest is primarily clinical may wonder why cultural practices concerning the body are important. I would suggest that clinicians must have a perspective that allows them the flexibility to understand each individual's motives and experiences as unique, yet always culturally conditioned. If we think of our efforts as a search for a more adaptive response under a given set of circumstances, it becomes clear that we must grasp the individual's context as fully as possible.

The first three chapters in this collection focus on the religious, moral, and clinical implications of attitudes toward the body. Philosopher Judith Andre explores the moral desirability of current attitudes toward the body. She questions the advisability of basing social status on socially constructed meanings for physical features and articulates a utopian view of a moral society in which we would appreciate our bodies as our selves and be willing to confer respect upon the diversity of human embodiments.

The pertinence of Andre's question is dramatically illustrated by Jean Goodwin, psychiatrist, and Reina Attias, psychologist. Using individual case material, these authors explore in careful detail a previously hidden realm of female experience. They outline the effects of sexual victimization on basic bodily functions, core self-image—especially body image—and fundamental elements of relational capacity such as self-control and the ability to communicate effectively. The chapter underscores the cultural resistance to the idea that girls are victimized and harmed in this way. This resistance appears both in the case material, as a reluctance to recall the victimization, and in the reader who recoils from the horrifying details of such victimization.

Allison Moore describes the recovery of battered women in a shelter, where treatment includes redirecting and refining skills of self-denial these women had previously developed in the process of adapting to their abusive mates. Moore argues that these skills are partial and distorted ascetic practices involving the capacity to deny and sacrifice oneself. The shelter builds on this capacity, encouraging women to develop ascetic practices that are constructive and lead to self-definition, self-assertion, and self-respect. Interestingly, the skills developed by battered women are similar to those used in fourth- and fifth-century monastic communities to reorient members' actions "toward ever more abundant life in God."

Margaret Miles' chapter expands our perspective on the Western social construction of desire and its goal, pleasure. She places the lack of authorization for female desire and its symbolic representation at the center of the current epidemic of fasting. She grounds her argument that desire is a gendered construct in an examination of St. Augustine's Confessions, an influential text in the construction of the dominant Western Christian understanding of desire. Miles maintains that since the third century of the Common Era, desire has been viewed as a male prerogative and argues that Augustine's explication of desire is based on his specifically male experience. Miles explains ascetic practices as efforts to achieve pleasure by giving definition to the self. In this way she expands our understanding of the potentially harmful practices of anorexic girls and women.

The second part continues the emphasis on the cultural construction of ideas about the body, exploring the influences of medicine and government on predominant notions of the "good body." Estelle Cohen traces the discovery of reproductive anatomy and describes the reluctance of the Christian, male European medical community to accept the facts determined by careful scientific research, sometimes even their own research.

Both Mary Brown Parlee, psychologist, and Arthur Leccese, pharmacologist, consider specific instances of contemporary cultural construction by focusing on the dynamic interplay between scientific discourse and dominant cultural categories. Parlee defines the nonscientific forces influencing the activities of contemporary scientists and their scientific discourse. She argues persuasively that the biomedical version of premenstrual syndrome has emerged as uncontested truth, not because it is supported by an overwhelming preponderance of empirical data and effective arguments, but because it is simply incontestable given the current structure of the scientific domain.

Leccese suggests that contemporary culture equates the "good body" with the "drug-free body." Using the example of anorexiant stimulants (drugs that have stimulating and appetite-suppressing effects in the brain), he argues that current prohibitionist notions are influencing scientific discourse and may result in the withholding of potentially beneficial pharmacologic treatment from the obese.

Part three explores the impact of cultural constructions on the experience of individuals. Using the words of her anorexic patients, psychiatrist Janet de Groot expands our appreciation of the actual experience of the body for individual anorexic women. She brings together somewhat disparate lines of thinking in the psychological literature to enhance our appreciation of the psychological factors influencing the development of this primarily female disorder.

Sara van den Berg, a professor of English literature, considers the narratives of Freud's hysterical patients, highlighting his appreciation of the hysteric's use of the body as a form of symbolic communication, "a language that linked mental and physical pain, past and present life, experience and fantasy, denial and desire." In doing so she traces Freud's discovery of psychoanalysis as a form of ascetic practice that can transform hysterical misery into common unhappiness. This can ultimately be seen as the continued, though more adaptively expressed, struggle between denial and desire.

William Monroe's paper on Flannery O'Connor's "celebration of embodiment" in her final novel, Parker's Back, integrates many of the ideas contained in the previous chapters while elaborating on the spiritual dimension of asceticism. Monroe describes the Gnostic movement as influential in early Western religions; thereafter Gnosticism serving as a countervailing theology "beneficially subversive of the masculine monotheistic orthodoxies of the West." The understanding of the gnostic as the knowing one among the unknowing, at war with the world, can be seen as "the assertion of the authentic freedom of the self" and is consistent with the preceding papers describing the ascetic practices of people with eating disorders. These practices can be looked upon as "a mode of alienation from the enculturated world motivated not by a desire for acceptance or esteem, but by a recurrent need for isolation and control" (as a means of expressing one's desire as different from that of the dominant culture). Monroe explores Flannery O'Connor's last novel as a rejection of gnostic asceticism through an affirmation of the profound goodness of the body as an incarnation of suffering and redemption.

The final section explores the practice of constructing the body in a wide range of cultures, including contemporary consumer culture. Anthropologist David Gilmore's examples of standards of attractiveness in many cultures emphasizes the extreme variety of cultural definitions of masculine/feminine, beauty/ugliness, activity/passivity, power/weakness. These examples suggest that culture mirrors the multipotentiality of biological forms as represented in studies of evolution. Gilmore's examination of the impact of cultural ideals on individual men further supports the notion that cultural expectations may limit and negatively affect individual experience in a manner that is only beginning to be appreciated.

By examining the predominant images in popular advertisements, Mary Winkler explores the messages we see daily on television and at the grocery checkout counter. She posits that the predominant images of women impede the development of an integrated womanhood by offering "only a choice between mirror-gazing Venus and destroying Medusa." Her essay brings us full circle, back to the idea that a healthier culture, by symbolizing desire in its myriad forms both gendered and otherwise, will be a culture that encourages respect for all.

In the afterword, Winkler notes the coincidence of popular concern with ascetic practices in pursuit of the "good" (feeling, self, body) and the resurgence of scholarship on the history of Christian asceticism. She ponders the connection between "spiritless specialization and heartless sensuality, and the passion for self-control" in contemporary society. Winkler makes a strong case for changing "the terms of our culture's conversation about the body." To avoid distorted ascetic practices that restrict rather than enhance our embodied life, Winkler suggests, we need to overcome contemporary American culture's medicalized neopuritanism, to find alternate ways of understanding our needs and desires.

This book grew out of an interdisciplinary conference held at the Institute for the Medical Humanities at the University of Texas Medical Branch in Galveston, Texas, in 1991. The conference, supported by the Institute's Jesse Jones Memorial Research Fund, was designed to explore the relationship between the current cultural idealization of control of the self and environment through ascetic practices and the apparent rise in the prevalence of eating disorders. As the conference developed and finally took place, the work presented suggested a much broader cultural concern with the body and the notions of denial and desire than even we who planned the conference had expected. Contributions from fields as disparate as anthropology, psychology, literature, philosophy, history, history of art, gender studies, and medicine revealed a preoccupation with cultural norms of bodily appearance and practice that represent moral and aesthetic standards.

We hope and believe that these essays will be useful to those who are interested in cultural practices, their evolution and meaning, and their influence on the development of personal ascetic practices. Scholars will find aspects of the book enlightening and useful in developing ideas within their respective fields. For the clinician, this volume provides compelling evidence of the importance of understanding personal ascetic practices as culturally conditioned.

The book suggests that we have reached a new developmental stage in our cultural history, one that readies and requires us to develop cultural norms for the "good body" that transcend the historically predominant categories linking certain physical characteristics with moral and aesthetic superiority.

Part One

Religious
and Moral
Implications
of the
"Good Body"

1

Respect for
Bodies

Judith Andre

There are various ways of attending to bodies, one's own or others'. Some are sad: the self-hatred of a fat child, for instance. Some are inadequate: what the philosopher Gilbert Ryle, in *The Concept of Mind*, called "ghost in a machine" theories, which treat the body as an inanimate tool.[1] Some are demeaning: much of pornography expresses contempt for women. My purpose in this chapter is to delineate a morally desirable attitude toward bodies, an attitude of respect.

I begin by sketching a kind of metaphysics of the human body. I talk about some ways in which our bodies are ourselves, a relationship I take to be central and wholesome, and I include in this discussion the ways in which parts of bodies (sperm, blood, kidneys) and aspects of bodies (slenderness, muscle tone, grace) are connected with personhood. I then talk about the socially

1. Gilbert Ryle, *The Concept of Mind* (New York: Barnes & Noble, 1949), 15ff.

constructed meanings of physical features, such as the construction of race. Finally I consider ways in which these connections can be treated with respect, or without it, and whether physical features are the proper occasions for constructions of social status.

Our Bodies, Our Selves

Metaphysics

Descartes described the essence of the mind as thought, and thought as something with no spatial characteristics. My memory of breakfast has no weight; my hopes for tomorrow have no physical dimensions. In contrast, Descartes said, matter has only physical properties: it takes up space, it has weight—but has no thoughts, memories, or desires.[2]

As P. F. Strawson has pointed out, however, most human qualities fit in neither of Descartes's categories.[3] Imagine someone who is relaxed, talkative, skilled at needlework, and knowledgeable about wine. Not one of these attributes is possible for pure spirit or for inanimate matter. Without bodies we could not be persons: beings who have consciousness and take up space. Persons can be clumsy, observant, or musical; stones and angels cannot.[4] Walt Whitman knew all this; he wrote "I am the poet of the Body and I am the poet of the Soul," finding no difference between them.[5]

A full description of ourselves—a metaphysics of personhood—is largely made of characteristics that are neither purely spatial nor purely intellectual.

Phenomenology

Our experience is as embodied as this description implies. Usually our bodies are a way of being in the world: of being some-particular-where; of taking in that place by seeing it, hearing it, and touching it. (Notice that our perceptual organs are particular to our species. Unlike the frog, we see stationary as well as

2. René Descartes, *Discourse on Method and Meditations or First Philosophy* (New York: Bobbs Merrill, 1960 [1641]), Meditation VI.

3. P. F. Strawson, "Persons," in *The Philosophy of Mind*, ed. V. C. Chappell (Englewood Cliffs, N.J.: Prentice Hall, 1962), 127–46.

4. There are other philosophical senses of "person" in which angels (should they exist) do qualify, as would God.

5. Walt Whitman, "Song of Myself," 1892 version, section 21, in *Whitman's "Song of Myself"—Origin, Growth, and Meaning*, ed. James E. Miller, Jr. (New York: Dodd, Mead & Company, 1964), 33.

moving objects; unlike a dog, we cannot smell in any detail.) As embodied beings we change our world by making things, moving them, and altering them—again in the limited, specific ways of which our species is capable.

A body is not just a perceptual tool. We are aware of it as well, especially of its boundary, our skin, although our awareness is usually latent; what we are most conscious of is the world, perceived by means of our exquisitely sensitive perimeter. Drew Leder delineates three ways in which the body, in ordinary experience, "disappears"—fails to appear. "Certain modes of disappearance are essential to the body's functioning." The first disappearance he calls focal. When I stroke a kitten, I feel the fur, not my own fingertips; my focus is outward. The second disappearance consists in becoming background rather than foreground: if the kitten scratches me, everything else momentarily disappears from my awareness. Finally Leder describes depth disappearance: we are normally unaware of the inner workings of our body. Our organs function without our attention, a helpful and perhaps essential autonomy that frees our attention for other things.[6]

Aware of our bodies or aware of the world through them, we are our bodies. They are not the res extensa of Cartesian thought. It follows that the human body has a different moral standing than a tool.

Body Parts and Aspects: Also Ourselves

Our bodies have parts and aspects, however, to which these remarks do not unambiguously apply. Without my body I would not be myself; but without my hair, or a few of my gallstones, or one pint of blood, I would still be myself. We can pay full respect to someone while ignoring the shape of her ears or her nose. Perhaps respect even requires ignoring the color of her skin or the shape of her breasts—but I am not convinced of that. Let me set forth some of the ways in which the elements of our bodies are aspects of ourselves.

Body Parts Are Parts of a Person

The body can be understood as a complex physiological machine, whose parts—blood, bones, cells—have no subjectivity. For this reason the human body, if not an object itself, at least seems to be composed of objects. But this is an illusion. Even these parts cannot be fully understood without paying atten-

6. Drew Leder, The Absent Body (Chicago: University of Chicago Press, 1991), 69, 11–102.

tion to the feelings and fears of the whole person. Only these, for instance, can explain why someone's muscles are tense and certain glands active. To understand the causes and the effects of, say, a low hemoglobin count, one must often consider the whole person. When we treat the body as only a physical machine—in the way physicians sometimes do—we can fail to understand it and hence fail to treat it effectively.

Some Bodily Aspects Express the Self

Some physical qualities tell us immediately about a person. Age, for instance, shows in the body, and age is part of who one is. A woman of sixty sees the world differently than one of twenty. She is likely to have more perspective, to be more sure of herself, to have less energy and fewer illusions—all important in understanding who she is.

Other physical qualities tell us about a person by telling us what choices she has made. Straight hair and crooked teeth can be changed; some of the marks of age can be erased for a while. These choices are not exactly "free," of course: the set of options from which we choose is utterly beyond our control. We do not create the menu from which we choose, nor the prices on it. The chemicals used to curl hair are not benign, and finding a flattering cut will (for some) be tricky and time-consuming. The alternative, not making the effort, has its own clear social cost (for the genetically unlucky, which is to say most of us). Knowing whether someone has permed her hair, lifted her face, or straightened her teeth tells us something about how she ranks such things as physical attractiveness, monetary cost, physical pain, and danger.

And then there is weight. Does weight tell us anything about the person—about her choices, or her fears, or her values? Can we deduce, for instance, that an overweight person eats more than a thin person or exercises less? The research on this is mixed, but the answer is generally yes. Suppose for a moment that the answer is simply yes. From that many people would conclude that the overweight person lacks self-discipline; therapists may infer repressed anger or something gone wrong in infancy. But these are not the only possible conclusions. Other cultures have seen instead a richer sensuality. Suppose that heavy people move less and sit more than slender people. Is sitting still a sign of inertia or of inner quiet?

In trying to lessen the cruelty that fat people suffer we may sometimes understandably overreact and claim that weight has nothing to do with personhood. I would argue that the connection is real but insist that it is various and individual. A friend of mine, for instance—call her Jane—has struggled all her life with being fat. Only recently has she surrendered her conviction that her body misfit her Mozart-loving soul. She no longer thinks that she is "really" an elegant, thin woman, accidentally lodged in a chunky body. Instead she now thinks that her body expresses her self. She eats much as she approaches her job: with energy and dispatch, with a desire to secure things, to "clear her plate," to get them "under her belt."[7] Her mother was also overweight. Jane now sees in her body the efficient daughter of a much-loved mother. She is able to see her body as herself—at least sometimes.

The Body Reveals Social History

There is another connection between aspects of the body and subjectivity: Any visible trait may have powerful social meanings. Height and the color and shape of one's eyes are interesting examples. In Toni Morrison's The Bluest Eye a black child longs for blue eyes. In Japan after the war, some Japanese women had the folds in their eyelids surgically altered. In the early 1970s an English woman who was six feet six inches tall had about six inches of bone removed from each of her legs. All of these concerns involve power. Round eyes belong to those who defeated Japan; blue eyes to the privileged classes in America; height to the gender that has power. A certain eye color and shape signify membership in a despised class—and so earn social punishment. Height is deemed inappropriate in a member of a subordinate group—and so earns social punishment. Looking at an unusually tall woman or anyone of African descent, one sees not just physical characteristics but social status.

I will call such attributes "bodily status-characteristics." Social standing molds us; it shapes our self-concept, our opportunities, and our worldview. The hero of Ursula LeGuin's The Lathe of Heaven dreams into existence many alternate worlds. He is white, the woman he loves is black. Once he creates a world without race: he and she both turn grayish-beige. The change in color changes her personality because it changes her history. In this world she lacks the toughness she had to have in ours.

Some bodily status-characteristics connect people with powerful or powerless groups. Others are anomalies like Cyrano's nose or a cleft palate—features sufficiently unusual that they are labeled deformities. Their bearers suffer, and we know this as soon as we see them. The opposite is also true: the

---

7. What Jane has managed is something like what Janet de Groot suggests therapy should do: she has gotten in touch with her subjective experience (chapter 7, this volume)

beautiful and handsome have privileges and perhaps confront prejudices that others do not.

Many parts and aspects of the body, then, have some connection with the person who, shall we say, wears them. They tell us about a person's personality, her taste, her values, her stage in life, her social history and standing. Morality entails valuing people as the uniquely embodied subjectivities that they are. We cannot do so while ignoring their bodies.

Moral Failure: Estrangement from One's Body

There are ways of attending to the body which, paradoxically, estrange it from oneself. A society that induces the wrong kind of attention is morally objectionable. Where only beauty matters, and where standards of beauty are impossibly high, suffering and alienation result.

In *The Absent Body*, Drew Leder devotes a chapter to the "dys-appearing" body: the body that enters our consciousness because of distress. I will use Leder's phenomenology of physical pain to describe the psychological pain of believing one's body is not good.

In earlier chapters Leder had described the ways in which we normally ignore our bodies. We focus through them, not on them; they are often merely background; our visceral depths function without us. The "ecstatic" body engages with the world: "The very nature of the body is to project outward from its place of standing."[8] In illness and disability, however, that outward focus lessens or disappears—as it also does for people who despise their own bodies.

Leder describes a tennis player who suffers a sharp chest pain. "The player is called back from ecstatic engagement to a focus upon the state of his own body.... Pain can thus overcome focal, background, and depth disappearance alike." How? Leder teases out the details. First, there is a "*sensory intensification*." "A region of the body [once silent] suddenly speaks up." Furthermore, it speaks up insistently, again and again. While "feelings of general neutrality or well-being are typically amorphous, marked neither by definable beginnings and ends nor abrupt transformation . . . even [chronic] pains participate in this *episodic temporality*" by continually reasserting themselves.[9]

8. Leder, *Absent Body*, 21.
9. Ibid., 71–72.

The result is an "*affective call.*" "One's attention is summoned . . . it is as if a magnet had reversed poles, reorganizing the experiential field inward." And "pain, like any other experiential mode, cannot be reduced to a set of immediate sensory qualities. It is ultimately a manner of being-in-the-world. . . . [It] reorganizes our lived space and time, our relations with others and with ourselves."[10]

This reorganization includes *intentional disruption* and *spatiotemporal constriction.* The player is unable to focus outside himself and may be immobilized ("frozen in agony"); even if he could resume the game, he might not want to take the risk. "Finally he may simply lose interest in the game. The . . . call of pain renders unimportant projects that previously seemed crucial," including connections with other people. Pleasures, in contrast, are more often "tied to a common world. . . . [They] tend to maintain our intentional links with other people. We feast and drink with friends . . . enjoyment . . . is our means of connection. . . . [But] pain tends to induce self-reflection and isolation." Further, it cuts us off from the past and future: "Severe pain summons us to the now."[11]

Still, "the very aversiveness of pain may also lead to a counteraction . . . a 'centrifugal' movement in which we seek to escape . . . by focusing outward upon the world, or dwelling in our past or a hoped-for future. Yet even such a movement outward bears witness to the original constrictiveness of pain. The body is no longer a nullpoint but an active presence whose call we must resist."[12] The body has become *an alien presence.* Patients "almost universally describe their pain as an 'it,' separate from the 'I.'" This attitude can yield some relief and help in reestablishing one's integrity.[13] Finally, "pain exerts a *telic demand* upon us." We feel impelled to *do* something, to make sense out of the pain and to get rid of it.[14]

Leder's description of pain illuminates what it is like to hate one's body. The major difference is that Leder is describing a new pain, while many people who hate their bodies cannot remember ever feeling otherwise.

Here are the elements of the experience. *Sensory intensification:* one is acutely

10. Ibid., 73.
11. Ibid., 74–75.
12. Ibid., 76.
13. Ibid., 76–77. The patient reports come from the work of J. C. White and W. H. Sweet, *Pain: Its Mechanisms and Neurosurgical Control* (Springfield, Ill.: Charles C. Thomas, 1955), 108, as cited in David Bakan, *Disease, Pain, and Sacrifice,* (Boston: Beacon Press, 1971), 74–75.
14. Leder, *Absent Body,* 77–78.

aware of a flat chest or a protruding belly. *Episodic temporality*: the awareness constantly reasserts itself, with every movement, in every mirror. An *affective call*: the awareness compels concern. *Intentional disruption*: one has difficulty focusing outward; the "game"—any of life's activities—may be abandoned, out of misery or fear. What cannot be abandoned is at least experienced differently: a meal becomes, not a necessary pleasure, but a dance with danger. I once read of women who could not achieve orgasm because they felt they had to "hold their stomachs in" during sex. *Spatiotemporal constriction*: to paraphrase Elaine Scarry, either the universe contracts to the size of the body, or the body swells to fill the entire universe.[15]

The body becomes an *alien presence*: not myself. My friend Jane, desperately hoping that her body had no connection with her person, had dressed in nondescript tents, had cringed from mirrors. When what is alien is one's age (rather than, or in addition to, one's size), what is feared and rejected is the accumulation of experience and memory, one's place in life. "I cannot be the mother of this adult; I hate being able to remember postwar Europe." The enemy can be one's race, one's genes: in the movie *Imitation of Life*, a light-skinned black woman rejects her darker mother: "Do I look as if I could be her daughter?"

Finally, one hears a *telic command*: do something. Make sense out of the misery (Am I lazy or gluttonous?) and get rid of it. (Stop eating. Buy new clothes. Restyle your hair. See a surgeon.) Virtually every magazine aimed at women offers "help" with the all-important project of looking better.

We see hundreds of advertisements a day, most with pictures of impossibly beautiful women, many now also with pictures of implausibly attractive men. It is no wonder that for so many of us our bodies "dys-appear": appear as sources of misery, as impediments to ecstasy, as reasons to abandon the game; not really ourselves, yet compelling our constant, frustrated attention. Many scholars describe religion as a response to suffering; it is not surprising, then, that Margaret Miles finds a religious dimension within anorexia.[16] A society that leads to this experience of the body is not admirable, not desirable. It is morally defective.

15. Elaine Scarry, *The Body in Pain* (New York: Oxford University Press, 1985), 35.
16. Margaret Miles, chapter 3, this volume. Miles sees anorexia, however, not as an escape from pain but as a route to pleasure. Her anorexic seeks, not escape from an unbearable body, but the expression and development of a self, in a society offering only male images of the inner life.

A Moral Ideal: Respect

The alternative, however, is not to deny the body, but to attend to it with respect. As I see it, respect has two components—acknowledging the existence of something and appreciating its value. A moral society would appreciate all the ways in which our bodies are ourselves. In it, as a result, people would easily own their bodies—as my friend Jane is trying to do. Furthermore, any constructed social meanings would be positive. This may be a tall order, but less formidable than a competing principle: that no social meanings whatever should attach to unchosen physical attributes. I will reject this principle.

Respecting Embodiment

Earlier I described three ways in which our bodies are ourselves. Respect and its lack take different forms for each.

First, every aspect of a body is a part of a person. What affects the body affects the person. Even investigating it can affect the person. Forgetting this, or not caring about it, can be both a moral failure and an epistemological one, since one's understanding will be limited and one's interventions likely to misfire. This kind of failure is objectification, and it is the occupational hazard of medicine among other fields.

To objectify is to treat as an object. As I use the word, an object is by definition not a subject. It has no desires, goals, or thoughts. As a result, it can be fully known from outside: there is no experience to fail to understand. (This marks the difference between the human and the physical sciences.) Objects also have different moral standing than do subjects, which may not be treated merely as means. An unusual cancer or challenging fracture is part of a person and may not be treated merely as an opportunity for practice.

Second, many physical aspects of a person reflect and express that person. Age certainly does so, and weight may—but not in the ways our society tends to assume. We draw erroneous conclusions about what a person is like, and these erroneous conclusions punish overweight people. But I suggest that we respond to these prejudices not by denying the connections between, say, age and personality, but by emphasizing how varied and individual they are, and by stressing the obvious but unnoticed connections. What do thinness and fitness, for instance, tell us about someone? Some people are thin because they are self-disciplined, some because they are genetically lucky, some because they are obsessed, some because they have what Aristotle called "rightly ordered desires." A moral stance toward body weight, or any other physical characteristic, would be realistic: noticing but not overdrawing the varied ways in which body shape expresses personhood.

And what about age? Youth has its special beauty; but so does maturity. An older face can manifest realism, experience, stubbornness, and kindness in a way a younger face cannot. And age also offers more purely physical beauties: in one short story, the skin of an old woman is compared to crumpled linen. Of course our belief that only young women are beautiful is not some accidental lapse of attention; it flows from our belief that the ideal woman is childlike, strong enough to serve a man but not strong enough to challenge him. Otherwise admirable traits become suspect if they threaten the subordination of women to men. Since this attitude discourages women from becoming mature, independent adults, it is pernicious and inconsistent with full respect. What we have is not just failure to notice, but a refusal to respect, the values of maturity.

So a second failure of appreciation involves partial vision, seeing only some of the ways in which bodies express selves, or seeing connections that are not there (for example, equating obesity with laziness or assuming that anything alterable but unaltered has therefore been "freely" chosen), or seeing the connections without valuing them. In the case of women and age, this failure of respect could be called infantilization. But there should be other names for other sets of blinders.

Finally, bodies tell us something about what a person's social history has been. At a minimum we need to be aware of this (and of our own complicity in it). We also need to value it properly—not pitying, not averting our eyes from, not sentimentalizing, but *respecting* people who have surmounted obstacles. And of course we need to see the evil in some social arrangements and try to change them. Which leads to my final question: in a just world, would unchosen physical characteristics like race and gender have any social meaning at all? The answer, I think, is not obvious.

The Social Construction of Race and Gender

The human meanings of physical characteristics are not found but created—by the domination of one group by another, sometimes; until wars end and economic inequalities subside, this kind of social meaning will endure. Furthermore, physical anomalies will be considered deformities until we accept more fully the risks inherent in life. (I say this because I believe that we shrink from the handicapped because we repress our fear of what might happen to us.)

What kind of society should we be working toward? It might seem wrong per se for a society to attach meaning to physical characteristics—when those characteristics are not an expression of individual personality and history. Most enlightened people find it self-evident that skin color, for instance, should have nothing to do with one's social place.

But the problem, I think, is subtler than that. Attributing meaning to our more physical aspects is necessarily suspect—so suspect that in practice, now, we simply should not do it. But there is an important theoretical point to be considered: such constructions are only suspect, not necessarily bad.

Both race and gender provide interesting illustrations. As Richard Wasserstrom argues in a profoundly insightful paper, the problem is not that blacks are treated differently; it is that they are treated badly. A racist society is not one where people are simply treated differently on account of race (whatever race is), but one where the different treatment is motivated by fear and contempt.[17] As a society, we are deeply racist, and so our racial classifications are always suspect. But as the struggles within feminism indicate, many people can conceive of a good and just world in which not everyone is treated alike, and where the differences are not just responses to individual differences (such as caloric requirements) but to group membership. I would argue that different treatment, even on account of purely physical features, is not bad per se (although different treatment in a racist and sexist society is dangerous). What is bad per se is treating people as if they do not matter, and whether the basis for distinguishing between people is physical difference, intelligence, or class does not change the nature of the offense. The moral problem, then, is not undue attention to physical characteristics but injustice and a failure of respect.

Not recognizing that leads us to be unduly anxious about our physicality. We insist that "it's not how old you are, it's how old you feel"; we point out the social origins of gender difference. If I am right we need not fear claims that some gender differences are genetically based—or even that some racial differences are.[18] At least in principle we need not worry, since the real problem is

17. Richard Wasserstrom, "Racism and Sexism," in *Today's Moral Problems*, ed. Richard Wasserstrom, 3d ed. (New York: Macmillan 1985), 1–28.

18. Something may be genetically based without being inevitable. Differences in physical strength between men and women, for instance, are clearly genetically based. But that would only mean that if both had identical environments, there would be a statistical difference in achievements. If men trained for a sport, say swimming, as everyone did fifty years

not whether people differ, or even why people differ, but how to treat people, each of whom is unique, with respect. Claims about race and intelligence, for instance, are dangerous not only because we are a racist society, but also because of an assumption we never think to question: we take it for granted that more intelligent people deserve power and privilege. It is probably not the case that any "race" (a socially constructed category) is less intelligent than any other. But some individuals are clearly less intelligent than others; where is the principle that says that less intelligent people can be deprived of basic security, of material pleasures, of equal respect? If blacks were less intelligent than whites on average in some genetically unalterable way—which is profoundly unlikely—would the lives they are forced to lead suddenly become acceptable? Of course not; no more than the holocaust would have been justified if the Nazis' vicious propaganda about Jews had been true. Racism usually depends upon such false empirical claims, but these are its more obvious (if still deadly) element. The less obvious, and equally deadly, element is the assumption that people different from the dominant group have a different, lower, moral standing.

We have not even begun to imagine a society in which everyone—regardless of ability, race, gender, beauty—is treated with genuine respect. Equality of respect does not entail identical treatment; in fact, since each person is unique, equality of respect entails different treatment. What differences require which response is the important question. Denying our bodies is not the answer.

Still an objector might persist: isn't there something inherently disrespectful about attaching social significance to an aspect of ourselves that does not express our person? On some important theories that would be so, especially on what might be called Kantian liberal grounds. But this conception of a person is notoriously disembodied, notoriously acultural. Communitarians point out that we are, and need to be, not just humans but members of smaller groups with individual histories and ways of living. This points out the theoretical possibility of a society where people live in groups and have different social roles and where some of the groups and roles may depend upon the more physical of our bodily attributes.[19]

---

ago while women trained as people do today, the fastest swimmers would be women. And, of course, even in equal environments, any given man may be outdone by a given woman.

19. I have argued elsewhere that not all morally binding roles are voluntarily assumed. Judith Andre, "Role Morality as a Complex Instance of Ordinary Morality," *American Philosophical Quarterly*, 28, no. 1 (January 1991): 73–80.

The Social Construction of Beauty

Standards of beauty are also socially constructed, but raise quite different questions. Race is beyond one's choice; beauty is not. With enough money, time, and energy most people can approximate what society wants. As one ages, greater and greater efforts are required; plastic surgery will eventually be necessary, and may be helpful from the beginning. So add pain and risk to the cost. Add as well a loss of experience: after breast surgery many women lose sensation in the nipple, an important source of sexual pleasure. They also lose the ability to nurse their babies.

For these reasons, one's appearance *does* express personhood. It expresses one's choices, one's values, one's taste. Standards of beauty can nevertheless objectify women: the altered breasts that cannot nurse a child nor pleasure their owner, that are of value only for the way they look, are more like objects than like parts of the body. Other standards infantilize (the emphasis on youth) and immobilize (high heels, short or tight skirts). Some beauty experts advise against smiling or frowning too much, since facial expressions eventually leave lines. Standards like these lead women to deny or to sacrifice important ways of being in the world.

Then there is the cost. Meeting contemporary standards of beauty often demands an undue amount of time, money, and attention. More important aspects of personhood may have to be curtailed. The resources put into hair, makeup, clothing, and fitness cannot also be put into friendship, work, and reflection. Of course we all know women who manage to do it all. On closer acquaintance, however, we sometimes find they manage to do everything but sleep. Life need not be so hard.

Finally there is the alienation I mentioned earlier. Ideally our bodies are ourselves and that is the way we experience them. But when the attention of others to our bodies is defective in some of the ways I've just analyzed, our experience is different. We want to deny, reject our weight and our age, because we have no support in seeing either as a neutral or good aspect of ourselves. And since our bodies are that with which we live, alienation from them is alienation from our life. Furthermore, the very attempt to deny the body can lead to an inability to forget the body and to live in the world.

A morally desirable standard of beauty would be multifold and achievable, consistent with different colors, sizes, and ages; it would not be at odds with movement, strong feeling, important work. It would be a source of joy, for its impulse would be to celebrate and decorate something that is seen as intrinsically attractive: the ordinary, individual human body. That we find such a thought strange, even counterintuitive, indicates how far we are from knowing that the body is good.

Conclusion

Walt Whitman knew how good the body is, and I will borrow some of his words for this conclusion. "I am the poet of the Body, and I am the poet of the Soul. . . . Seeing, hearing, feeling, are miracles, and each part and tag of me is a miracle. / Divine am I inside and out, and I make holy whatever I touch. . . . The scent of these arm-pits is aroma finer than prayer. . . . I dote on myself, there is that lot of me and all so luscious."[20] He knew that his body was himself; he honored it. But Whitman was a giant and a male; he knew what many men and most women cannot.[21]

Further, Whitman's body linked him with every human being. "Whoever degrades another degrades me / And whatever is done or said returns at last to me. . . . By God! I will accept nothing which all cannot have their counterpart of on the same terms. / Through me many long dumb voices, / Voices of the interminable generations of prisoners and slaves, / Voices of the diseas'd and despairing and of thieves and dwarfs. . . . Of the deform'd, trivial, flat, foolish, despised . . . voices veil'd and I remove the veil, / Voices indecent by me clarified and transfigur'd."[22] If we can learn to love our own bodies and to form a society in which that is possible, perhaps we can learn to love others as well: with no need to believe that we are all alike, perhaps we can begin to appreciate that each person is limited, particular, and precious.

20. Whitman, "Song of Myself," sec. II, ll. 422, 508–26, 544; pp. 33, 39, and 41.

21. Margaret Miles finds only male images in Augustine's *Confessions*, a normative spiritual journey. Whether the same is true of Whitman I do not know. Often, at least, he speaks of men and women with true grammatical equality: "The married couple sleep calmly in their bed, he with his palm on the hip of the wife, and she with her palm on the hip of the husband. . . . The female that loves unrequited sleeps, / And the male that loves unrequited sleeps . . ." (Walt Whitman, "The Sleepers," section I, in *Leaves of Grass, The 1892 edition* [New York: Bantam Books, 1983]).

22. Whitman, "Song of Myself," sec. II, ll. 503–19, pp. 37–39. Note the similarity to what William Monroe finds in the dying Flannery O'Connor (chapter 9, this volume).

2

Eating Disorders in
Survivors of Multimodal
Childhood Abuse

Jean M. Goodwin and

Reina Attias

The feminist revolution provoked many reluctant discoveries about previously hidden realms of female experience. One of the most difficult areas concerns the female experience of victimization, particularly sexual victimization. In this realm, both abuse experiences and their consequent symptoms have existed as closely guarded secrets. There is resistance both to the idea that girls are victimized in this way and to the idea that the victimization harms them. As secrecy diminishes, evidence is emerging that this harm affects basic bodily functions; core self-image, especially body image; and fundamental elements of relational capacity, including self-control and effective communication. The examples of eating disorders described in this chapter illustrate

Reprinted from *Clinical Perspectives on Multiple Personality Disorder* edited by Richard D. Kluft and Catherine G. Fine (Washington, D.C. and London: American Psychiatric Press, Ltd., 1993), with the kind permission of American Psychiatric Press.

newly emerging connections between victimization of children and distortions in body experience and body image.

Many classic clinical descriptions of multiple personality disorder (MPD) and incest contain accounts of disordered eating behaviors. The extreme multimodal childhood abuse that is almost invariably present in these patients may involve abnormal eating experiences, including starvation, force-feeding, forced ingestion of nonfood substances, and emotional abuse around eating or weight, in addition to oral rape and forced fellatio.[1]

Cornelia B. Wilbur's eleven-year treatment of "Sybil" dealt with several types of disordered eating. Dr. Wilbur traced the origins of these symptoms to specific characteristics of Sybil's childhood abuse. Neither "eating disorder" nor "anorexia" appears in the index of Sybil.[2] Close reading, however, reveals that this patient was twenty-two years of age, weighed 79 pounds, and was five feet five inches tall when she first met Dr. Wilbur. Her ideal body weight would have been 123 pounds. At 65 percent of her ideal body weight, she fell well within the Diagnostic and Statistical Manual of Mental Disorders, IIIR guidelines defining anorexia nervosa.[3] The text leaves it unclear whether "Sybil" ate too little, simply fasted, or found some other way to achieve this low weight. At least three other alters—one child alter and two adults who enjoyed eating—complained that Sybil was not feeding the body. The body images of the sixteen alters in Sybil's system ranged from "plump" and "chunky" to "willowy," "small," and "pale and thin." They ranged in age from toddler to middle-aged. Two male alters complained about looking like a girl; they wanted male genitals and bodies. Although repetitive vomiting is not described in this account, Sybil did complain of difficulties swallowing. Another somatic symptom, massive diarrhea, probably also interfered with her ability to gain weight. Conflicts about eating and about body image became more intense as treatment progressed and alters became more co-conscious.

As Sybil recovered memories of her childhood, it became more understandable why eating and swallowing were so difficult for her. Because of daily physical and sexual abuse in childhood, she was often too angry, frightened, humiliated, or depressed to feel like eating. In addition, her mother insisted on

1. W. H. Dietz and D. Bienfang, "Obesity, Family Violence and Medicine," in Unhappy Families: Clinical and Research Perspectives on Family Violence, ed. E. H. Newberger and R. Bourne (Littleton, Mass.: PSG, 1985).

2. F. R. Schreiber, Sybil (New York: Warner Books, 1974).

3. G. W. Thorn and G. F. Cahill, "Gain in Weight, Obesity," in Harrison's Principles of Internal Medicine, ed. M. Wintrobe, G. Thorne, R. Adams, et al. (New York: McGraw-Hill, 1974).

absolute control of Sybil's body. She imposed force-feeding on her daughter and induced defecation through the use of enemas and laxatives. Sybil's diarrhea may have been a somatosensory memory of those episodes. Her difficulty swallowing related not only to the force-feedings but also to being gagged by having rags stuffed into her mouth and being hit in the throat. One time she was struck so violently that her larynx was fractured. By refusing to eat, Sybil avoided memories of the abusive feeding and elimination practices and of the assaults on her mouth and throat. Her very low weight also avoided the secondary sexual characteristics that might have panicked child and male alters as well as those alters who were phobic of sexuality because of sexual abuse.[4]

Other therapists working with patients with multiple personality and related dissociative states have documented other eating disorder behaviors: binge eating, induced vomiting, fear of food, and laxative abuse.[5] Torem treated two patients with bulimia nervosa whose altered states of consciousness during episodes of binging and purging were the clue to the fact that these behaviors were part of a dissociative disorder. One of these bulimic patients gorged when in an ego state that had been starved by the mother. The patient's purging, on the other hand, was the adaptive effort of an ego state that had been forced to eat rotten food and vomitus. In this case, each limb of the bulimia represented both sensations related to a dissociated memory of abuse and behaviors that constituted realistic but displaced efforts to defend against parental assaults.[6]

Early clinical accounts of eating disorders and of incest victimization syndromes occasionally describe patients with both conditions. Bruch described a fourteen-year-old girl with abdominal pain, anorexia, vomiting, aphonia, anger, and sexual preoccupations who revealed genital fondling by her father.[7]

Crisp described a sixteen-year-old girl with both anorexia and bulimia whose symptoms had begun subsequent to her widowed father's first frank

4. H. Bruch, *Eating Disorders: Obesity, Anorexia and the Person Within* (New York: Basic Books, 1973).

5. E. L. Bliss, *Multiple Personality, Allied Disorders and Hypnosis* (New York: Oxford University Press, 1986); R. Kluft, "The Natural History of Multiple Personality Disorder," in *Childhood Antecedents of Multiple Personality Disorder*, ed. R. P. Kluft (Washington, D. C.: American Psychiatric Press, 1985).

6. M. S. Torem, "Dissociative States Presenting as an Eating Disorder," *American Journal of Clinical Hypnosis* 29 (1986): 137–42.

7. Bruch, *Eating Disorders*.

sexual advances. She also became alcoholic.[8] Eating disorders have been described acutely in other survivors of childhood sexual abuse.[9] Annie Katan treated an adult woman who presented with agitation, anxiety, and depression. This patient had been genitally fondled by her father from about age two; at age five, she had fellated an unknown adult male who approached her at school. After the episode of fellatio, she had problems involving gagging, vomiting, and an inability to swallow, and she could eat only a few special foods.[10]

The current view of both anorexia and bulimia is that they are complex disorders that probably include many subgroups. Some patients have coexisting major affective symptoms; some have borderline personality disorder; some cases develop after a traumatic event, such as a rape or attempted rape.[11] For many patients with eating disorders, this is part of a more extensive syndrome of psychological suffering. Among the patients described in the first nineteenth-century English accounts of anorexia nervosa, one refused to speak and was enuretic and encopretic; another had intense headaches and shivering.[12] Bruch estimated that 10 percent of anorexic patients have an atypical "hysterical" pattern that includes a later age at onset, conversion symptoms, sexual preoccupation, and dysphoria about weight loss.[13] Among patients with bulimia, the lifetime rates of additional psychiatric disorders are high, not only for mood disorders but also for substance use and anxiety disorders. Studies of family patterns of these patients are just becoming available.[14]

8. A. H. Crisp, "The Psychopathology of Anorexia Nervosa: Getting 'Heat' Out of the System," in Eating and Its Disorders, ed. A. L. Stunkard and E. Stellar (New York: Raven Press, 1984).

9. C. Bagley, "Mental Health and the In-the-Family Sexual Abuse of Children and Adolescents," Canada's Mental Health 32 (1984): 17–23; J. Conte and J. R. Schuerman, "Factors Associated with Increased Impact of Child Sexual Abuse," Child Abuse and Neglect 11 (1988): 201–11; P. S. Jorne, "Treating Sexually Abused Children," Child Abuse and Neglect 3 (1979): 285–90; J. J. Peters, "Children Who Are Victims of Sexual Assault and the Psychology of Offenders," American Journal of Psychotherapy 30 (1976): 398–421.

10. A. Katan, "Children Who Were Raped," Psychoanalytic Study of the Child 28 (1973): 208–24.

11. S. Abraham and P. J. V. Beaumont, "Varieties of Psychosexual Experience and Patients with Anorexia Nervosa," International Journal of Eating Disorders 1 (1982): 10–19; N. F. Damjouli and J. M. Ferguson, "Three Cases of Posttraumatic Anorexia Nervosa," American Journal of Psychiatry 142 (1985): 362–63; D. B. Herzog and P. M. Copeland, "Eating Disorders," New England Journal of Medicine 313, no. 5 (1985): 295–303; W. J. Swift, D. Andrews, N. E. Barlage, "The Relationship between Affective Disorder and Eating Disorders: A Review of the Literature," American Journal of Psychiatry 143, no. 3 (1986): 290–99.

12. J. A. Silverman, "Anorexia Nervosa in 1888," Lancet 1 (1988): 928–30.

13. Bruch, Eating Disorders.

14. J. I. Hudson, H. G. Pope, D. Yurgelum-Todd, et al., "A Controlled Study of Lifetime Prevalence of Affective and Other Psychiatric Disorders in Bulimic Out Patients," American

Preliminary data suggest that survivors of childhood abuse may be more likely to fall into that subgroup of patients whose eating disorders are accompanied by other severe symptoms. One study described ten adult incest survivors whose severe symptoms had led to multiple psychiatric hospitalizations. All had been physically and emotionally mistreated and sexually abused. Seven had eating disorders, all involving purging with anorexia, normal weight, or obesity; four had been hospitalized because of their eating disorders. Five of the seven connected their purging with prior fellatio experiences. Two additional survivors had episodes of either fasting or vomiting that had not been previously diagnosed as eating disorders. Associated symptoms, present in more than half of these survivors, included dissociative symptoms, borderline personality disorder, legal difficulties (particularly loss of child custody), alcohol and substance abuse, rape victimization, spousal abuse victimization, multiple suicide attempts, major affective disorder, and somatic complaints.[15]

Some statistical studies of incest survivors and of patients with eating disorders have begun to quantify this area of overlap. Sedney and Brooks surveyed a nonclinical population of college women for both childhood sexual experiences and symptoms. They found higher percentages of both weight loss and being overweight in those subjects with a history of intrafamilial or extrafamilial childhood sexual abuse. These differences were not statistically significant, however. Finn and colleagues also failed to find significant associations. However, Runtz and Briere, in a similar study of 278 undergraduate women, found that eating problems were more likely to be found in the group with prior sexual abuse. The sexually abused group admitted to problems with both overeating and undereating more frequently than the nonabused group, but only the undereating item reached significance. Other questionnaire items on which abused and nonabused women differed significantly included school problems, conflict with authority, early sexual behaviors, dissociation, somatization, anxiety, and depression.[16]

Journal of Psychiatry 144 (1987): 1283–87; Swift, Andrews, Barlage, "Relationship between Affective Disorder and Eating Disorders"; C. Johnson and A. Flach, "Family Characteristics of 105 Patients with Bulimia," American Journal of Psychiatry 142 (1985): 1321–24.

15. J. Goodwin, K. Cheeves, and V. Connell, "Defining a Syndrome of Severe Symptoms in Survivors of Extreme Incestuous Abuse," Dissociation 1, no. 4 (1988): 11–16.

16. M. A. Sedney and B. Brooks, "Factors Associated with a History of Childhood Sexual Experiences in a Nonclinical Female Population," Journal of the American Academy of Child Psychiatry 23 (1984): 215–18; S. Finn, M. Hartman, and G. Leon, et al., "Eating Disorders and Sexual Abuse: Lack of Confirmation for a Clinical Hypotheses," International Journal of Eating Disorders 5 (1986): 1051–60; M. Runtz and J. Briere, "Adolescent 'Acting-Out' and Childhood History of Sexual Abuse," Journal of Interpersonal Violence 1, no. 3 (1986): 326–34; J. Briere and

Oppenheimer and colleagues reported that 31 percent of patients with anorexia nervosa and 42 percent of patients with bulimia described experiences of childhood sexual abuse. Pyle and colleagues report an identical percentage, 42 percent in fifty-eight patients with bulimia nervosa. In addition, 74 percent reported enduring prior physical abuse and 94 percent psychological abuse. In this sample, 30 percent reported self-mutilation. Powers and colleagues found a higher percentage of childhood sexual abuse in patients with morbid obesity (37 percent of 27) than in those with bulimia nervosa (29 percent of 31) or anorexia nervosa (27 percent of 15).[17] Other estimates of the frequency of childhood sexual abuse in patients with eating disorders range from 29 to 82 percent.[18] It is unclear, however, whether these percentages are higher than expected, because 44 percent of women in the general population have experienced rape or attempted rape before age eighteen.[19] Also, because we are postulating child abuse as only one of many possible etiologies for eating disorders, a simple comparison of raw frequencies of prior abuse is not the definitive test of the hypothesis. More detailed qualitative data are needed describing both the nature of the childhood sexual abuse and the development of the eating disorder. If further studies support the finding of a childhood sexual subgroup among patients with eating disorders, this would fit with other findings:

1. High hypnotizability in bulimic and anorexic patients.[20]

2. The presence of dissociative symptoms in as many as 75 percent of bulimic patients.[21]

M. Runtz, "Symptomatology Associated with Childhood Sexual Victimization in a Nonclinical Adult Sample," *Child Abuse and Neglect* 12 (1988): 51–59.

17. R. Oppenheimer, K. Howells, L. Palmer, et al., "Adverse Sexual Experience in Childhood and Clinical Eating Disorders: A Preliminary Description," *Journal of Psychiatric Research* 19 (1985): 357–61; R. L. Pyle, T. Perse, J. E. Mitchell, et al., "Abuse in Women with Bulimia Nervosa" (Paper presented at the annual meeting of the American Psychiatric Association, Montreal, May 1988); P. S. Powers, D. L. Coovert, D. R. Brightwell, "Sexual Abuse History in Three Eating Disorders" (Paper presented at the annual meeting of the American Psychiatric Association, Montreal, May 1988).

18. M. P. Root and P. Fallon, "The Incidence of Victimization Experiences in a Bulimic Sample," *Journal of Interpersonal Violence* 3 (1988): 161–73; G. Sloan and P. Leightner, "Is There a Relationship between Sexual Abuse or Incest and Eating Disorders?" *Canadian Journal of Psychiatry* 31 (1986): 656–60.

19. D. E. H. Russell, "The Incidence and Prevalence of Intrafamilial and Extrafamilial Sexual Abuse of Female Children, *Child Abuse and Neglect* 7 (1983): 133–46.

20. Bliss, *Multiple Personality*; Torem, "Dissociative States."

21. Abraham and Beaumont, "Varieties of Psychosexual Experience."

3. Minnesota Multiphasic Personality Inventory and other test similarities between incest survivors and anorexic patients.[22]

Sexual dysfunction is yet another symptom associated with traumatic
child abuse.[23] In a study of twenty-seven males with bulimia and anorexia,[24] 26
percent were homosexual, and almost all had problems with sexuality and
sexual behavior. Because males are less pressured toward abnormal eating by
societal preoccupations,[25] all-male samples may include higher percentages of
patients whose eating disorder reflects childhood trauma.

A Theoretical Framework for Exploring Connections between Child Abuse and Eating Problems

Goodwin, Cheeves, and Connell proposed that some self-abusive behaviors in
adulthood represent a continuation of childhood abuse, with the survivor
now incorporating the role of the parent-perpetrator.[26] Thus, the child who
has been thrown into walls later throws himself into them or walks into them
"accidentally." "Stripes," originally the result of lashings, are reenacted as the
thin cuts of the delicate self-mutilator. Sexual abuse becomes promiscuity,
often with sadistic partners. In this model, starvation of the child, labeled
earlier as failure to thrive, would become self-starvation; force-feeding could
be reenacted as gorging; and compulsive laxative use could take the place of
parental overcontrol of elimination.

Case studies already cited indicate the situation is even more complex,
however. Reenactments are only one way in which fragments of dissociated
memories of childhood abuse resurface. Braun has proposed a model describing four separate aspects of memory that can be dissociated or retrieved:
behavior, affect, sensation, and knowledge. Braun uses the mnemonic BASK to

22. S. R. Hathaway and J. C. McKinley, Minnesota Multiphasic Personality Inventory, rev. (Min-
neapolis, Minn.: University of Minnesota, 1970); R. Scott and G. Thoner, "Ego Deficits in
Anorexia Nervosa Patients and Incest Victims: An MMPI Comparative Analysis," Psychological
Reports 58 (1986): 829–46.

23. J. Goodwin, "Developmental Impacts of Incest," Handbook of Child Psychology, vol. 5.,
ed. I. Noshpitz, J. Berlin, R. Call, et al. (New York: Basic Books, 1987).

24. D. B. Herzog, D. K. Norman, C. Gordon, et al., "Sexual Conflict and Eating Disorders in 27 Males," American Journal of Psychiatry 141 (1984): 989–90.

25. C. Steiner-Adair, "The Body Politic: Normal Female Adolescent Development and
the Development of Eating Disorder," Journal of the American Academy of Psycho-Analysis 14, no. 1
(1986): 95–114.

26. Goodwin, Cheeves, and Connell, "Defining a Syndrome."

represent these four aspects. Within this model, enactments—gorging, self-starvation—are only one mode in which traumatic memories can resurface. Feeling states are another. Another mode is the sudden experiencing of sensations—such as the difficulty in swallowing experienced by Sybil—which are recognized as memory fragments only later.[27]

Another way in which eating behaviors function in the life of an abuse survivor is to defend against the initial assaults or the memories of them. Thus, Torem's patient ate greedily because in the displaced time of her memory she was being starved; she purged to rid her system of poison. Sybil avoided disruptive flashbacks by staying away from kitchens and food and the act of swallowing.

Still another way eating disorders can emerge in these survivors is as a secondary effect of the posttraumatic and dissociative disorders that are the primary results of the abuse. The chronic anxiety, depression, hostility, and guilt that characterize posttraumatic stress disorder are not conducive to normal enjoyment of food. When dissociation has split the body image into multiple fragmentary identities, the tasks of identifying and achieving an ideal weight become hopelessly complicated. This is the case with MPD patients. With alters eating different menus at various times of day, often unbeknown to each other, good nutritional control becomes the exception rather than the rule. When leaving the body is the preferred defense against abuse and flashbacks, the normal triggers of hunger and satiety are left behind.

Multiple Eating Disorders in a Patient with MPD

In the case of Anita, multiple forms of disordered eating illustrate all three categories of impingements from prior child abuse: reenactment or reexperiencing of abuse, displaced defenses against abuse, and secondary effects on eating due to other sequelae of abuse.

Anita is thirty-three years old, single, obese, and a chronic mental patient whose multiplicity was diagnosed only one year ago. At nineteen, she was hospitalized for anorexia nervosa. At present she weighs 220 pounds and has had multiple emergency room visits for vomiting and dehydration. At one point Anita explained her vomiting: "We're sick. Someone's been beating us up." A persecutor alter was reenacting (via self-mutilation) the genital mutila-

---

27. B. G. Braun, "The BASK (Behavior, Affect, Sensation, Knowledge) Model of Dissociation," *Dissociation* 1, no. 1 (1998): 4–23; 1, no. 2 (1998): 16–23.

tion that her grandfather had practiced, leaving her with pain, nausea, and vomiting. The vomiting was complicated by fasting related to several fragmented affective aspects of the memory. Nine-year-old Maggie was too angry to eat. Three-year-old Caroline was too sad: "She only cries; she doesn't drink." Betty was too anxious, and her hyperventilation made the nausea worse. Helen fasted "to get closer to God." A "psychotic" alter saw food "as bugs." One alter was specialized to do all the vomiting for the system; she smelled the stench of the outhouse in which she had been locked at age three by her grandfather as punishment for refusing his sexual advances.

Anita's disturbed eating is entwined with every aspect of her dissociative disorder. Among her twenty alters are infants, animals, demons, and spirits whose "nutritional requirements" vary as greatly as do their body images. This symptom complex, in addition to being a container endlessly repeating various dissociated fragments of the memory, could also be used as a powerful obstacle to remembering. When reconstruction was proceeding rapidly, Anita would often call to cancel a treatment session, saying, "They've made me too nauseated to go in today." At other times, the vomiting alter rescued the system from potentially lethal overdoses and illegal drugs (grandfather, too, had given Anita substances to sedate her).

Eating Disorders in Incest Survivors with Mixed Posttraumatic and Dissociative Symptoms

Whereas in patients with MPD one finds multiple eating disorders as a response to multiple types of child abuse, in less disturbed incest survivors, it is more possible to focus on single eating dysfunctions and single types of child abuse.

Disordered Eating as Memory Equivalent

Ann is a twenty-seven-year-old woman who entered psychotherapy to explore emerging memories of incest with her father. Her diagnostic exploration revealed beatings by both parents from an early age; sexual abuse, including genital touching and fellatio between ages seven and twelve; emotional abuse, including overcontrol of eating and excretion; and exploitation of her capacity to work. From the age of seven she was making meals and caring for younger siblings.

Although her cognitive memories of the incest seemed clear and complete, she usually showed very little feeling about the abuse. Feelings tended to surface for her around 4:00 P.M., when she would experience anxiety and dysphoria and stuff herself with food. Further exploration of this experience revealed that it contained cognitive and behavioral aspects of her childhood experience, as well as some of her feeling states. She realized that stuffing herself with food was how she comforted herself after the fellatio with her father, which generally had taken place about 4:00 P.M.

We have seen other instances in which abnormal eating represented a fragment of a dissociated memory. One patient remained unaware of her incest pregnancy until delivery, then rerepressed the entire experience after the baby died. During the years when she was amnesic—both concerning the incest and the traumatic delivery—she remained severely obese and vomited secretly every morning. She had also concealed her morning sickness during pregnancy. During this period when she was unable to access knowledge and memory, her overeating, vomiting, shame, and obesity represented behavioral, affective, and sensory fragments of the lost memory.

Some incest survivors who have been diagnosed as bulimic describe certain foods as triggering intense nausea, dysphoria, and the feeling that they are choking. Often they can control their bulimia by avoiding foods such as milk, tapioca pudding, rice pudding, mayonnaise, and egg whites. Some of these survivors state clearly that these foods reevoke the somatic sensations they felt when the abuser ejaculated into the mouth.

Disordered Eating as Defense against Memory

Once we understand that eating behaviors and associated sensations can contain dissociated memories and trigger flashbacks, it becomes more understandable how eating in all of its aspects, like sexuality in all of its aspects, can become the focus of multiple secondary posttraumatic symptoms as the patient attempts to use numbing mechanisms to avoid remembered pain. In addition, body weight is a powerful tool for changing body image. Thus some survivors are able to become grossly obese to escape any identification with the childlike body image that would trigger flashbacks to the abuse. Other survivors become thin, maintaining a prepubertal or quasimasculine low body weight, to avoid fears of rape or impregnation that might erupt, together with memories of the abuse, if their body image were that of a young adult woman.

Ann's weight remained normal until her marriage. She found that she was able to enjoy sex with her husband, but she experienced vivid visual flashbacks of her father after intercourse. As her weight climbed, the flashbacks decreased in number. Although her current weight of more than 200 pounds is seriously interfering with her health, she is afraid that if she complied with medical recommendations to lose weight, she would no longer be able to have sex with her husband.

Barbara entered treatment at age twenty-five because of extreme dysphoria and the intrusion of disorganized memory fragments whenever she saw her father. In psychotherapy she was able to reconstruct extreme incestuous abuse by her father between the ages of three and eleven. This included fellatio and forced vaginal intercourse. There was physical abuse (including strangulation) and emotional abuse around eating. Barbara's weight fluctuated. At one point she became thin and obtained work as an artist's model. She became increasingly panicked at the attention men gave her and began to mutilate herself.

Christine is a twenty-two-year-old woman who was subjected to physical and sexual abuse from her father, her mother, two uncles, and a cousin between the ages of four and seventeen. From age eight to seventeen, she had regular vaginal intercourse with her father. Although she has never been diagnosed with an eating disorder, she says of herself, "I never eat and I never have periods." She maintains her weight between 80 and 90 pounds. She says that she was terrified of pregnancy from the time oral sexual contact with her father progressed to vaginal intercourse, at age eight. She did not menstruate until age sixteen and still has only one or two menstrual periods each year.

Darlene is a twenty-six-year-old woman who has been diagnosed with bulimia nervosa. She was sexually abused by her father and her brother between the ages of two and sixteen. She describes her purging as follows: "It's like cleaning out your system. If I can get the semen out of my system, I feel better. Sometimes I eat and think about the guys who raped me. Afterward it's like I pretend I'm purging all over them."

For Darlene the eating disorder functioned both as a healing ritual and a revenge fantasy. In the other cases, a shift in self-image is important in the defensive strategy. For those survivors of multimodal childhood abuse who do not have access to the alters available in MPD, different weight and body images seem to offer ways to change state in order to avoid the unpleasant cognitive or affective aspects of dissociated memories. For example, the two patients who became obese (Anita and Ann) not only distanced themselves from the child body image that inhabited their flashbacks but also decreased courting advances and sexual triggers from men. Anita describes her obesity as a comprehensively numbing state. She feels that all sensations and some affects, especially anger, are muted by her encasing layers of fat. This parallels recent physiologic studies finding depressions in both sympathetic and parasympathetic activity associated with increasing body fat.[28] Where a weight state has become an important mechanism for numbing, it becomes as conflicted as other such mechanisms, such as substance abuse or anorgasmia. The patient needs it but hates needing it.

Understanding the meanings of weight and eating as they relate to dissociated memories of abuse and defenses against them can help the therapist understand the intense preoccupation with weight and eating of some incest survivors. For a survivor desperately attempting to avoid flashback images of his or her body, it can be helpful to substitute more abstract elements of body image, such as weight or clothing size, for the dangerous visual images that would otherwise be used to represent the self mentally. These patients may become obsessed with attaining a certain body weight or wearing a certain outfit because their real aim is to attain a particular ego state. A therapist who grasps this aspect may be able to help the obese patient reduce to a compromise weight that allows some further exploration of sexuality without producing so many sexual triggers that the patient becomes frightened and more symptomatic. The female anorexic patient, too, may be able to reach a compromise weight that is physically safer but still allows her long periods of amenorrhea.

Conclusions

Nurturance comes from the Latin word for "suckling," so it is perhaps not surprising that survivors of inadequate or distorted nurturance have difficulty feeding and swallowing. The concept of orality is based on this analogy but may be too abstract and metaphorical to capture the concrete eating disabilities we are describing here. Nor is it surprising that those who feel powerless and betrayed turn to eating as the last bastion of autonomy and self-expression. Centuries of fakirs, saints, and "hunger artists" have taught us to expect this, too.[29]

28. H. R. Peterson, M. Rothchild, C. R. Weinberg, "Body Fat and the Activity of the Autonomic Nervous System," New England Journal of Medicine 318 (1988): 1077–83.

29. F. Kafka, "A Hunger Artist," in The Penal Colony, trans. W. and E. Muir (New York: Schocken Books, 1975 [1948]); R. M. Bell, Holy Anorexia (Chicago: University of Chicago Press, 1985): H. Bruch, Eating Disorders; S. T. Mogul, "Asceticism in Adolescence and Anorexia Nervosa," Psychoanalytic Study of the Child 35 (1980): 155–75.

Reviews of the literature and case studies suggest that childhood abuse survivors might present a qualitatively different picture from some other sub-groups of patients with eating disorders. Some possible distinguishing charac-teristics are later age at onset, greater conflict about eating, greater variety of disordered eating practices, the presence of altered states of consciousness, and the presence of associated severe symptoms, including borderline person-ality disorder, other family violence problems, alcohol and substance abuse, self-mutilation and suicidality, flashbacks, and somatization, including conver-sion disorders.

The therapist should remain alert to the possibility that abnormal eating behaviors represent fragments of dissociated memories or ways to defend against those memories or that they occur as epiphenomena related to post-traumatic or dissociative sequelae of child abuse.

Previous investigators have described distorted body images in some patients with eating disorders. Our experience indicates that this disturbance may be even more profound than previously thought, extending to absent body image or multiple body images.[30] Such disturbance may be an inevitable consequence of overusing dissociative exits from the body. "Who would not leave a burning house?" asked one of our patients. Another described being oblivious to both her ongoing anorexia and her previous sadistic child abuse until she caught sight of her reflection in a subway window. "That looks like someone who just got out of a concentration camp," she thought, and then recognized the reflection as her own. The preoccupation with weight seen in some patients may be like the preoccupation with clothes shown by H. G. Wells's *Invisible Man* (1897/1987); he was not trying to cover up a wounded or deformed body image, but one that was not there at all. Further study of this disrupted population may help us learn more about the construction of body and self-image during normal child development. The developmental linkages between autobiographical memory and self-image may turn out to be so numerous and intricate that we will learn to look for gaps in memory when-ever we find disturbances in self-image, and vice versa.[31]

30. L. Bienz and F. Irigoyen, unpublished data, October 1985.

31. K. Nelson, "The Ontogeny of Memory for Real Events," in *Remembering Reconsidered: Ecological and Traditional Approaches to the Study of Memory*, ed. U. Neisser and E. Winoyrod (New York: Cambridge University Press, 1988); S. W. Touzz, P. J. V. Beaumont, J. K. Collins, et al., "Body Space Perception and Its Disturbance in Anorexia Nervosa," *British Journal of Psychiatry* 144 (1984): 167–71.

The Good Woman:
Asceticism and Responsibility
from the Perspectives
of Battered Women

Allison M. Moore

I am a social ethicist who works daily with battered women who seek shelter and support services from Sanctuary for Families, a shelter for battered women and their children in New York City.[1] The shelter provides a unique perspective on two contrasting understandings of asceticism in the lives of battered women, asceticism as self-denial and asceticism in the service of recovery from

1. Sanctuary for Families is a not-for-profit agency funded by public and private sources. It provides temporary shelter for battered women and their children and services for residents and nonresidents including individual counseling, support groups, and advocacy to help women find employment, housing, legal protection, child care, medical care, and other resources necessary to establish a safe life for themselves away from their abusers. Most of the residential clients earn less than $25,000 a year in jobs or receive public assistance; nonresidential clients come from all economic groups. Residential clients are predominantly black and Latina, but nonresidential clients are from all ethnic groups, religious traditions, and ages.

abuse. In this chapter, I will share some of my observations and discuss their implications for theories of asceticism and responsibility.

Asceticism is often understood as a discipline of self-denial, rejection of physical and emotional needs for the sake of a "higher goal" of salvation. Many women I work with have spent years denying their own needs in the hope of remaining safe in an abusive relationship. Battered women often allow their abusers to dictate their activities and friendships.[2] They put lots of energy into trying to figure out what their abusers want, to please them, or to change themselves so that their abusers will stop insulting or hurting them. As girls, many of them learned that grown women should deny themselves for the sake of their male partners and their families. Battered women thus endure physical and emotional pain and constant fear in order to hold the family together. By the time women come to a shelter, it seems they have only the weakest sense of themselves left. This understanding of self-denial is a dangerous distortion of asceticism that progressively restricts battered women's lives.

Margaret Miles offers a more positive understanding of asceticism that illuminates women's work to find healing from abuse.[3] For her, Christian asceticism is a response to aspects of contemporary culture that distract people and societies from the abundant life God intends for all. Early Christian monastics challenged their culture's norms governing family life, possessions, and sexuality and developed mental and physical disciplines to help monks find salvation. In a similar way, counselors at Sanctuary for Families challenge battered women to understand that they have the right to attend to their own needs, to develop their own skills, and to build a life free of abuse for themselves and (often) their children. Counselors encourage battered women to question current expectations of "good women's" responsibility to care for others at the expense of their own well-being. Performing daily affirmations, participating in weekly counseling sessions and support groups, securing an order of protection or negotiating with lawyers, establishing a reliable source of economic support, and finding safe, affordable housing can all be seen as ascetic practices through which women find healing. Understanding asceti-

2. In this chapter, I focus on men's abuse of women since this constitutes 95 percent of the violence in adult couples. This focus in no way denies that some men are abused by women or that a small percentage of gay and lesbian relationships may be abusive.

3. See Margaret Miles, *Fullness of Life* (Philadelphia: Westminster Press, 1981), 141–46 for her discussion of the Rules of Basil and Benedict. I will return to this theme later in this chapter.

cism as a discipline that retrains women to believe in themselves and their ability to act effectively in the world can provide a holistic framework for the practical work of recovery from abuse and the intellectual development of theories of empowerment.

Asceticism as Self-Denial

Generally speaking, women learn to deny themselves in patriarchal families. The family is perhaps the most universal and powerful of all institutions—a place where infants are cared for and children learn what is expected of them, how to participate in society, how to distinguish right from wrong. As historian Carl Degler points out, "the equality of women and the institution of the family have long been at odds with one another. The historic family has depended for its existence and character on women's subordination. . . . The family's existence assumes that a woman will subordinate her individual interest to those of others—the members of her family."[4]

If these expectations characterize relationships grounded in respect and some degree of love and mutuality, then the tendency to deny oneself, focus on others, and try to obey the male is even more pronounced for battered women who live in fear. In the past fifteen years many people have documented the effects of violence against women on these women's sense of self-respect, accomplishment, and self-assertion.[5] They have recognized patterns of behavior for both abusive men and battered women. Any woman can be battered. A relationship that begins with expectations of mutuality and support may quickly become a fairly systematic experience of domination and control of women by the men they love.

Abusive relationships have several identifiable characteristics. First, the man characteristically lacks respect for the woman and her needs. This can be communicated through insults and constant criticism, lack of acknowledgment of the woman's emotional or material needs, isolation, threats, and various forms of violence and threats of violence. Violence and fear become a constant part of the woman's experience.

Second, both people center their attention, consciously and uncon-

4. Carl Degler, *At Odds: Women and the Family in America from the Revolution to the Present* (New York: Oxford University Press, 1980), vi–vii.

5. See Lenore Walker, *The Battered Woman* (New York: Harper and Row, 1979; Del Martin, *Battered Wives* (New York: Simon and Schuster, 1983); and Ginny NiCarthy, *Getting Free* (Seattle: Seal Press, 1986) or *The Ones Who Got Away* (Seattle: Seal Press, 1987), among others.

sciously, on the abuser's perceived needs, wants, and moods. Battered women learn to pay attention to the needs of their partners (husbands or boyfriends) instead of to their own needs, in the hope of pleasing their abusers and reducing the violence. Many battered women perceive themselves to be primarily dependent on their abusers for physical, emotional, and financial support, even when this may not be true. This sense of dependency and powerlessness is increased when women are isolated from family and friends who might provide reassurance or a different perspective, or remind them of skills they exercise daily.

Third, abused women begin to distrust their own judgment and sense of themselves. They come to accept some of the belittling, critical, and fearful things they are told repeatedly by their abusers. This pattern is exacerbated when family, friends, and social institutions trivialize battered women's experiences or blame women for their situation and do not respond to their appeals for help. Many women come to believe that the abuse is their fault. Most abuse increases in severity and frequency over time and can result in the woman's death.

Battered women develop a series of strategies to cope with abuse and try to minimize it. The process of learning to live with abuse is gradual, so that habits which gradually erode self-respect and self-assertion become second nature. Strategies of self-denial include denying bodily needs in order to survive, deferring to the abuser's authority, believing that abuse is punishment for one's sins, and trying to change the abuser's behavior by changing one's own actions and attitudes.

Some women who have been physically or sexually abused become numb to the needs of their bodies. Others try to second-guess their partner's needs and fulfill them as a way of reducing tension and minimizing violence. Women who are successful in work, at school, or in community activities may not tell their partners for fear the men will become jealous or make them stop the activity. By denying their body's needs or hiding their abilities, these women hope to make themselves invisible to their partners. Gradually, these women's needs and abilities become invisible to themselves as well.

Self-denial may take the form of deference, an echoing of the abuser's voice. Abusers often argue that they know what is best because they have more work experience or knowledge, because they are older, or because they are male. In some cases the man may well have greater knowledge or experience. Yet the authority that batterers claim and that women sometimes grant is based not on relevant expertise in particular situations but on fear of the violent exercise of the abuser's power. Many abused women defer to their partner's decisions and stop insisting on their own needs, goals, and plans for their family. Believing that "he knows what is best for me" can become a habit that leads women to distrust themselves.

One of the most frequently asked questions in initial interviews and support groups is what did I do to deserve this? It is part of the human condition to feel guilty for our shortcomings, and punishment is a logical corollary to guilt. For battered women, these feelings of guilt are reinforced by abusers who explicitly tell them they are bad and "punish" them for their "wrongdoing." For many women, the belief that suffering is God's punishment for wrongdoing reinforces their sense of guilt. They may feel that the abuse must be endured until they have learned whatever message God has to teach them.

Another strategy of self-denial encourages a battered women to feel that her actions are under her control and that she can make the abuser change if only she "gets it right." Elaine Pagels suggests that one reason Augustine's theory of original sin was so readily accepted by fourth-century Christians was that it seems easier to accept responsibility for some flaw in human nature than to live with the fact that nature itself has limits and brings pain.[6] Some battered women seem comfortable accepting the idea that they are inadequate and that the abuse is their fault. This idea implies that if the woman can rectify the inadequacy, she can stop the abuse.

For some women, self-blame takes the more subtle form of hoping that they can heal their partners. They blame their partners' abuse on their difficult childhoods or their sense of powerlessness at work. Some battered women believe that if only they can care for their abusers adequately, they can heal their partners' old hurts and the men will no longer abuse them. Since caretaking is a primary part of women's identity in prevailing social norms, some women assume that the abuse indicates they are not fulfilling their role properly and are not meeting their abusers' needs. Either form of assuming responsibility for stopping male violence—caretaking or seeking to rectify some personal inadequacy—is an indirect way for women to try to control their partners or their situations. These efforts are usually unsuccessful because the man, not the woman, is responsible for the abuse.

Precisely because the abuser is unable to assume responsibility for his abuse, he blames the woman for "making him do it." This can range from the

6. Elaine Pagels, *Adam, Eve and the Serpent* (New York: Vintage Books, 1988), chapter 6.

abuser's believing that his partner deliberately provoked him to hit her to much more subtle blaming: "She knows I have to have quiet when I get home but the children are still up"; "If you weren't so stupid you'd know what I want"; or "Why do you have to spend money all the time?" when the woman buys food or pays the bills. The abuser's litany of blame reinforces the self-blame women already experience.

Unfortunately, women often hear a similar litany when they seek help from family, friends, or public officials. More than one client has talked about going to her minister for support and having him or her ask, "What did you do to provoke his violence?" Similar responses are fairly common among marriage counselors or therapists who do not understand the dynamics of abuse. Especially if a woman has previously left her abuser and then returned to him, family members may blame her for weakness or imply that the abuse can't be so bad if she returned to it. When I give presentations about domestic violence, audiences always ask why women stay. Many fewer people listening to presentations ask why men batter.

Asceticism in the Service of Healing

Fourth- and fifth-century men and women joined monastic communities in the desert in order to reorient their actions, attitudes, and emotions toward ever more abundant life in God.[7] Battered women come to shelters to find healing for body, mind, and spirit, which necessarily entails a reorienting of actions, attitudes, and emotions toward safety and a more satisfying life. Asceticism illuminates the connections between mind, body, and spirit more clearly than much of the psychological literature concerned with battered women's healing. Ascetic disciplines developed to purify believers' souls have parallels in the daily activities of women in shelter who seek to strengthen their self-respect and their ability to act effectively in the world.

Miles distinguishes three attitudes about the human body in the history of Christian asceticism: "the body as foil for the soul, the body as problem, and the body as human condition." Many battered women have come to see their bodies either as a "foil for the soul," when the body is ignored or denied for the sake of the soul's health, or as a problem, when the body is blamed for the soul's "lack of integrity."[8] For instance, many women who have been physically

7. Miles, *Fullness of Life*, 137.
8. Ibid., 135.

or sexually abused learn to ignore their bodies as a way of coping with physical pain and violation. They may minimize the risk of threatened abuse or the severity of physical injuries ("He only punched me a few times," even though those punches resulted in hospitalization for internal hemorrhaging). Some women feel their bodies have betrayed them, and think that if only they can ignore their bodies' needs they can continue to hold the relationship together. Another response among women who are seen primarily as sex objects is to stop caring for their appearance or physical needs in hopes that their aspirations, fears, ideas, needs—their "souls"—will be taken seriously. Counselors try to help women recognize that their "whole selves," bodies and souls, are valuable, have been hurt by abuse, and are in need of healing.

"Christian asceticism takes the body as a condition when it makes it the intimate partner of the soul in learning, suffering, and salvation" and assumes that the way believers care for their bodies and address material needs "orients the entire human being toward the source of life itself."[9] Desert mothers and fathers carefully explored how certain physical disciplines such as fasting, continence, solitude, sleep deprivation, and sometimes physical pain could help believers in their quest. The plans for establishing safe lives that counselors work out with clients also contain physical and mental disciplines that will orient clients toward greater life. Body and soul are intimate partners in the quest for healing: no amount of skillful counseling to develop self-respect or recognize patterns of abuse will help a woman remain safe unless she also provides for her body's needs for safety, food, medical care, and so on. No provision for physical needs or change in environment or activities will keep a woman from returning to an abusive situation unless she also develops psychological insight into her situation.

Miles sees fourth-century monastic life as a counterculture to the secular world's orientation toward sex, power, and possession. "Secular culture both provides conditions for the pursuit of sex, power and possessions and limits the destructiveness of infinite demand."[10] Yet according to such theologians as Basil, Benedict, and Cassian, in organizing society around these instincts, secular culture deadens participants to the true source of life in God. Miles writes: "If one of our priorities is to locate our cultural conditioning so as consciously either to act out of this conditioning or to begin to modify it; and if we see that monasticism was a creative and skillful resolution of precisely this social condi-

9. Ibid.
10. Ibid., 143.

tioning, so that men and women were able to make choices in the direction of more love and more life than their cultural options offered, then we must recognize that the asceticism advocated by monastic authors was essential to achieving freedom from that conditioning."[11]

Counselors at Sanctuary for Families try to help battered women begin to modify the cultural and interpersonal conditioning that keeps them trapped in abusive relationships. They offer clients education about the political, economic, and social structures that maintain patriarchy, condone violence against women, and discourage the development of self-assertive women. By providing support groups and communal living and by making statistics about the prevalence and severity of domestic violence available, they help battered women recognize that they are not alone. Education about the dynamics of oppression helps counteract the effects of racism, economic exploitation, and sexism. Counselors hope that in a countercultural environment women will learn to respect themselves and acknowledge their needs.

The development of self-respect and self-assertion provides the foundation for battered women's healing, or "salvation" in the language of asceticism. Self-respect includes a will to live that involves social as well as biological aspects. The will to live is a motivating factor seen in women's desires to develop their abilities, to care for themselves, and to keep struggling. Self-respect is often what leads a woman to flee from her abuser and enables her to respond to actions of affirmation and support. Self-respect also includes acknowledgment of the characteristics that make each person unique.

Self-assertion depends on self-respect but is not reducible to it. Self-assertion depends on a fundamental sense of competence: the ability to identify one's own needs and to actively seek ways to meet those needs. This sense of competence is exactly what abusers try to question or eliminate in the women they abuse. Self-assertion includes the ability to make plans and carry them out, to envision new possibilities for one's life, and to begin to realize some of these plans. Self-assertion entails learning to ask for help when necessary, a skill that contradicts what many women have been taught about ignoring their own needs and caring for others. By asking for help, battered women discover options and begin to trust their own abilities.

How can self-respect and self-assertion be nurtured? Miles describes four goals of ascetic practice as formulated by Christian monastics and theologians: (1) the intensification and concentration of consciousness which increase the

11. Ibid., 155.

capacity to love and work, as described by Ignatius of Loyola; (2) the self-understanding of psychological dynamics that impede or nurture the quest for salvation; (3) the gathering and focusing of physical and psychic energy, as described by Augustine; and (4) the facilitation of personal growth through rules of community life formulated by Basil, Benedict and others.[12] Each of these has parallels in the lives of battered women, and counselors in battered women's shelters have developed particular techniques to help clients attain these goals.

Miles describes Ignatius's technique to intensify consciousness as "a series of mental and physical exercises that effectively break both habitual thought patterns and habitual treatment of the body [so that these] then can be reintegrated in more productive directions" in a fairly concentrated period of time.[13] Most battered women do not call a shelter until they are desperate, often literally frightened for their lives. Women find themselves involuntarily in a crisis that often requires an "intensification and concentration of consciousness in order to make life choices."[14] The time women spend in a shelter, far away from the usual routine of violence and perceived failures, offers them the opportunity to explore their traditional thought patterns and their habitual treatment of their bodies, to decide whether they really want to stay away from the abuser, and to discover how they could accomplish that within a relatively short period of time (because of funding restrictions, most shelters have to limit the length of time women may stay in a shelter).

Solitude; reflection on emotions, thoughts, and actions; advice from a spiritual guide; and then particular exercises that "address the exact nature of spiritual distraction"[15] are methods of achieving self-understanding that work for monks in the Egyptian desert and for women in shelters. Women must leave familiar neighborhoods, jobs, friends, and family in order to keep their abusers from finding them. Many women experience great loneliness even in a relatively crowded shelter because they are surrounded by strangers. The loneliness provides time for reflection on the life they have left, on their hopes and fears, and on the new life they could begin. Counselors are the contemporary equivalent of spiritual guides. In individual counseling sessions, clients have a counselor's undivided attention and help in identifying healthy and unhealthy patterns in their lives.

12. Ibid., 136.
13. Ibid., 150.
14. Ibid.
15. Ibid., 136

Ascetic monks developed rigorous techniques of watchfulness to observe and interpret "the demons and passions that deflect the soul from its purpose."[16] Once particular issues were identified, monks and guides adopted specific physical and mental disciplines to redirect the soul. In shelters, counselors may work with battered women to develop daily disciplines to help them resist internalized and external pressures to remain in the abusive relationship. Self-help books and counseling exercises for battered women suggest specific techniques that challenge these women's sense of themselves as worthless or bad. Ginny NiCarthy's Getting Free is a classic in the battered women's movement. NiCarthy asks women to reflect on their priorities, dreams, and values for marriage and family life; to identify their rights; to make lists of pros and cons of leaving the abusive relationship; to write out affirmations and say them to a mirror (for example, "You are beautiful, smart, capable, wonderful, a child of God"). Books for African-American and Latina women include exercises that help them identify ways of remaining true to their culture in a racist society.

Daily practices that enhance self-understanding are physical as well as psychological. Women in shelter have very concrete changes to make in the way they schedule their days. In an abusive relationship, women's routines are usually dictated by the abuser's needs and demands. In shelter, women must create new daily routines that meet their own goals and needs. These new routines orient women's behavior toward healing, sometimes even before they can recognize the positive effects of the choices they have made. Women who have been abused have often learned to ignore their bodies or reject them as ugly and painful. Activities such as taking bubble baths regularly, or getting their nails or hair done, or caring for their bodies in some other tangible way help women value their bodies more positively. Some women get very sick after a week or so at the shelter as their bodies recover from fear and shock. Many women move differently after they have been in a shelter for a while; they are less nervous; they are not constantly looking over their shoulders; they no longer sit on the edges of chairs. These more subtle signs of physical healing also indicate the body's role in the development of self-respect and self-assertion.

For Augustine, bodily practices were meant to gather and focus the soul's energy. Fasting, for example, could increase the soul's hunger for God. Clients in shelter can benefit from focusing their energy on their own healing, which is

16. Ibid.

developed through the concrete steps they take to secure housing, income, child care, and other material resources. Battered women often have to negotiate with unfriendly bureaucracies where persistence and meeting all sorts of inconvenient requirements are key. More important, clients have to shift their attention from trying to please or care for everyone else to identifying their own needs and limits. In asking other people to help her meet her needs, a battered woman can become her own, often forceful, advocate. Activities that address battered women's physical and material needs slowly affect their emotions, thoughts, and self-understanding and lead both body and mind to a new life.

Monasteries were established to challenge the way secular society understood sex, possession, and power and to provide a retreat from contemporary culture. Battered women's shelters were established to provide a safe refuge for battered women and to challenge cultural norms that condone abuse. Yet just as Basil, Benedict, and other founders of religious communities recognized the instrumental value of fostering community life for monks' search for personal salvation, shelter staff found that rules for community life enable some clients to make positive changes in their own lives.

For instance, many clients who first questioned the need for attendance at support groups and "house meetings" later commented that they found these events invaluable and would never have attended unless they were required to do so. Women who thought that they could never be friends with other women find themselves making friendships in spite of themselves. Communication and sharing in a supportive community is a vital step in reducing a battered woman's sense of dependence on her abuser.

Support groups offer another example of the ways life in community helps women find personal healing. In support groups women describe their lives in their own words, far from the critical voices of abusers. Clients can reinterpret their experiences in the presence of people who will affirm their being and well-being. Clients may come to realize that some of the actions they take for granted, such as getting the children off to school in the morning, attending night classes, or getting a promotion at work, are proof that they are able to take effective action in the world. Stories of "the ones who got away,"[17] battered women who successfully escaped abusive situations, offer hope that women currently in shelter can also live in safety and realize some of their own

17. See NiCarthy, *The Ones Who Got Away*, for personal accounts of several women who successfully established safe lives.

desires. Women who may have mentioned only the ways they failed to please their partners or make them change have a chance in the presence of supportive others to re-evaluate their actions in terms of their own well-being. The discipline of community life in support groups and in interactions with other shelter residents promotes the healing of each woman.

A comparison between the monastic goals and techniques of intensification of consciousness, enhancing self-understanding, gathering and focusing energy, and learning to live in an alternative community and the goals and techniques of women in a battered women's shelter can illustrate the positive role of asceticism in helping women recover from abuse. Ascetic practices that acknowledge the interaction of body, mind, and culture enable women to replace habits of self-denial with habits of self-assertion and self-respect. The "reconstitution" of a woman's life ultimately depends both on the presence of supportive others and on her decision to take control of her life. The shelter as counter culture, a space dedicated to women's needs, hopes, and problems, inspires movements for changes in political, economic, and social institutions that would promote and reinforce women's self-assertion and self-respect.

Asceticism and Responsibility

Two goals of shelter staff help illustrate two components of a definition of appropriate responsibility for battered women, which has broader implications for all women. First, each woman needs to recognize that she is responsible for her own well-being. This includes identifying her needs and goals and trusting that she has the abilities to work to meet those needs. Second, each woman must recognize the extent and the limits of her responsibility to others. This includes assessing the contributions and responsibilities of all people involved in a particular situation and then working to hold both individuals and, with the help of movements for social change, social, political, and economic institutions accountable for failing to provide women with what they need to live in safety.

Taking responsibility for one's own well-being means that "good women" must: (1) identify their needs and goals; (2) acknowledge their power as well as the extent and limits of their ability to work toward those needs and goals; (3) recruit help at times from other people and institutions to meet their needs and goals. A willingness to accept responsibility for oneself is grounded in a sense of self-respect and self-assertion, strengths that many women have to work very hard to develop. Ethicists who have based their theories implicitly and explicitly on the experiences of privileged males tend to assume that it is easy to assume responsibility for oneself. They ignore important nuances of responsibility. It is often difficult for women in general, and for battered women in particular, to believe that they can and should accept responsibility for their own well-being when central social, political, and economic structures assume both that women will be taken care of and that women ought to care for everyone else first. These assumptions are rooted in the expectations that women's primary contributions occur in the private world of the family and that the family, in turn, fulfills women's needs.

When I think of responsibility to others, my first image is of increasing obligations to more and more people in more and more ways. While there is truth in the idea that responsibility depends on recognizing our interdependence on each other and on the planet, an important element of responsibility from the perspectives of battered women is evaluating and letting go of some of these obligations. To whom should women be responsible and in what ways? Women can choose how they will respond to others; they can acknowledge the relations of dominance and oppression that influence their actions and their evaluation of the world; they can analyze their ties and commitments to children, lovers, friends, employers, family of origin, and others; they can assess their own talents and limits and choose how they will contribute to the well-being of others. Women cannot change other people, or provide for all their needs, or change many aspects of social organization. "Good women" may need a new image of responsibility that includes letting go of obligations imposed on them and of the expectation that they can control other people's behavior and that allows them to choose obligations that honor everyone involved.

By contrast, reflecting on what men and women can contribute to a relationship and acknowledging that both men and women have needs, desires, preferences, faults, and abilities and are capable of caring for themselves and of recruiting the help they need can help women attribute responsibility more accurately. In addition, reconsidering what social, political, and economic institutions owe children and other dependents would also keep mothers and other women from being held solely responsible for the well-being of children. By challenging existing expectations and reevaluating the underlying institutional framework, we can make it possible for battered women, and indeed all women, to develop stronger and more assertive personalities.

4

Textual Harassment: Desire
and the Female Body

Margaret R. Miles

In his *Lives of the Most Eminent Philosophers*, the Roman author Diogenes Laertius made the puzzling observation that "even the despising of pleasure is pleasurable."[1] The fourth-century Christian Gregory of Nazianzus referred to "the pleasure of no pleasure."[2] More recently, in *Middlemarch*, George Eliot had Celia say that Dorothea "likes giving up."[3] In what sense is "giving up"—asceticism—pleasurable? In this chapter I will suggest that it is necessary to entertain the odd notion that what might be interpreted as "negative" or destructive behavior could have not merely productive but even pleasurable effects.

1. Diogenes Laertius, *Lives of the Most Eminent Philosophers* VI.2.70, trans. R. D. Hicks (New York: Putnam, 1925).
2. Gregory of Nazianzus, *De oratione* 6, cited by Herbert Musurillo, S. J., "The Problem of Ascetical Fasting in the Greek Patristic Writers," *Traditio* 12 (1956): 6.
3. George Eliot, *Middlemarch*, ed. David Carroll (New York: Oxford University Press, 1986), 42.

How would contemporary understandings of eating disorders change if this complex phenomenon were described as a kind of perverse pleasure, the amazing, poignant, sturdy pleasure of a plant seeking light in a crowded forest? If theorists and clinicians attend only to potential or actual destructive effects, I am persuaded, we will fail to identify useful strategies for addressing those less-than-desirable effects. When eating disorders are understood as a dangerous, "kinky" pleasure, the clinical task will be to identify and cultivate more direct and unambiguous satisfactions. In short, effective treatment of the 90 percent of anorexics and bulimics who are women will involve exercising and strengthening female desire, providing it with the support of multiple and diverse models, symbolic authorization, and a repertoire of textual warrants. Examining the social construction of desire and its goal, pleasure, will therefore be central to my argument.

I believe there is an important connection between the social construction of female desire in middle-class North American society and asceticism, "the pleasure of no pleasure." I understand desire not only as sexual desire but also as including a broader repertoire of desire for particular social roles and achievements. Desire is preliminary to pleasure and integrally entailed in its production. Recently, Teresa de Lauretis remarked on the "weakness" of female desire, "its lack of authorization, symbolic representation, support and encouragement."[4] This observation is an important one: if female desire— eros—is not cultivated, or if it is construed merely as the complement to male desire, this could help to explain why so many young women practice and enjoy the asceticism of fasting.

There are two fundamentally different approaches to thinking about desire. Forty years ago Herbert Marcuse pictured sexual desire as radically at odds with the constraints of societies, a wild card, undomesticated, on which the individual could base rebellion against society; one's sexuality organized the "true," uncolonized "self."[5] More recently, Michel Foucault argued against Marcuse's model in which an untouched, pristine, free, stock of desire—an individual property—is appropriated by society, trained to serve its economic,

4. Teresa de Lauretis, "The Essence of Triangle or, Taking the Risk of Essentialism Seriously: Feminist Theory in Italy, the U.S., and Britain," in *Differences: A Journal of Feminist Critical Studies* 1, no. 2 (Summer 1989): 22.

5. Herbert Marcuse, in *Eros and Civilization* (Boston: Beacon Press, 1955), extended Freud's analysis of civilization as based on instinctual renunciation and the sublimation of sexuality, in *Civilization and Its Discontents*, trans. J. Riviere (London: Hogarth Press, 1930) and *The Future of an Illusion*, trans. W. D. Robson-Scott (London: Hogarth Press, 1928).

emotional, and social ends. Rather he pictured individual desire as socially produced and conditioned, as *called into existence* as well as shaped by society.

Using Foucault's model, Frigga Haug, a German feminist, has analyzed female sexualization. She discusses the complex and intricate process by which women learn to please others, to attract the male glance and gaze. Female sexualization, a crucial aspect of socialization she says, is intimately concerned with achieving the right body parts—the right hair, breasts, legs—and behavior—the right walk, the right eye movements. Female desire, then, is socially constructed as the passive complement of male desire rather than as a distinctive female "I want."[6] If a strong and centered desire is not primarily a personal attribute or capacity but is produced by one's socialization, it is evident that the lack of an active, effective, distinctive female desire is the result of a "lack of symbolic authorization" combined with a lack of institutional recognition and confirmation. So women's longings never take form—individually or collectively—as a powerful force. Moreover, if Western societies fail to provide authorization and symbolic representations of positive pleasure, the practice of refusing the problematic pleasures "provided" is likely to become pleasurable. "No pleasure," not only as a refusal of the pleasures to which one is socialized but also as a set of performative practices, can develop a "personalized" desire.

Understanding eating disorders as, in some sense, pleasurable provides a conceptual handle that is useful for clinical as well as for theoretical purposes. I will contest both the understanding of eating disorders as an attempt by the powerless to control *something*, and the suggestion that young women starve themselves in order to look like the models they see in the media. Anorexia nervosa will, I think, prove impervious to understanding or treatment until they can be seen as a female strategy for imagining and achieving pleasure. That the range of behavior labeled eating disorders is also dangerously self-destructive and that it also punishes families, communities, and society is evident. But theoretically positioned as *effects* rather than as causes or motivations, punishment of self and others appears as secondary to its production of pleasure.

Asceticism, then, not only *expresses* desire; it also acts to resist socialization. Resistance, we should note, assumes an unwanted socialization to resist. Asceticism is an alternative to the pleasure of assuming the roles and capabilities established by one's society. Unlike that of the person who accepts socializa-

6. Frigga Haug et al., *Female Sexualization*, trans. Erika Carter (London: Verso, 1987).

tion, the ascetic's desire refuses socially designated objects and instead seeks its object in an activity of alternative self-construction. In its practical strategies for resistance, asceticism exposes the social construction of the gendered "I," challenging and subverting the illusion of naturalness that characterizes the socialized self. Consciously chosen and practiced, asceticism is pleasurable. It becomes counterproductive—more painful than pleasurable, even potentially physically destructive—when fascination with practices and their effects assumes centrality. Asceticism in itself, then, is not inevitably "positive" or "negative." In the abstract it is neutral—simply a methodology or tool; close examination of particular practices in specific contexts is required to determine whether ascetic practices accomplish the purposes for which they are intended and, if they do, whether the cost to the individual or to society seems to outweigh the benefits.

I will first consider some descriptions of the connection between desire and pleasure in the dominantly Christian West, examining one influential textual construction of (male) desire, St. Augustine's *Confessions*, in order to demonstrate the specificity of desire as gendered. Then I will sketch an understanding of eating disorders that provides incentives for women to seek and to create more direct and effective pleasures than the "pleasure of no pleasure."

I

In the Christian West, a myth of individual autonomy, self-directedness, a chosen self that is cultivated, exercised, trained and has articulated and examined values continues to exert attractive force. This myth may have a corrective function in societies that are deeply embedded in traditional ideas, practices, and social arrangements. It may also function to encourage individuation in societies in which mass communication media socialize under the guise of entertaining or informing. However, the accuracy and specific productivity of orienting myths as well as their effects in particular social contexts must be continuously examined. If the myth of autonomous individuality has indeed reflected anyone's experience in North American and Western European cultures, it has seldom been true for women. Linked to other people by kinship, marriage, and reproduction, women have rarely represented themselves as solitary "self-actualizing" entities.

As early as the third century of the Common Era, self-shaping desire was recognized to be a male prerogative. In the late Roman period, women who resisted traditional roles in order to create and cultivate a religious "self" whether in one of the philosophical schools, in Christianity, or in Judaism, were spoken of as "becoming male." Chosen, intentional behavior was clearly understood as a male prerogative. Nevertheless, countercultural religious and philosophical communities recognized—had a context for understanding— these women's behavior.

In societies that lack symbolic representations of female aspiration, women who have dared to formulate distinctive desires and to act these out in a deliberately chosen life-style have usually encountered scorn, misunder-standing, and, often, violence.[7] Throughout the West, folktales, novels, and— more recently—films depict the flamboyant life of Joan of Arc, or Anna Ka-renina, Madame Bovary, Isadora Duncan, or Camille Claudel only to conclude with a narration of their alcoholism, insanity, or painful and ignominious death in youth or early middle age. Indeed, these stories can often claim the status of biography—real life—thereby reinforcing their effectiveness as cautionary tales and illustrating again Antigone's observation: "As in the past, this law is immutable: for mortals greatly to live is greatly to suffer."

It may be true that to disregard the conventional wisdom advocating a life of moderation and obedience to one's socialization is dangerous to "mortals." Nevertheless, there has been, and currently is, in late twentieth-century North America and Western Europe, social tolerance for the possibility—even the expectation—that young men will enjoy a more or less extended period of social rebellion and sexual experimentation. In the male-designed and admin-istered societies of the West, however, women who attempt to behave in unconventional ways inevitably meet myriad covertly and overtly powerful strategies of restraint and opposition. Through socialization, female desire is strongly directed to traditional roles, roles that are crucial to the reproduction of society, especially in the bearing and rearing of children. Multiple rewards and punishments reinforce this socialization with precisely the necessary amount of forcefulness. The sensory and emotional pleasures entailed in resisting socialization can be considerable.

7. Differences according to class and race need, of course, to be taken into account; it has certainly always been more likely that a wealthy noblewoman of a dominant race could act as she chose than that a working-class woman could. Nevertheless, women of all classes who resisted female socialization to conventional marriage and motherhood have fre-quently met dramatic and untimely ends, both in life and in literature.

II

What are the pleasures of "giving up"? The relief of psychic pain can be one such effect. Because body and psyche are interconnected, the psyche's pain can be reproduced in the body, bringing it to the surface where it can find expression. For example, the starving psyche might be acted out as a starving body, replacing involuntary pain with voluntary—chosen and controlled—pain. Asceticism may be, in fact, the most direct way to vent the psyche—a democratic, accessible method of relieving psychic pain. It was Karl Marx who said: "There is only one antidote to mental suffering, and that is physical pain."[8]

Asceticism also offers some sensory pleasures of which historical authors have been well aware. Thomas Aquinas spoke of a "renewal of the senses" that occurs as a result of sensory deprivation. Augustine also acknowledged that the sense of taste, for example, is dehabituated by a fast. He even warned against fasting for what he considered the questionable purpose of clarifying the palate! From Catherine of Genoa, with her predilection for maggots, to the twentieth-century manic depressive John Custance, with his fascination with dirt and excrement, ascetics have repeatedly insisted that ordinarily common or repugnant objects become almost unbearably sensuous when, through various ascetic practices, the senses are stripped of their conditioning to aversion and attraction.[9] In fact, the perennial claim of ascetics is that asceticism creates more—not less—pleasure.

The common core of these claims for the "pleasure of no pleasure" is that asceticism dehabituates and sensitizes the senses, forging a permeable and vivid connection between the living body and the psyche. Perhaps the question ultimately is: "What sets the body thinking?"[10] In health and ordinary circumstances, psyche and body seem to maintain a tenuous connection at best; one's body comes to be noticed only when it "acts up." Ascetic practices, however, alter the body world and make the mind notice that it feels, not more-of-the-same, but different and differently.

Moreover, asceticism and hedonism have much in common. In hedonism, the discipline is excess rather than deprivation, but in either case the

8. Karl Marx, *Herr Vogt*, trans. Stanley Edgar Hyman, as quoted in *The Tangled Bank: Darwin, Marx, Frazer and Freud as Imaginative Writers* (New York: Grosset and Dunlap, 1966), 118.

9. The inversion of socialization is itself pleasurable. In *The Powers of Horror*, Julia Kristeva has observed that "one of the insights of Christianity . . . is to have gathered in a single move perversion and beauty as the lining and the cloth of a single garment" (New York: Columbia University Press, 1982), 125.

10. Drew Leder, *The Absent Body* (Chicago: University of Chicago Press, 1990), 171.

body is *worked*. Just as asceticism can be pleasurable, hedonism can be the sternest asceticism of all;[11] addiction to pleasures regularly requires the renunciation of comfort and security. Hedonism's effects on the body can even parallel those of the harshest asceticism in causing pain and disease; hedonism can be *hard on the body*. Moreover, asceticism can be more erotic than hedonism: instead of creating fatigue and habituation, asceticism saturates the denied object with affect so that it becomes magic.

In *The Ascetic Imperative in Culture and Criticism*, Geoffrey Galt Harpham made a breakthrough identification of the powerful dynamic at work in asceticism.[12] Working on the literature of the fourth-century ascetic movement in Christianity, he asked himself why men who had left the sexual stimulation of cities for the isolation of an eremitic life in the Egyptian desert should constantly be preoccupied with "demons" in the guise of beautiful and lascivious women. Nor could he doubt that many of these authors—like Evagrius Ponticus—were highly sophisticated in psychology. To be sure, they had not read B. F. Skinner's experiments, but they knew that the best way to avoid temptation was simply to busy oneself with other matters. Given their sophistication *and* their preoccupation with sex, Harpham deduced that the dynamic of temptation and resistance was the method by which these ascetics "took hold on their souls"—as one fourth-century ascetic put it. Strong desire, powerfully evoked but denied its object, brings desire to consciousness, makes it accessible. Desire can then be worked with, pointed toward an object of choice, *designed*. Indeed, the primary pleasure of asceticism may be the dynamic of temptation and resistance that enables the ascetic to create a countercultural "self," a consciously chosen and cultivated interior life.

III

What would "authorization" of desire look like?[13] In order to convincingly support my claim that women lack such authorization, I will discuss the gender specificity evident in one of the "great Western texts" on desire, Au-

11. As Epicurus clearly saw when he defined pleasure as the absence of pain, rather than the more "positive" pleasures of sumptuous and excessive diet and drink, parties and lovemaking, since these inevitably entail physical and emotional pain.

12. Geoffrey Galt Harpham, *The Ascetic Imperative in Culture and Criticism* (Chicago: University of Chicago Press, 1987).

13. This section is adapted from my book *Desire and Delight: A New Reading of Augustine's "Confessions"* (New York: Crossroad, 1991).

gustine's Confessions.[14] The Confessions centrally and primarily concerns satisfying desire, getting—and keeping—the greatest pleasure. It is explicitly about desire, longing, and passion—both physical and spiritual—and both most evidently when Augustine most intends to distinguish spiritual from physical. It is an erotic text, a book preoccupied with bodies, pleasures, and pains. It is not, however, as is usually claimed or assumed, about "human" desire; it is about its author's desire—Augustine's desire.

It is instructive to analyze why and how Augustine became a model of physical and spiritual desire. Having deconstructed this powerful (male) model, we can begin to construct other models more consonant with women's experiences, more challenging and supportive of women, and—not incidentally—more responsive to the desperate need of our endangered planet for more responsible models of subjectivity and desire.

The Confessions narrates Augustine's life story in order to demonstrate the mysterious path by which, by pursuing the objects of his desire most aggressively (and destructively, to himself and other people) he was led unerringly to an expansive, intense, and fruitful desire, which he names as the desire for God. Augustine's autobiography has been powerfully influential in constructing what is recognized and authorized as desire in Western societies. The influence of books and ideas should not be exaggerated; "great ideas" do not, of course, explain why the world is as it is and why people act as they do. Nevertheless, the Confessions contributed to shaping Western values and therefore to designing social arrangements and institutions, especially heterosexuality, marriage, monasticism, and the church.

It is important to acknowledge at the outset that my "reading" of the Confessions is necessarily and inevitably affected by my own social location as a late twentieth-century academic Anglo-Saxon woman. It is, moreover, a disobedient reading because I notice and note features of the text that—although there—would, perhaps, be overlooked by an ancient reader or a twentieth-century male reader. In recognizing and acknowledging my perspectival reading, however, I admit only what any honest reader must acknowledge—that is, the lack of a universal, transcendent, or God's-eye perspective from which to interpret.

The strange discovery I made recently in rereading the Confessions is that, in my former readings, I had obediently assumed the position of the sympathetic

14. Augustine, The Confessions of St. Augustine, trans. Rex Warner (New York: New American Library, 1963).

male colleague for whom Augustine wrote. The *Confessions* was not written to be read by a woman; to read it with "understanding" is to read it as a man—an educated skill. The difficult and interesting task, then, is to produce a gendered reading: not only to notice Augustine's actual and textual treatment of women, but also to recognize that the metaphor that dominates his construction of pleasure is male sexuality. Furthermore, Augustine's sexual experience is not accidental or incidental to the primary concerns of the *Confessions*. In spite of his loud and frequent disclaimers, Augustine learned more than he acknowledged from his own experience of sex; he learned what Audre Lorde has called "the deep and irreplaceable knowledge of [his] capacity for joy" from his sexual experience.[15]

In his *Confessions*, Augustine narrates his own desire from infancy forward as a compulsive grasping at every object that crossed his path in the fear that something would be missed—his word for his anxious rapaciousness is concupiscence. From stealing pears from a neighbor's tree, to professional success as a teacher of rhetoric, to sexual experience, Augustine energetically pursued sex, power, and possession until he pushed himself to the point of intellectual and emotional collapse.

He did not recount the destructive effects of his aggressions on other people. My curiosity about the woman with whom he lived for thirteen years and who bore their son—a woman whose name he never mentioned—is not satisfied in the *Confessions*. He did give a rather more ample account of his mother, Monica; he described her as focused single-mindedly on himself, his happiness, and his salvation through Catholic Christianity. Though Monica had a husband and other children, her son pictured her as completely and passionately attached to himself, following him from North Africa to Milan, praying continually for him with tears "which fell streaming and watered the ground beneath her eyes in every place where she prayed." Monica was, according to Augustine's report, a passionate woman, but her passion was confined to her relationship with God and Augustine. Augustine placed her on a pedestal, a model of selfless female desire: "I cannot express how she loved me and how she labored with much greater pain to give me birth in the spirit than she had labored when giving birth to me in the flesh." We learn little of her own subjectivity or of any woman's subjectivity from Augustine's heroic epic. The women of the tale are only there as part of Augustine's support system.

The central moment in Augustine's autobiography, the moment for which

15. Audre Lorde, *Sister Outsider* (Freedom, Calif.: Crossing Press, 1989), 57.

the book is famous, is that of Augustine's conversion. Curiously, it was not a moment of intellectual insight, religious ecstasy, or belief or faith. Augustine described this experience quite explicitly as a conversion from compulsive sexual activity to continence.

Prefiguring and mirroring his conversion, Augustine, juxtaposed images of himself as alternately distracted or dispersed among pleasures or gathered and collected in a disciplined "return" to himself and to God throughout the *Confessions*. His model of the spiritual life as re-collection has become the dominant model of Western Christian subjectivity and spirituality and has, in the twentieth century, passed into secular culture in the form of numerous varieties of psychotherapy and secular spirituality. The model is one of centering, of arresting the hemorrhage of energy and attention that flows out of the self toward other human beings and objects of all sorts and pulling that energy within, collecting, focusing, centering. This was Augustine's model. It is based on Augustine's sexual experience, and I question its usefulness as a model for women and for late twentieth-century people in general. Augustine's clearest definition of the model occurs in the following passage:

> I have been spilled and scattered among times whose order I do not know; my thoughts, the innermost bowels of my soul, are torn apart with the crowding tumults of variety, and so it will be until all together I can flow into you [God], purified and molten by the fire of your love.

Re-collection, continence was, for Augustine, both a literal practice, a renunciation of sexual activity, and his model of the spiritual life. His image of sin as "turning away from you, God, toward lower things—casting away, as it were, its own insides, and swelling with desire for what is outside," being "spilled and scattered" are almost embarrassingly direct and literal allusions to male orgasm. Continence, on the other hand was, for Augustine, the pivotal point of change. Again, his model was concrete and explicit, based on retention of seminal fluid:

> The Word calls you to come back . . . you will lose nothing. What is withered in you will flower again, and all your illnesses will be made well, and all that was flowing and wasting from you will regain shape and substance and will form part of you again.[16]

16. Augustine, *Confessions* XI.29.

In Augustine's physical and spiritual universe, the hoarding of seminal fluid became both practice and paradigm for an integrated life. My intention in calling attention to the physical model of Augustine's subjectivity is not to discredit or minimize his powerful description of the inner life. It is, however, to help us see that the re-collected life is but one form of interior development; it is not the only or the necessary form. Other models of subjectivity need to be imagined, fleshed out, and embodied.

As his own writings demonstrate, Augustine was well aware of the danger of his construction of desire and subjectivity; he knew that he must *keep* insisting that he intended no disparagement of the objects of the sensible world in urging detachment from them. Yet his formulation of the inner life as a withdrawal from attachment to the world of senses and objects, from other people and the natural world, has played a role in creating the present condition of the earth and of human society. Alternatives to Augustine's model are desperately needed, models that respond to the crises of our own day by emphasizing attention to, and affection for, the vulnerable and threatened earth, by energizing committed labor for peace and justice, and by illuminating the spiritual discipline of loving relationship and community.

As a "great text of the Western world," the *Confessions* has played a role in the social construction of desire. This powerful statement of desire and fulfill-ment has formed and informed Western people's amorphous, polymorphous, multiple, and inarticulate longings. But what we have thought of as "human" desire is always marked by the particularities of individual lives, by socially constructed gender assumptions, expectations, and roles, by social location, institutional affiliation, class, and race. If the claim that desire is socially con-structed and differentiated according to these factors seems farfetched, attempt to imagine a female protagonist of the *Confessions*. Could Augustine's demand-ing, energetic, aggressive passion have occurred—much less been admired and become a classic formulation of physical and spiritual desire—in a woman, in his time or in ours?

I am envious of the social construction and support of Augustine's pas-sion, both his relentless pursuit of worldly satisfaction and his latter passionate love of God, combined with institutional authority. To search frantically, des-perately; to long restlessly, lustfully, feverishly; to embody the kind of consum-ing and complex desire that knows its object when it touches it; few women have sustained such uncompromising desire, at least partly because women have had few literary paradigms, few images, few models. In the societies of the

Christian West, women's desire has been constructed to serve male desire as its mirror and counterpart.

The lack of female models does not mean, of course, that no women have managed to formulate and pursue a distinctive desire; it does mean that it is immensely more difficult for women to do so in societies that have no female epic heroes, no models but male models for passionately seeking women. Many—though not most—women have learned to use male models, to adopt, adapt, or rebel against these models of heroic hunger. Educated women have learned to read as men, blind to the biology and socialization, the institutions, and the legal and social arrangements that have *authorized* the author.

A gendered reading of the *Confessions* is attentive to who speaks and who listens; it reveals the myriad ways that the male author's experience informs and gives body to his text. It is certainly significant that Augustine critiqued his society's construction of male sexuality, equating tumescence and the myth of male helplessness in the face of sexual urges with pride and sin. He experienced, he says, a vast relief and freedom in the practice of continence. Later in his career he formulated a model of sexuality based on principles of complementarity and responsibility. This was not a model he had ever lived, and it did not go as far as to imagine equality and mutuality, but it became an enormously influential model. No alternative model could hope to produce the social effects of a model of heterosexual relationship that enjoyed the institutional and personal authority of Augustine himself.

IV

Let us return to the "pleasure of no pleasure." How can a fruitful approach to eating disorders be sketched? Let us first consider briefly two contemporary authors who have addressed the problem. Caroline Walker Bynum, in *Holy Feast and Holy Fast*,[17] explores the food attitudes and practices of medieval religious women, concluding that they were often able to gather social and religious authority by their abstinence from food. Bynum, who is an insightful and perceptive historian, understands the social and religious context in which these medieval women lived. In an epilogue, however, she argues that there is no connection between medieval women who fasted for religious reasons and contemporary women who fast, she says, simply in order to achieve the

17. Caroline Walker Bynum, *Holy Feast and Holy Fast: The Religious Significance of Food to Medieval Women* (Berkeley: University of California Press, 1987).

slender boyish body that is repetitiously reiterated in fashion magazines, on television, and in films.

I question whether Bynum's medieval women are as unrelated to contemporary fasting women as she claims. Common to both medieval and twentieth-century North American middle-class women is the fact that they lived—and live—in male designed and administered societies. Both groups of women operate in societies that deny them collective power in the public sphere, societies in which they are largely unable to affect the institutions that legislate and enforce the particular social arrangements that shape their lives.

Bynum misses the opportunity of demonstrating that modern anorexics who starve themselves, complaining that their bodies are "too big" might, like medieval women, be describing an unbearable asymmetry between their cultural provisions and support, and their personal yearning. Twentieth-century women are socialized to confine their longings to concern for physical attractiveness—that is, to anxiety regarding their value as commodities in a consumer culture. Like medieval women, twentieth-century women live in a culture that neglects to incite, encourage, and provide support for women's intellectual, psychological, and spiritual development. Eating disorders might be seen as a form of resistance to a society in which the bodies of young women are "too big" a focus of attention in relation to intellectual, psychological, and spiritual aspects of women's lives. By contrast to her society's attention to her body, a young woman experiences her subjectivity as too small, underdeveloped, unable to balance the body whose social significance is so huge. Bynum finds in medieval women's food practices a "resonance and complexity" that emerges only when these practices are placed in their "full context."[18] A similar study of twentieth-century anorexics might fruitfully identify the full context of modern women's use of food as tool or weapon, seeking in it the "range and richness" that Bynum finds in medieval women's food practices.

The problems of women who live in societies designed and administered by men have some fundamental similarities, despite enormous differences in particularities. These problems revolve around two foci: first, the cultivation of a subjectivity that is *defined* neither by social conditioning nor by rebellion from the normative male subjectivity, and second, imagining and constructing social roles that are not *assigned* by male projection, language, economics, and pleasure. In my book *Carnal Knowing: Female Nakedness and Religious Meaning in the Christian West*, I proposed three conditions I consider essential for progress

18. Ibid., 298; Bynum's emphasis.

toward equitable social arrangements between men and women.[19] Women must have (1)access to public space—in media and institutions—in which to (2)develop a collective voice that will enable them to (3)represent themselves as subjects of their own experience rather than as objects of male projections.

Susan Bordo's article "*Anorexia Nervosa*: Psychopathology as the Crystallization of Culture"[20] identifies a grid on which the "control axis" and the "gender/power axis" intersect to produce the phenomenon of anorexia nervosa. Bordo's complex analysis enables her to glimpse the dynamic of temptation and resistance in the behavior of fasting women. Anorexic women, she says, "are as obsessed with *hunger* as they are with being thin." She quotes women who describe their *pleasure* in fasting—what I have called "the pleasure of no pleasure." Bordo's analysis suggests that what must be asked is how eating disorders are produced by constraint, that is, by the foreclosure of more directly pleasurable routes.

I will close by suggesting that the primary pleasure of asceticism is the development of a centered, chosen self, built up gradually from the many decisions, the many choices, the many disciplines occurring over a period of time. In eating disorders the issue is not control but the shaping of a self that is nowhere required, supported, or suggested in values circulated in the public sphere of a media culture. The crucial question is this: what feature(s) of human experience does a society designate as symbolic of self, revelatory of the truth of who-one-is?

In Augustine's world, sexuality played this role so that the way to develop subjectivity was to scrutinize and manage sexual activity. That arena of self-expression, however, seems presently to be exhausted, enervated, perhaps, by the public circulation of a hedonistic rhetoric that promotes sex as good, healthy, invigorating, and recreative—even though the reality of many people's experience may be otherwise. The early medieval ascetic's imaginative dynamic of sexual temptation and resistance and the later medieval women's abstention from food has been superseded by the anorexic's preoccupation with food. In a consumer society, the arena of struggle and self-definition chosen by many young women is food, a commodity that is everywhere,

19. Margaret R. Miles, *Carnal Knowing: Female Nakedness and Religious Meaning in the Christian West* (Boston: Beacon, 1989; New York: Vintage, 1991).

20. Susan Bordo, "*Anorexia Nervosa*: Psychopathology as the Crystallization of Culture," in *Feminism and Foucault*, ed. Irene Diamond and Lee Quinby (Boston: Northeastern University Press, 1988).

requiring constant opposition. And this *activity* of desire, temptation, and re-sistance can be intensely pleasurable.

This analysis suggests that clinical approaches to treatment must identify more direct, more complex, and polymorphous—more *satisfying*—pleasures that could effectively create, focus, and direct desire around less dangerous self-definition than that achieved by eating disorders. Individual therapy, how-ever, is only part of the solution. Until women can define their distinctive desires and pleasures and gain symbolic representation and support for these desires in the public sphere, the private and privileged reeducation of desire can never hope to help more than a few; it cannot alter the epidemic of fasting women.

Part Two

Authority

and Cultural

Constructions

of the

"Good Body"

5

The Body as a Historical Category:
Science and Imagination,
1660–1760

Estelle Cohen

More than forty years ago, Simone de Beauvoir reminded us that Aristotle had taught many generations of scholars that "the female is a female by virtue of a certain lack of qualities."[1] Missing from her analysis, and even more tellingly

This chapter is an abbreviated version of several chapters of my forthcoming book, *Gender and the History of Gynecology: Constructing Biology as Social Knowledge ca. 1660–1860.* Since I began working on this paper, it has become almost commonplace to think about the body as a historical category. Therefore, it is only apt that I declare my debt at the outset to Jean-Pierre Vernant, who used the expression first (see note 50 for the complete reference): perhaps it is not such a new idea after all.

Financial support from The John Rylands Research Institute of the University of Manchester made preparation of this manuscript possible; I particularly wish to acknowledge the generous assistance of David Miller and Valerie Ferguson. It is a pleasure to thank Monica Green and Helen King for their learned and thoughtful comments.

1. Simone de Beauvoir, *The Second Sex* (Harmondsworth: Penguin Books, 1972), 15–16; first published in 1949 as *Le Deuxième Sexe*. Contemporary scientific literature on sex determi-

from those of recent, better informed historians of science and medicine, is an appreciation of the powerful alternative traditions of thought that have remained largely hidden from history. Study of comparative anatomy intensified around 1660, with results that sometimes have had to be recovered in recent years because of the neglect, indifference, or, more often, downright hostility of contemporaries and succeeding generations. My interest in the matter relates to my growing conviction of the selection of traditions in the history of medicine, as in other kinds of history, and my interest in the wider social and political debates that help explain why particular medical views and technologies have either prevailed, been lost, or been deliberately discarded at particular times. As a gender historian I am drawn especially to debates about sexual difference, to arguments about gender that attempt to ground social distinctions on alleged biological distinctions, and therefore to the cultural and social significance that controversies regarding female biology acquired during the centuries after 1660.

Attempts to ground social differences between the sexes on presumed natural differences were widely disparaged during the century after 1660. Significant numbers of informed commentators contested the view that female biology provided a sound basis for female subjection, arguing instead that women's "understanding appears in every way similar to that of men," that there is "no natural impediment in the structure of our bodies" either, and that "all the researches of anatomy have not yet been able to show the least difference [apart from reproductive organs] between Men and Women."[2] One physician urged women to read medical books, claiming that knowledge of their own anatomy would permit "inward government" of their bodies.[3] Another, however, noting the lack of agreement among physicians and their tendency to perpetuate myths about women, exclaimed with undisguised glee that fables abound about the menses, which "tho' recounted by many grave and some great Authors, I reject, . . . and have only recited . . . to shew what things have been superstitiously credited without sufficient examination by

nation similarly tells a tale in which the female is defined by an *absence*, although other narratives based on the same facts could be constructed. See, for example, the discussions of this literature by Anne Fausto-Sterling, "Society Writes Biology/Biology Constructs Gender," in *Learning about Women*, ed. Jill K. Conway et al. (Ann Arbor: University of Michigan Press, 1987), 64–69; and Judith Butler, *Gender Trouble* (New York: Routledge, 1990), 106–11.

2. Emilie du Châtelet, from the preface to her translation of Bernard Mandeville's *Fable of the Bees* (1735), quoted in translation in Esther Ehrman, *Mme. du Châtelet: Scientist, Philosopher and Feminist of the Enlightenment* (Leamington Spa: Berg, 1986), 61; Judith Drake, *An Essay in Defence of the Female Sex* (London, 1696), 12; "Sophia," *Woman Not Inferior to Man* (London, 1739), 24.

3. Bernard Mandeville, *The Virgin Unmask'd* (London, 1709), 123.

men of great Authority who have been prevailed upon to believe what the women at all times would laugh at."[4]

Medical arguments about female anatomy and physiology in the period around 1700, so far from supporting dominant social attitudes, often contested them; that is, an important body of medical opinion rejected both old and new theories, both popular and learned traditions which continued to represent women as inferior and defective versions of men. One reason why attempts to account for women's subordination in household and society chiefly by reference to female biology ran aground in this period was the general failure to agree on the presumed natural differences between the sexes. On the one hand, among the diversity of opinions respecting female bodies current at the time, none commanded immediate assent. Examination of a range of medical texts suggests that scientific writings, like other kinds of public discourses, offered different, often ambivalent, and sometimes contradictory ways of construing female nature. Well-known, highly regarded, and widely read medical writers confessed that there were a number of important questions about women's bodies that they could not answer, indicating their uncertainty, for example, about how conception takes place as well as the causes of menstruation. A considerable and growing number of writers now argued that the multitude of disorders traditionally ascribed to the uterus by scores of learned authorities were probably due to factors that had little if anything to do with the uterus. Although increasing numbers of physicians were clearly distinguishing between the functions of male and female sexual organs, they did not yet differentiate the sexual needs and experiences of men and women. Unable to confirm the truth of a particular theory by a variety of empirical tests then available, many concluded that the current state of medical knowledge often did not allow unambiguous resolutions of particular problems.[5]

For all these reasons, among others, recent work in the history of science and medicine probably exaggerates the extent to which new research in comparative sexual anatomy and embryology influenced social attitudes in this period. For one thing, unless the sheer range and downright uncertainty of medical opinions were either misrepresented or overlooked—as indeed they

---

4. James Drake, *Anthropologia Nova; or, A New System of Anatomy* (London, 1717; also 1707, 1727, and 1750), I, 176–77. This two-volume text was posthumously published and edited by his sister, Judith Drake (see note 2), who was also an unlicensed medical practitioner.

5. For example: Michael Ettmueller, *Etmullerus Abridg'd; or, A Compleat System of the Theory and Practice of Physic* (London, 1699 and 1706); M. de la Vauguion, *A Compleat Body of Chirugical Operations* (London, 1699, 1707, and 1716); *Riverius Reformatus ; or, The Modern Riverius*, trans. Bernard Mandeville (London, 1706, 1713).

were in the popular sex manuals appearing on all sides from the end of the seventeenth century—they could not be used to confirm social and cultural assumptions about female inferiority.[6] It may also be the case that the teachings of biology and medicine were only occasionally taken as sources of authoritative social knowledge before the end of the eighteenth century.

In a curious set of dialogues between a maiden aunt and her niece published in 1709, women were advised to study their own anatomy: after all, we are told, it takes no more time, skill, or effort to read an anatomy text than to complete an intricate piece of filigree.[7] This, in a book by a Dutch doctor practicing in London, which also warned graphically of the legal penalties and physical disabilities women suffer in marriage and childbearing, particularly in England, and which most unusually featured an informed political discussion between the two women, all under what I take to be a deliberately misleading title, The Virgin Unmask'd. Even the volume's table of contents proves untrustworthy: for it lures the reader into expecting a tale of illicit sex, which in the event the author, Bernard Mandeville, apparently forgets to tell. Although he promises at the book's end to continue the narrative in a succeeding volume, the sequel in fact never appears.

If words are clearly so deceptive, are images any less so? Indeed, do readers and writers around 1700 expect them to be reliable, to accurately depict some actual reality however that is understood? Does a strictly literal reading of texts in this period help us to understand their meaning? To what extent is the presumption that seeing is believing useful in any attempt to reconstruct widely shared cultural beliefs and assumptions in the century after 1660? In particular, I wish to argue that new optical instruments, new medical practices, and new technologies associated with print that both enhanced and extended visibility—indeed brought the body's interior as well as its surface into view in ways never possible before—did not yet enjoy the confidence and

6. Popular compilations falsely attributed to Aristotle, such as Aristotle's Masterpiece, began to appear in the 1670s. On vernacular medical texts in eighteenth-century England, see Mary E. Fissell, "Readers, Texts, and Contexts," in The Popularization of Medicine, ed. Roy Porter (London and New York: Routledge, 1992), 72–96; and Charles E. Rosenberg, "Medical Text and Social Context," Bulletin of the History of Medicine 57 (1983): 22–42.

7. Bernard Mandeville, The Virgin Unmask'd (London, 1709), 123. I have traced this theme to François Poullain de la Barre's De l'égalité de deux sexes, discours physique et moral, où l'on voit l'importance de se défaire des préjugez (Paris, 1673; English translation: The Woman as Good as the Man: Or, The Equality of Both Sexes [London, 1677]). There are two modern editions of this important work in the history of feminist thought: by A. Daniel Frankforter and Paul J. Morman for The Edwin Mellen Press, Lewiston, Lampeter, Queenston, 1989; and by Desmond M. Clarke for Manchester University Press, Manchester and New York, 1990.

status as reliable sources of scientific knowledge that technologies currently used in medical imaging, for example, apparently enjoy today. Quite the contrary. The new interest in acquiring and displaying vast collections of anatomical specimens, the growing obsession with preserving body parts, particularly parts of the female sexual anatomy, were suitably mocked by a noted Italian physician early in the eighteenth century. Giovanni Bianchi claimed to have collected whole shelves of jars filled with hymens—at a time when scores of reputable investigators doubted the actual physical existence of the hymen. He was of course also mocking the obsession with female virginity in a superbly ironic tale of a female cross-dresser.[8]

Persistent doubt about the usefulness of the new visual techniques was explained in a variety of ways. Physicians who found the microscope irrelevant to an understanding of the human body argued that microscopy gave no indication of function, was worthless as a diagnostic aid, and that the causes of diseases were invisible in any case. The microscope was a mere plaything, large numbers of the learned declared. No doubt, their assessment of its value was influenced to some extent by the easy availability and apparent popularity of portable microscopes among the less learned.[9]

As one would expect, skepticism about the ocular evidence or, more precisely, about the interpretations erected upon the data had much to do with what one was prepared to see. Therefore, we learn a good deal about specific medical controversies and about social and cultural theories that sought scientific foundation during this period from examining the debates about new medical practices. Often explicitly and unabashedly ideological, physicians and others denounced particular procedures and their practitioners in terms that suggest that their hostility may have derived from resistance to the lessons that microscopy and recent anatomical research could be said to have taught. Given present-day use of visualization and surveillance techniques to scrutinize, to exert authority, and to ground and communicate scientific opinions,

8. Giovanni Bianchi, *Historical and Physical Dissertation on the Case of Caterina Vizzani* (London, 1751). See also Giulia Sissa, "The Seal of Virginity," in *Zone 5: Fragments for a History of the Human Body*, part 3, ed. Michel Feher et al. (New York: Urzone, 1989), 143–56, especially 152–54 on the *Encyclopédie* article on "Virginitié."

9. See Kenneth Dewhurst, *Dr. Thomas Sydenham (1624–1689): His Life and Original Writings* (Berkeley and Los Angeles: University of California Press, 1966), especially 64–65 and 85–93; Dewhurst, *John Locke (1632–1704): Physician and Philosopher* (London: The Wellcome Historical Medical Library, 1963), especially 272–73; Lester King, *The Road to Medical Enlightenment, 1650–1695* (London: Macdonald, 1970), 119–20; Marjorie Nicolson, *The Microscope and English Imagination*, Smith College Studies in Modern Languages (Northampton, Mass.: Smith College, 1935).

we are understandably inclined to associate observation and experiment with a knowing that seeks to control, dominate, and displace. Therefore it is instructive, certainly surprising, to consider the quite different consequences that new ways of seeing—and naming—women's bodies appeared likely to produce in the view of feminist writers in the decades either side of 1700.

Controversies about female anatomy and physiology during the century after 1660 were often sparked by new ways of seeing women's bodies. The widespread skepticism that accompanied claims to knowledge based on the new medical practices of dissection and microscopy demonstrates that the link between visualization and knowledge widely presumed to exist in later periods was still vigorously contested.[10] My examination of these disputes refers to texts by medical practitioners that were widely read in their own day. Written in the vernacular and produced in small-format editions, they were almost certainly intended for a lay as well as a professional readership. Moreover, these texts (and a good many others) offer evidence of the extent to which powerful, enduring ideologies and images of women were being challenged in a range of discourses, including medical discourse. Analysis of this literature clearly offers evidence as well of distortions and omissions in the transmission of traditions in the history of medicine. Therefore, I wish to emphasize the need to analyze, not assume, the importance of medical arguments for social and cultural constructions of gender. Accepting that gender is a social fiction, I propose to ask: to what extent was this fiction constituted by medical theories and reinforced by medical practices in the period circa 1660 to 1760?

René Descartes's mind-body dualism was interpreted by his own and succeeding generations as legitimating the public careers of learned women, who then went on to argue, with others, that recent anatomical findings confirmed women's intellectual equality with men. That is, Cartesian women, and numbers of Cartesian men as well, took the separation of mind and body as a way of making physical differences between the sexes less significant and of asserting the equality of the sexes in rationality and will. They further pointed out that the new anatomy (as it was sometimes called) thoroughly

10. Among recent studies that explore the controversies associated with the new visual techniques, see Catherine Wilson, "Visual Surface and Visual Symbol: The Microscope and the Occult in Early Modern Europe," *Journal of the History of Ideas* (1988): 85–108; Michael Aaron Dennis, "Graphic Understanding: Instruments and Interpretation in Robert Hooke's *Micrographia*," *Science in Context* 3, no. 2 (Autumn 1989): 309–64; Steven Shapin and Simon Schaffer, *Leviathan and the Air-Pump* (Princeton: Princeton University Press, 1985), 36–40 and 55–79.

discredited inherited scientific traditions cited in defense of arguments for female inferiority and infirmity.[11]

Feminist discourse has long resisted claims that to be equal, men and women must be the same. As far back as the late seventeenth century, feminist writers recognized that male and female were not fixed or stable identities but relational and constructed.[12] Similarly, seventeenth-century accounts of the differences between male and female sexual anatomy, by Reinier de Graaf, a Dutch physician, and Jane Sharp, an English midwife, for example, clearly did not conclude that their views offered any basis for social and cultural arguments about female inferiority. On the contrary: like feminist writers from around 1670 (François Poullain de la Barre, Judith Drake, Catherine Macaulay, and Olympe de Gouges, for example), who labored to ground claims for equality on the recognition of differences, not sameness, they stressed that women's anatomical differences did not in any way diminish their worth. In other words, seventeenth-century medical opinions were sometimes cited in attempts to *collapse* traditional social and cultural hierarchies still being defended by reference to alleged natural differences between the sexes as well as to biblical teachings.

At the end of the eighteenth century, de Gouges reiterated the view that the sexes were differentiated only for the purposes of reproduction, that all members of a species had been endowed by "nature" with similar, but not necessarily identical, faculties.[13] By that time, however, the medical opinions that could have supported her rejection of fixed, categorical distinctions between male and female, opinions that had been widely publicized in a variety of texts up to about 1760, had already been submerged. Was there, then, a period when female was not defined by absence and passivity in important

11. Ruth Perry, "Radical Doubt and the Liberation of Women," *Eighteenth-Century Studies* 18, no. 4 (Summer 1985): 472–94; Erica Harth, *Cartesian Women* (Ithaca and London: Cornell University Press, 1992); Carolyn C. Lougee, *Le Paradis des Femmes: Women, Salons, and Social Stratification in 17th-Century France* (Princeton, N.J.: Princeton University Press, 1976); Catherine Gallagher, "Embracing the Absolute: The Politics of the Female Subject in 17th-Century England," *Genders* 1 (Spring 1988): 24–39.

12. See, for example, Mary Astell, *Reflections upon Marriage* (London, 1700, 1703, 1706, and 1730), now available in a modern edition, edited and introduced by Bridget Hill (Aldershot: Gower/Maurice Temple Smith, 1986); Anon., *Female Rights Vindicated; or the Equality of the Sexes Morally and Physically Proved* (London, 1758); Catherine Macaulay, *Letters on Education* (London, 1790).

13. On Olympe de Gouges, see especially Joan Wallach Scott, "French Feminists and the Rights of 'Man': Olympe de Gouge's Declarations," *History Workshop Journal* 28 (Autumn 1989): 1–21; and Harth, *Cartesian Women*, 213–39.

medical and scientific texts, when male and female were construed as neither homologous nor mutually exclusive, neither different versions of the same model nor oppositional yet complementary?[14] If there was such a time, and I obviously believe that there was, why have we learned so little about it from historians of medicine and science?

Investigation of medical debates about female biology in the period up to about 1760 establishes that new anatomical findings appeared to significant numbers of anatomists and physicians to challenge received ideas about the female's role in reproduction, the causes and nature of menstruation, and even the vexed question of the hymen's physical existence—a question increasingly regarded as distinct from the issue of virginity. Given the range of arguments on all these matters, it is perhaps not so surprising that Louis de Jaucourt, in his *Encyclopédie* article dealing with the wife's position in law, ambivalent though it may be, nevertheless concluded that positive, or man-made, law had misinterpreted biological evidence insofar as it invariably subjected the wife to her husband: as he put it, "It would be difficult to demonstrate that the husband's authority comes from nature." Similarly, William Alexander, an Edinburgh physician, queried male assumptions about female inferiority in his two-volume history of women: "This boasted preeminence of men is at least as much the work of art as of nature; [for] women in those savage states where both sexes are alike unadorned by culture are, perhaps, not at all inferior in abilities of mind to the other sex, and even scarcely inferior to them in strength of body."[15]

It is especially instructive to examine the controversies relating to generation, in particular the ongoing concern to pinpoint the relative contribution of the male and female to conception and heredity. Although these problems had been vigorously debated for more than a century, largely on the basis of human dissections and microscopic study, no resolution of the matter had emerged by the middle of the eighteenth century.[16] At that point, many of the protagonists

14. I take this model from Thomas Laqueur's provocative and useful study, *Making Sex: Body and Gender from the Greeks to Freud* (Cambridge and London: Harvard University Press, 1990), which in my view overlooks many of the complexities, varieties, and continuities in debates about women's bodies before the nineteenth century.

15. Louis, Chevalier de Jaucourt, "Femme (Droit Nat.)," in *L'Encyclopédie*, VI (Paris, 1756), 471–472. A translated excerpt is offered in the splendid collection of documents edited by Susan G. Bell and Karen M. Offen, *Women, the Family, and Freedom*, vol. 1, 1750–1880 (Stanford, Calif.: Stanford University Press, 1983), 34–36; William Alexander, *The History of Women*, 2 vols. (London and Edinburgh, 1779, 1782), II, 39.

16. On theories of generation in the seventeenth and eighteenth centuries, see Jacques Roger, *Les Sciences de la vie dans la pensée française du XVIIe siècle* (Paris: Armand Colin, 1963 and

impatiently sought clarity elsewhere, having convinced themselves of the insolubility of human reproduction.

In 1660 the teachings of Hippocrates, Aristotle, and Galen, as they were then understood, on conception and embryological development remained largely intact, although recent study of the structure of the ovaries suggested potentially subversive alternatives. From Aristotle (384–322 B.C.), early modern anatomists and physiologists learned a theory of conception that posited the idea of the female as providing merely the soil in which the male seed could grow. In Aristotle's view, the egg that developed into an embryo was a product of conception and could arise only out of the union of seed and soil (which was the catamenia, or menstrual coagulum). This view survived into the eighteenth century at least, although effective challenges to its ability to account for observable data began to be mounted from the sixteenth century onward. Galen (A.D. 129–ca. 210), aware of Herophilus' discovery of the ovaries around 300 B.C., transmitted to successive generations the view that women contribute a kind of seed that is also relevant to reproduction. Although Galen's two-seed theory holds that both the male and the female contribute to the matter of the fetus, he insisted that the female's seed is imperfect, scantier, colder, wetter, and less active than the male's. Some of the Hippocratic texts, on the other hand (late fifth and fourth centuries B.C.) clearly offered alternatives to ancient biological theories that supported the view of female inferiority. According to G. E. R. Lloyd, these writings "represent . . . important dissenting voices against the notion of the essential disparity between the contributions of the two parents."[17] Moreover, we know that these views found influential support throughout the ancient period. In other words, classical medical traditions respecting women's bodies were neither as uniformly misogynist nor as consensual as later generations would have us believe.

A significant change occurred from the late seventeenth century with the reemergence of contending theories of preformation and the scornful rejection of both theories by significant numbers of scholars. Preformationist hypotheses argued that the fetus preexisted in either the female egg or the male seed. The former view, ovism, developed from the analogy with egg-laying

---

1971), especially chapter 2; Elizabeth Gasking, *Investigations into Generation, 1651–1828* (Baltimore, Md.: Johns Hopkins University Press, 1966); L. W. B. Brockliss, "The Embryological Revolution in the France of Louis XIV: The Dominance of Ideology," in *The Human Embryo*, ed. G. R. Dunstan (Exeter: Exeter University Press, 1990), 158–86.

17. G. E. R. Lloyd, *Science, Folklore and Ideology: Studies in the Life Sciences in Ancient Greece* (Cambridge: Cambridge University Press, 1983), 94.

animals and the recent presumed discovery of ova in human females; the latter view, animalculism, received much of its impetus in this period from Antoni Leeuwenhoek's discovery of microscopic "animals" (that is, spermatozoa) in semen. The animalculists regarded the female as a kind of nest for the develop-ing embryo; some even denied the existence of eggs in female ovaries. The ovists, on the other hand, among whom were a number of influential teachers of anatomy and midwifery in the eighteenth century, while accepting that the female played a role in reproduction insofar as the infant was presumed to preexist in the ovum, nevertheless stressed the animating responsibility of the male semen. Thus, Marcello Malpighi (1628–94), for example, explained, "The egg is weak and powerless and so requires the energy of the semen of the male to initiate growth." Others imagined that the relatively inert egg was "shaken" into life by the sperm, whose intervention allowed it to "escape" into the fallopian tube.[18] Therefore both versions of the preformationist theory slighted women's role in conception. As in the ancient period, so too in the seven-teenth and eighteenth centuries, even those who acknowledged the female's contribution to biological reproduction did not necessarily accept that her role was equal to that of the male. Moreover, even knowledge of the function of the ovaries, as it developed in the early modern period, did not preclude belief in the male's fundamental superiority.[19] But such knowledge was sometimes interpreted as offering the possibility of contesting that assumption, as appar-ently frantic statements around 1700 to the effect that ova are fictitious or at best useless ornaments make only too clear.

Recent studies of ancient biology and medicine teach us that the question of women's role in reproduction was debated as far back as the Pre-Socratics and that a Hellenistic anatomist practicing in Alexandria around 300 B.C. dis-covered the ovaries, explained their function correctly, and went on to argue that the female, like the male, secretes seed. Herophilus, author of the earliest known treatise on midwifery, is thought to have initiated the systematic dissec-tion of humans in the ancient period. Only fragments of his writings remain, and he was known to later generations largely through Galen's references to his work until physicians in sixteenth-century Padua rediscovered him.[20] It

18. Marcello Malpighi and William Smellie, cited by Angus McLaren, *Reproductive Rituals* (London and New York: Methuen, 1984), 23 and 25.

19. The form of my argument is indebted to Lloyd's account of these matters for an-cient Greece in *Science, Folklore and Ideology*, 109–11.

20. Heinrich von Staden, *Herophilus: The Art of Medicine in Early Alexandria* (Cambridge and New York: Cambridge University Press, 1989), 40–41, 233, xi.

would appear that a remarkably similar story needs to be told about the belated discovery among English readers of Reinier de Graaf's mid-seventeenth-century studies of the female reproductive system.

De Graaf was one of a circle of anatomists and medical students in several Dutch universities, the University of Leiden in particular, who in the 1660s undertook intensive study of female sexual anatomy. During this period, the Leiden group pioneered techniques for preserving specimens. Jan Swammerdam, for example, is credited with a new injected wax technique, which he demonstrated in his preservation of a human uterus. De Graaf made similar anatomical preparations and, in addition, invented a special syringe for the purpose. Frederik Ruysch, most famously, went on to develop a method which allowed him to preserve entire corpses for years. At the same time, improvements in the making and printing of copper plate engravings allowed these anatomists to faithfully reproduce details of their dissections; and microscopes, which had been available since around 1610, were only now beginning to be applied to a systematic investigation of anatomical specimens.[21]

Reinier de Graaf, who had dissected numerous female corpses over a period of twelve years in Utrecht, Paris, Leiden, and presumably Delft, where he had a busy medical practice, cheerfully disputed received opinions about female anatomy and physiology. In A Treatise on the Organs of Generation in Women (1672), he rejected attempts to explain menstruation either by reference to the moon's motions—so easy to disprove by daily experience, he retorted—or as an evacuation of a plethora, a view still widely held: "Completely disproved," he exclaimed, "not only by reasoning but also by frequent dissection." The notion that menstruation is a form of bleeding by which women rid themselves of excess materials represented women as inherently defective and easily disabled, often requiring medical or surgical intervention merely to fulfill their natural functions. This particular explanation of menstruation was in fact revived by an English physician, John Freind, in the early eighteenth century despite its powerful rejection by contemporary French, Dutch and German physiologists and physicians. Although apparently adopted in a number of popular publications, it was contested and ridiculed in lectures and textbooks on the subject in England as well as on the Continent that pointed out that the good doctor had not had much practice at the time he published,

21. For excellent brief studies of De Graaf, see Marc Klein, "Graaf, Regnier de," in Dictionary of Scientific Biography V, ed. C. C. Gillispie (New York: Charles Scribner's Sons, 1972), 484–85; and Hubert R. Catchpole, "Regnier de Graaf 1641–1673," Bulletin of the History of Medicine 8, no. 9 (November 1940): 1261–1300.

that he had foolishly relied on what ancient authors said, and that his claims could be easily disproved by reference to women's actual experience. De Graaf substituted for these inherited views the argument that menstruation was the result of a process of fermentation, itself the culmination of natural processes and natural laws "we have not yet discovered." He then went on to denounce the ancient source of so many myths about women's bodies. Galen, he declared, echoing Vesalius's view of the matter, must now be seen as the great dictator of medicine who "could never have seen, even in a dream, a female uterus."[22]

In common with growing numbers of his contemporaries, De Graaf distinguished the ovaries from the testes and emphasized their essential role in biological reproduction: "They should rather be called ovaries than testes because they show no similarity, either in form or contents, with the male testes properly so called. On this account, many have considered these bodies useless, but this is incorrect because they are indispensable for reproduction."[23] De Graaf's book contained a detailed description of the female sexual organs, accompanied by remarkably accurate diagrams; the fallopian tubes were described clearly and accurately, and his description of the ovaries included the first account of the glandular nature of the corpus luteum. His book was widely believed at the time to be superior to the accounts of all previous writers, and even today it is thought that "the physiology of the ovary can be illustrated by utilizing De Graaf's plates without modification."[24] Shortly after the publication of De Graaf's renowned treatise, his former teacher, Ysbrand van Diemerbroeck, announced that the presence of eggs in all kinds of animals was now "certain and unassailable."[25] De Graaf was known to the learned scientific community throughout western Europe through his Latin publications from around 1665. It was he after all who introduced his fellow townsman Leeuwen-

22. Regnier de Graaf, *New Treatise concerning the Generative Organs of Women* (1672), trans. and ed. H. D. Jocelyn and B. P. Setchell for the *Journal of Reproduction and Fertility*, supplement no. 17 (Oxford: Blackwell Scientific Publications, 1972), 119–20. John Freind's views, published in *Emmenologia* (English trans. by Thomas Dale, London, 1729), were mocked by William Osborn, among others, in his popular lectures on midwifery given in London in the 1770s. Students' notes of his lectures are widely available; I have consulted those in Marsh's Library, Dublin, and the library of the College of Physicians of Philadelphia.

23. De Graaf, *New Treatise*, 135.

24. Klein, *Dictionary of Scientific Biography* V, 485. In fact, a recent textbook has reproduced three of De Graaf's drawings: Lord Zuckerman and Barbara J. Weir, eds., *The Ovary*, 2d ed. (New York: Academic Press, 1977), 1: 17–19.

25. Ysbrand van Diemerbroeck, *The Anatomy of Human Bodies* (1672); English trans. by William Salmon (London, 1694), 158.

hoek to the Royal Society (just months before his own premature death in August 1673), calling attention to Leeuwenhoek's excellent microscopes.[26]

Four years later Leeuwenhoek used his superior instruments to observe semen, and then went on, in apparent ignorance of De Graaf's earlier anatomical research and the fragile consensus it had helped to produce, to declare in a series of letters to the Royal Society between 1685 and 1694 that "the mammalian ovaries were useless ornaments" and that "the sole function of the uterus and the female sex was to receive and nourish the masculine seed."[27] A scientist who visited him on behalf of the Royal Society reported that Leeuwenhoek was a "very civil" man but one who, "being ignorant of all other men's thoughts, is wholly trusting to his own," which, the visitor commented, "now and then leads him into extravagances, and suggests very odd accounts of things . . . such as are wholly irreconcilable with all truth."[28]

Leeuwenhoek interpreted his microscopic data within the theoretical framework of animalculism, a theory to which he stubbornly adhered despite his failure to find optical evidence to support it. And it would appear that some like-minded contemporaries, as well as several modern historians of science, have been more interested in his conclusions than in his experimental results. In letters to two English correspondents in 1678 and 1683, he declared that "it is exclusively the male semen that forms the foetus, . . . [which] originates not from an egg but from an animalcule that is found in the male semen." Despite repeated failures to find the figure of the animal within the spermatozoa, he remained convinced that it was there. Leeuwenhoek confessed in a letter to the Royal Society written in 1685:

> I have in fact imagined that I could say as I beheld the animalcules in the semen of an animal that there lies the head and there the shoulders and there the hips; but since these notions have not the slightest

26. De Graaf to Oldenburg, 28 April 1673, in Henry Oldenburg, *Correspondence*, ed. and trans. A. Rupert Hall and Marie Boas Hall (Madison: University of Wisconsin Press, 1965—), 9: 602–3.

27. For much of what follows, I rely on Edward G. Ruestow's authoritative essay, "Images and Ideas: Leeuwenhoek's Perception of the Spermatozoa," *Journal of the History of Biology* 16, no. 2 (Summer 1983): 185–223. I have also preferred Ruestow's translations of Leeuwenhoek's letters to those in the dual-language edition: *Collected Letters* (Amsterdam: Swets & Zeitlinger, 1939—). Here I have used Ruestow's summary of these letters, p. 198.

28. Thomas Molyneux, quoted by K. van Berkel, "Intellectuals against Leeuwenhoek," in *Antoni van Leeuwenhoek 1632–1723*, ed. L. C. Palm and H. A. M. Snelders (Amsterdam: Rodopi, 1982), 197.

shred of certainty, I will not yet put forward such a claim, but hope that we may have the good fortune to find an animal whose male seed will be so large that we will recognize within it the figure of the [male] creature from which it came.[29]

Edward Ruestow emphasizes that despite Leeuwenhoek's persistent efforts to disprove current ideas about the role of ova in generation, many of his contemporaries remained skeptical. It would appear that Leeuwenhoek's findings merely confirmed the views of those who still doubted that the fundamental processes of reproduction were yet understood.[30] Nevertheless, he attracted favorable attention from some quarters, and at least one English anatomist was moved to record his gratitude and relief now that Leeuwenhoek's microscope had restored male dignity. In 1698, in the introduction to his massive folio volume, *The Anatomy of Human Bodies*, William Cowper recalled the recent, mid-seventeenth-century discovery of ova by Dutch anatomists and physicians. He further noted how De Graaf and others,

> upon the Invention of these Ova, . . . began to erect an Opinion, that the Female only furnished the matter of the *Foetus*, and the Male serv'd [merely] to Actuate it. . . . This opinion, which derogates much from the Dignity of the Male-Sex, prevailed till Mons. Leeuwenhoek by the Help of his Exquisite Microscope . . . detected Innumerable small *Animals* in the Masculine Sperm, and by this Noble Discovery, at once removed that Difficulty, and added much to the theory of generation.[31]

Leeuwenhoek's lengthy reports of his microscopic findings and imagined vistas (published in the *Philosophical Transactions* of the Royal Society) may have settled the matter for Cowper—and no doubt for others, as we know—but certainly not for all medical writers. So far from resolving the question, the controversies in English medical discourse over the role of the female in biological reproduction and related issues appear to have flared up only during

29. Ruestow, "Images and Ideas," 207.

30. Ibid., 185. It is instructive to contrast Leeuwenhoek's reputation in his own day with modern appraisals of his stature as a scientist. See, in addition to the article by Van Berkel, "Intellectuals against Leeuwenhoek," Steven Shapin, "Closure and Credibility in 17th-Century Science," in *Conference Papers of the British Society for the History of Science and History of Science Society Anglo-American Conference* (Manchester, 1988), 149–51.

31. William Cowper, "The Introduction Explaining the Animal Oeconomy," in *The Anatomy of Human Bodies* (London, 1698).

the closing years of the seventeenth century. The terms of the debate in England, so far as I can tell, as well as many of the references and virtually all of the diagrams, can be traced to cognate medical disputes in the Netherlands beginning around 1665. The only plagiarism of which I am aware, though, is by the same William Cowper; that is, the plates used to illustrate Cowper's *Anatomy* were lifted without acknowledgment from Govert Bidloo's *Anatomia* of 1685.

Among a growing number of medical texts around 1700 that disputed a variety of opinions about women's bodies, James Drake's *New System of Anatomy* deserves to be singled out. Reprinted four times between 1707 and 1750, the two-volume text, which included some of De Graaf's diagrams of the female reproductive system, was recommended by Herman Boerhaave, teacher of anatomy and medicine to students from many western European countries and the North American colonies in the early eighteenth century on account of its accuracy. The text was posthumously published and edited by the author's sister, Judith Drake, who is also likely to have written at least the chapter on generation, which was never listed in the table of contents by the publisher. In this chapter Drake insisted that at present the causes of generation are not sufficiently understood. The author summarized recent developments in embryology, including Leeuwenhoek's microscopic findings, about which she remained skeptical. That is, like many others, Drake had confirmed the observation of microscopic organisms in seminal fluid which looked like tadpoles, but she was not convinced that these beings were preformed fetuses contained in the semen. On the contrary, Drake rejected both versions of the preformationist hypothesis; neither, she pointed out, accounts for mixed generation in animals or the fact that children often resemble both parents. Such observations, Drake argued, prove that both sexes contribute to conception and heredity. Moreover, the attempt to account for these facts by alleging that the uterus "may have so much effect on the fetus as to alter the figure of the animal" contained in the sperm (a position adopted by Leeuwenhoek among others) "is so poor, so unphilosophical a shift, that it is not worth an answer; and they might with as good Authority persuade me, that an Orange-tree transplanted from Sevill to England would bear Apples, and . . . vice versa." Drake further emphasized the contribution of the female to conception: "Generation cannot [take place] without an egg rightly disposed, . . . [a] concession which I think is at this time universal." Ignoring the representations by Leeuwenhoek and Cowper of ova as mere fantasy or sham, she declared that the existence of true ova in the ovaries of women is agreed on all sides, is indeed incontestable! Drake referred repeatedly to the writings of De Graaf, who she labelled "the most industrious and accurate enquirer" into the female body, both to affirm the existence of eggs in the ovaries of "all sorts of [female] animals whatsoever" and to cast doubt on the existence of the hymen. De Graaf, after all, "confesses that he always sought it in vain."[32]

In her *Essay in Defence of the Female Sex*, which went through three editions in 1696 and 1697, Judith Drake had argued that there was no basis in nature for women's subject status. She compared the experience of Dutch and English wives and also highlighted the apparently more equal condition of men and women among the rural laboring classes.[33] Her attack on male domination and on the prevailing social categories which distinguished men from women was a political critique that contested the alleged grounds of female subjection and powerlessness. That is, masculine identity in the early modern period was associated with particular social and economic opportunities from which women were often, perhaps increasingly, excluded, as well as with privileged access to a particular kind of education. For example, studying Latin became "a way of achieving masculinity."[34] The feminist critique of classical traditions in this period was, first of all, an attack on traditions that distinguished male and female social destinies: traditions of thought and language that after all represented women as naturally domestic and men as properly political. Drake engaged with revered traditions, with male intellectual authority, and then went on to ridicule male ideals, mocking the scholar and the country gentleman in particular. Her characterization of the uselessness of scholars was intended to deflate any pretensions they may have had to honor as well as to learning: "Talk to them of the present and their native country, and they hardly speak the language of it and know so little of the affairs of it that as much might reasonably be expected from an animated Egyptian Mummy. . . . They hang so incessantly upon the . . . strings of Authority that their Judgments . . . become altogether crampt and motionless for want of use." Arguing that male domination was secured by means of conquest, usurpation, and subterfuge, Drake further explained that one cannot learn anything about women from books,

32. James [and Judith] Drake, *A New System of Anatomy*, 2d and 3d eds. (London, 1717 and 1727), chapter 24 of "Generation"; pp. 184–88; p. 164 on ova; p. 150 on De Graaf and the nonexistent hymen.

33. Judith Drake, *Essay in Defence of the Female Sex*, 15–17.

34. Mary Ann Clawson, *Constructing Brotherhood: Class, Gender, and Fraternalism* (Princeton, N.J.: Princeton University Press, 1989), 48. On gender relations in seventeenth-century England, see Susan Dwyer Amussen, *An Ordered Society: Gender and Class in Early Modern England* (Oxford and New York: Basil Blackwell, 1988); Angeline Goreau, ed., *The Whole Duty of a Woman* (New York: Doubleday, 1985), a stunning collection of women's writings; and Elaine Hobby, *Virtue of Necessity* (London: Virago Press, 1988).

particularly history books, because their authors were men, and "as men are parties against us their evidence may justly be rejected." Thus did late-seventeenth-century feminist writers like Drake turn the tables on men who would scorn learned, unmarried, deviant women; where they really scored, of course, was in their contempt for the masculine models normally deemed most worthy.[35]

Ridicule of men's exclusive claims to intellectual authority was also developed in the writings of midwives in the seventeenth and eighteenth centuries. *The Midwives Book, or the Whole Art of Midwifery Discovered* by Jane Sharp was published in 1671 and had gone through four editions by 1725, when it appeared in a cheaper edition with a slightly altered title but identical contents. What is most obvious in this extraordinary book she addressed to her "sisters," the midwives of England, are the lengths to which Sharp was prepared to go to dispel the myths currently being purveyed in popular books, such as those falsely attributed to Aristotle. The ancients, she charged, Galen in particular, could not have had knowledge of human bodies that was dependent on dissection: "The inside of men or women they saw not, and so were ignorant of the difference between them;" she debunked the alleged authority of learned as well as popular traditions about multiple births; and she stressed the fact that women are not merely men turned outside in and inverted, contesting both the assumption of homologous structures, which represents women as defective men, and the recurrently popular myth of Tiresias, who, it was said, had been changed from male to female and back again, and who, Sharp explained derisively, "because he had been of both sexes, . . . was chosen as the most fit judge to determine the great Question, which of the two, Male or Female, find most pleasure in . . . copulation."[36]

The case of Pierre Dionis, a Paris surgeon who offered a series of apparently successful courses in anatomy and surgery between 1673 and 1680 (when he was awarded a court appointment), further illustrates the resistance to particular theories of generation and the equally fervent efforts to propagate the new anatomy in the period around 1700. From the time of Vesalius in the mid-sixteenth century, anatomy had relied more and more on public display, particularly on dissections in large theaters.[37] Dionis boasted that he had per-

35. Judith Drake, *Essay in Defence of the Female Sex*, 28–29, 23.
36. Jane Sharp, *The Midwives Book, or the Whole Art of Midwifery Discovered* (London, 1671), 68, 69–70, and 82.
37. On public anatomy in early modern European cities, see especially Giovanna Ferrari, "Public Anatomy Lessons and the Carnival: The Anatomy Theatre of Bologna," *Past and Present* 117 (1987): 50–106; and Toby Gelfand, "The 'Paris Manner' of Dissection: Student An-

formed his anatomies and surgical procedures before audiences of 500 or more, and called his public presentations "demonstrations" to distinguish them from the presumably more weighty—because derivative as well as authoritative—lectures of physician-professors. The term *demonstration*, moreover, had acquired particular significance in debates about knowledge in the second half of the seventeenth century.[38] Since Descartes, "demonstrable" could be used to denote propositions deemed self-evident, such as axioms in geometry. This did not, of course, deter philosophers from applying this designation to social and political principles which they thereby elevated to the status of universal truths. In this way John Locke and many others represented their class-specific and temporally specific opinions as beyond dispute.[39] Dionis, however, sought not to foreclose debate so much as to incite it—that is, to attract serious attention to points of view and empirical data that many of his contemporaries preferred to treat disdainfully. His views cannot have gone unnoticed, to judge from the multiple editions and translations of his books on anatomy, surgery, and midwifery in the eighteenth century. His widely available *Dissertation sur la génération de l'homme* (1698), included in all editions of his anatomy text from 1698 (which was translated in 1703 as *The Anatomy of Humane Bodies Improv'd*) found the notion of a social hierarchy that differentiated masculine from feminine worth "foreign to nature." He specifically denied on several occasions that the inherited conception of the natural infirmity of women had any basis in biology. Moreover, he characterized the Aristotelian view of generation, which denigrated women's contribution to conception and heredity, as "not only partial, but a groundless Fancy, . . . the vain Imagination of a certain sort of Men who would present Metaphysical Possibilities which appeal to them as Matters of Fact."[40] Like De Graaf before him (to whom he referred, and whose opinions and observations he repli-

---

atomical Dissection in Early 18th-Century Paris," *Bulletin of the History of Medicine* 46, no. 2 (1972): 99–130.

38. For the views of Thomas Hobbes and John Locke on "demonstration," see Tom Sorell, *Hobbes* (New York: Routledge and Kegan Paul, 1986), 43–45 and 137–40; Shapin and Schaffer, *Leviathan and the Air-Pump*, 19 and 23–24; and William Youngren, "Founding English Ethics: Locke, Mathematics, and the Innateness Question," *Eighteenth-Century Life* 16, n.s. 3 (November 1992): 12–45.

39. Most useful here are E. J. Hundert, "The Making of Homo Faber: John Locke Between Ideology and History," *Journal of the History of Ideas* 33 (1972): 3–22; and Joyce O. Appleby, *Economic Thought and Ideology in Seventeenth-Century England* (Princeton, N.J.: Princeton University Press, 1978), especially chapters 6 and 9.

40. Pierre Dionis, *The Anatomy of Humane Bodies Improv'd* (London, 1703), 222, 231, and 220.

cated), Dionis considered that his extensive experience of human dissection provided sufficient proof of an ovist hypothesis that argued that both parents contributed to generation. We need to understand why Dionis and De Graaf, among others, apparently failed to persuade—why seeing was not believing—in order to explain both the tenacity of inherited ideas being daily disproved by ocular experience and the appeal of new ideas which could not be demonstrated. A part of the explanation, to be sure, was already proposed by Dionis; after all, it cannot have escaped notice that at about the same time that the mammalian ovaries were rediscovered and renamed, microscopy revealed that the kingdom of the bees was ruled by a Queen: "the King . . . is female" was how it was announced when the French edition appeared in 1682: this at a time when the government of bees was widely believed to be "the perfect model of monarchical government."[41]

During the decades following publication of De Graaf's work, Charles Drélincourt, Professor of Medicine from 1668 to 1697 and personal physician to the Princess of Orange (later Queen Mary of England), published a series of treatises on female reproductive biology and the human fetus, lengthy reviews of which appeared in Pierre Bayle's *Nouvelles de la république des lettres* in 1684 and 1685, which would have assured their transmission to a large scholarly community. Drélincourt claimed to be refuting hundreds of errors on the subject of generation and insisted that current arguments about the role of ova and the ovaries in reproduction have ancient authority (referring to Herophilus, for example) as well as the evidence of recent anatomical research to support them. His publications studiously ignored Leeuwenhoek's ever more persistent efforts to demolish this point of view.[42]

41. The ovist hypothesis preferred by Dionis is the same version argued by De Graaf and Drake; Dionis explained his preference in *Anatomy* (1703), 210–11. There is now an immense literature on the family-state analogy in early modern states and the relevance of the bee metaphor to cultural anxieties about gender hierarchy. See, first of all, for the references in the text, Renato Mazzolini, "Adam Gottlob Shirach's Experiments on Bees," in *The Light of Nature*, ed. J.D. North and J.J. Roche (Dordrecht: Martinus Nijhoff, 1985), pp. 68–74. The broader debates are best approached through reading Sarah Hanley, "Engendering the State: Family Formation and State Building in Early Modern France," *French Historical Studies*, 16, 1 (Spring 1989), 4–27 and Jeffrey Merrick, "Royal Bees: The Gender Politics of the Beehive in Early Modern Europe," *Studies in Eighteenth-Century Culture*, ed. John Yolton and Leslie Brown, 18 (East Lansing, Mich.: Colleagues Press, 1988), 7–37.

42. Charles Drélincourt's Latin publications on embryology and female reproductive anatomy were widely known among the learned. Pierre Bayle sought to gain a wider audience for Drélincourt's provocative views by arranging for a French translation of one of his texts (later attributed to Bayle in some libraries!) and by "reviewing" some of the Latin works in his monthly journal.

One might well ask why there were no English translations of De Graaf's publication on the female sexual organs before 1848. At that time, only the chapter on ovaries was translated (by Robert Knox, notorious Edinburgh resurrectionist) for the British Record of Obstetric Medicine and Surgery, a short-lived Manchester journal edited by a physician, Charles Clay, noted for his pioneering interest in the surgical removal of ovaries.[43] A Dutch edition of De Graaf's complete writings appeared in 1686 and a French edition in 1699. The only references I know of to his work in English in this period, apart from the English translation of another Dutch text on anatomy (by his former teacher, Van Diemerbroeck) which cited De Graaf's experiments, is Andrew Snape's remark about De Graaf's "curious" work on rabbits in his book on The Anatomy of a Horse (1683 and 1687). A series of medical pamphlets dating from the final years of the eighteenth century (reprinted from the Philosophical Transactions of the Royal Society) indicate continued interest in the work of De Graaf, quoting from his Latin texts, as well as continuing controversy and uncertainty regarding generation. One of the physicians concluded, on the basis of his own replication of De Graaf's experiments on rabbits: "De Graaf had the fate of Cassandra, to be disbelieved even when he spoke the truth!"[44] The full text of De Graaf's Treatise on the Organs of Generation in Women has been available in English only since 1972, three hundred years after its initial publication![45]

Alexander Monro, who taught anatomy at the University of Edinburgh from 1719, had studied in London, Paris, and Leiden and therefore was unlikely to be uninformed about the work of De Graaf, Drélincourt, Drake, or Dionis. Therefore it is interesting to note that his lectures on the history of anatomy acknowledged that De Graaf "has given a most exact description of the parts of generation far exceeding anything either done before, or since his time," but then offered his students no detailed information whatever about the nature of De Graaf's discoveries or opinions. Given that a large proportion of Monro's students were probably local surgical apprentices, the unavailability of De Graaf's work in English most likely would have precluded access. He cited Diemerbroeck's anatomy text, indicating its continued use by medical

43. Charles Clay was a general practitioner who set up a vast private practice in Manchester in the first half of the nineteenth century. He claimed to have performed hundreds of ovariotomies at a time when such procedures were often life-threatening and therefore regarded as a form of vivisection. Because his journal apparently attracted few readers, the English translation of De Graaf's chapter on the ovaries is likely to have gone unnoticed.

44. William Cruikshank, "Experiments on Rabbits" (communicated to the Royal Society in March 1797) (London, 1797), 198.

45. Journal of Reproduction and Fertility, supplement no. 17 (Oxford: Blackwell Scientific Publications, 1972).

students in Holland and Germany over many years, but added that "it contains nothing new" and neglected to indicate either its availability in an English translation (1689 and 1694) or its usefulness as a source for De Graaf's opinions. His treatment of both Drélincourt and Drake was little short of libelous. He said nothing at all about Drélincourt's work, apart from references to two presumably satirical pieces, accepted that he was "certainly a man of great learning [who] made a great noise in the world," but portrayed him as one who "showed his reading a little too much"—on the whole, an arrogant and offensive fellow. His brief remarks on Drake appeared to take at face value the fairly obvious jokes directed at Cowper in the original preface by James and Judith Drake to the *New System of Anatomy*. Thus Monro credits Cowper with having written "the best part of [Drake's] book" and having made drawings of several of the figures with his own hand.[46] The Drakes had thanked Cowper for his chapters on the nose and the penis, and for the drawings made by his own hand—at a time when his plagiarism of Bidloo's plates was common knowledge, at least partly to call attention to the contrast between their production and his recent anatomy book. (Their publisher had purchased the plates of a Dutch anatomy text from the printer, and then proceeded to commission an accompanying text from James Drake.)

There are several possible explanations for Monro's shabby treatment of these writers. The one I find most persuasive relates to his clear bias in favor of an animalculist hypothesis, evident in both his physiology lectures and his directions for conducting a dissection. For example, minute attention to the male sexual organs included investigation of the animalcules in the semen "through a double microscope with a great magnifier." Nothing quite like that was prescribed for the female sexual organs: although the ovaries were to be dissected, Monro did not indicate any need for microscopy.[47]

Biological theories derived from the teachings of Aristotle and Galen, which retained their canonical status until the end of the sixteenth century, were sometimes used even beyond that date to underpin social and cultural arguments about female inferiority.[48] The powerful challenges to these systems

46. Alexander Monro primus, *A Short History of Anatomy*: lecture notes taken by David McBride, April 1750, at the University of Edinburgh. Edinburgh University Special Collections, MSS Lectures. See especially pp. 82–83, 88, and 95.

47. Christopher Lawrence, "Alexander Monro primus and the Edinburgh Manner of Anatomy," *Bulletin of the History of Medicine* 62 (1988): 205.

48. Robert Filmer, most notably, found uses for Aristotle's views on generation in his defense of absolute monarchy. See Gordon Schochet, *Patriarchalism in Political Thought* (Oxford: Basil Blackwell, 1975), and Carole Pateman, *The Sexual Contract* (Oxford: Polity Press, 1988), especially chapter 4.

of biological thought on the basis of both new knowledge and new doubts during the century after 1660, however, often derided dominant social attitudes as well. One wonders to what extent the diversity of medical opinions and pervasive uncertainty regarding what was known or knowable undermined attempts in this period to defend social and cultural differentiation by reference to natural differences. It is certainly not the case (as some recent work continues to argue) that despite disagreement about details, scholarly opinion in the seventeenth and eighteenth centuries did not contest classical traditions which represented the female as a lesser human. Therefore, what needs to be clarified is how far and in what ways medical writers may have contributed to the lively debates in various public discourses about woman's nature and appropriate social destiny at this time. As at other times, medical opinions respecting women's bodies in the period around 1700 were clearly not just statements about anatomy and physiology. Leeuwenhoek and Cowper are just two examples among many of the extent to which cultural and social assumptions "shape perception and influence reasoning," as Fausto-Sterling has so aptly put it.[49]

It is now a commonplace that medical texts, like any other, are culturally specific constructs. Since Foucault, it is no longer possible to deny that discourses about the body are one way of confirming dominant social values. On the other hand, my study of medical texts in the seventeenth and eighteenth centuries clearly demonstrates that discourses about the body can also contest prevailing social ideologies insofar as medical writers sometimes deliberately ridiculed inherited and popular attitudes toward women. This period was characterized by a multiplicity of discourses on gender and sexual difference, not least of all in the medical literature written for a nonprofessional as well as a professional readership. Although medical texts have indeed at times contributed to attempts to naturalize a particular ideal of femininity, to make the social appear natural, to ground social and cultural constructions of women's roles in society and household on the alleged facts of their natural differences, the absence of consensus regarding woman's nature in the seventeenth and eighteenth centuries calls into question the argument that medical writers in this period fostered an ongoing tendency to confuse social values with so-called natural facts. The proliferation of popular sex manuals from the end of the seventeenth century, which were prescriptively pronuptialist, pronatalist, and

49. Fausto-Sterling, "Society Writes Biology," 64. Edward Ruestow's article on Leeuwenhoek's perceptions illustrates precisely how far his preconceptions influenced his "findings" ("Images and Ideas," 233).

distinctly antifeminist, so far from representing the state of medical opinion at the time, may actually testify to a perceived need to reinstate a kind of biological determinism. In any case, assumptions of consensus in the period before the late eighteenth century are problematic, to say the least, based, as they often appear to be, either on limited reading of early medical texts or, worse, on histories of medicine that distort, disparage, or altogether ignore important earlier traditions of thought, such as those represented by the work of De Graaf, Diemerbroeck, Drélincourt, Drake, and Dionis, among others. The wide acceptance, particularly in the past 150 years or so, of the notion that a woman's social destiny can be grounded on the presumed facts of female biology in a way that a man's cannot should not lead us to infer that medical views about women's bodies have invariably or even overwhelmingly supported prevailing social attitudes about women in earlier periods. Too often, efforts to interpret medical opinions and texts in the early modern period have been either narrowly focused or largely uninformed about specific and changing historical contexts.

Recent work on the history of the body has emphasized the extent to which the body has a history: that is, we are learning to think about the body not as "a fact of nature, a constant and universal reality, but as an entirely problematic notion, a historical category, and one, moreover, steeped in imagination."[50] Dualisms that have become embedded in our language and thought since the late eighteenth century were still far from absolute in the early modern period. The reality of premodern cultures and societies was richer, more complex, varied, and fluid than our limited categories sometimes allow us to grasp.[51] For example, I have not discovered evidence of fixed categories and definitions of sexual difference in much of the medical literature published before the late eighteenth century. Quite the contrary: I would argue that an instability of categories respecting gender and sexual difference remained characteristic of the period up to at least 1760. Moreover, close study of the debates about female anatomy and physiology in the period after 1660, of the

50. Jean-Pierre Vernant, "Divine Body, Dazzling Body" in *Zone 3: Fragments for a History of the Human Body*, part 1, ed. Michel Feher et al. (New York: Urzone, 1989), 20. Also see Judith Butler, "Sex and Gender in Simone de Beauvoir's *Second Sex*," *Yale French Studies* 72 (1986): 35–49, especially 44–45 where she describes the body as "a cultural situation" or "a field of interpretive possibilities."

51. Caroline Walker Bynum, "The Female Body and Religious Practice in the Later Middle Ages," in *Zone 3: Fragments for a History of the Human Body*, part 1, ed. Michel Feher et al. (New York: Urzone, 1989), 162; and Elizabeth A Castelli, "Mortifying the Body, Curing the Soul," *differences* 4, no. 2 (1992): 134–49.

disputes about women's role in reproduction in particular, offers powerful evidence of the existence of widely publicized alternative traditions of medical thought and practice in the seventeenth and eighteenth centuries, traditions that have been slighted or suppressed in modern histories of medicine.

It is equally clear that the new anatomy and the new body images, whose meaning and impact remain far from self-evident, did not in the end dislodge deep-rooted social and cultural prejudices about women—or indeed alter women's experience of subjection and inequality. As in the ancient world, so too in early modern Europe, research in anatomy and physiology produced empirical data that contradicted notions of women's essential inferiority and "otherness." However, despite sustained challenges, even ridicule, such long-standing assumptions survived the discursive battles of the seventeenth and eighteenth centuries, indeed seemed to be "immune to refutation."[52] At the end of this period, gender was inscribed more confidently and systematically than ever, not only in anatomy and physiology but in pathology as well: therefore the need for a special branch of medicine to treat diseases peculiar to women. The rediscovery of ovaries in mid-seventeenth-century Leiden elicited a variety of responses, some of them quite hostile; but none quite compares with the view of the mid-nineteenth-century physician who redefined "woman" as "a pair of ovaries with a human being attached" while describing "man" as "a human being furnished with a pair of testes."[53]

52. I borrow the phrase from G. E. R. Lloyd's description of a comparable situation in ancient Greece (*Science, Folklore and Ideology*, 111).
53. Rudolf Virchow, cited by Anne Fausto-Sterling, *Myths of Gender* (New York: Basic Books, 1985), 90.

6

The Social Construction of
Premenstrual Syndrome: A Case
Study of Scientific Discourse
as Cultural Contestation

Mary Brown Parlee

During the past twenty years, premenstrual syndrome (PMS) has emerged as a topic in scientific publications and conferences, advertisements for over-the-counter drugs, women's magazines, trade books, greeting cards, cartoons, sweatshirt slogans, jokes, everyday talk among and about women, and conversations between women and men. PMS is now a repository of widely shared cultural understandings that social actors use to make sense of (some) women's words and actions. Twenty-five years ago practically no one in the United States had heard of PMS; today many people have.

Why? What does this striking example of the formation and spread of a cultural concept mean? Can it tell us anything about how and with what effect gendered notions of health and illness are formed and how they function, about how and with what effect biomedical discourses about female bodies serve to advance and contest claims about social relations of gender, about how women collaborate with and resist cultural constructions of themselves as social actors when the technologies of the "good body" are at work? These are some of the questions I want to begin to explore in this chapter.[1]

It seems possible to identify four interrelated phenomena that contributed to the emergence of PMS as a new concept in the culture, a biologically based illness only women can have: feminism, the challenge by the women's health movement to the medicalization of menstruation, the dramatic increase in popular and scientific writing on menstruation from a biomedical perspective, and the embrace by many women of PMS as a meaningful label for their experience.

Feminism became part of public discourse and individual consciousness for the second time in this century. Although feminists and the meaning of "feminism" vary and continue to change, the common core challenges existing gender relations, their economic bases, and the ideologies supporting them. Within the framework of liberal political theory, which permeates public political discourse in the United States, this media-mediated version of feminism translates into a demand for equal opportunity with white men in paid work. A central tenet of liberal theory is that justice demands equal treatment for persons who are equal in relevant respects; if individuals are not "really" equal, then arguments for equal treatment may be harder to sustain within this framework.[2]

A feminist women's health movement emerged, claiming that women have the right to name and define their bodily experiences.[3] It radically challenged medical definitions and control of pregnancy and birth, menstruation,

1. During the time PMS was coming into existence as a concept in the scientific and public domains, I was engaged as a feminist in biomedical research on menstruation. My background in biology and experimental psychology equipped me to do research from within a biomedical perspective but failed to enable me to understand the social and cultural phenomena I observed and participated in as the research developed. Part of the power of biomedicine as an interrelated set of social institutions and knowledge is that its perspective is taken by scientists and many in the broader culture to be "obvious," its assumptions invisible and unquestionable, its notion of what is "real" uncontestable. I had to get outside my discipline socially and intellectually in order to begin to understand how these assumptions work, how they are enacted as situated practical accomplishments, how they function as forms and effects of power. Because this is work in progress, I try here to distinguish insofar as possible between descriptions of events in the cultural construction of scientific discourse on PMS as I experienced them and interpretations and explanations of these events. The former can be persuasively documented, I believe, but the latter are more arguable.

2. I. M. Young, Justice and the Politics of Difference (Princeton, N. J.: Princeton University Press, 1990); E. Weed, Coming to Terms: Feminism, Theory, Politics (New York: Routledge, 1989).

3. Boston Women's Health Book Collective, Our Bodies, Ourselves (New York: Simon & Schuster, 1973; subsequent editions published in 1976, 1979, 1984, 1992).

menopause, aging, disability, and ideal body shape. It traced links between macro-social processes constituting class-modulated social relations of gender and some of the micro-social processes through which medicalization occurs: doctor-patient interactions, representations of women in the medical literature, research and teaching organized around the equation of male bodies with the norm and the normal.[4]

With increasing frequency during the 1970s and 1980s, both the scientific literature and the popular (or elite, opinion-setting) media carried articles describing women's experiences of menstruation from a biomedical perspective. In these scientific and popular representations of women's menstrual experiences, menstruation was almost invariably pathologized and medicalized, with a focus on negative emotions in the premenstrual phase of the cycle and on impaired performance of paid work and family responsibilities.[5]

In the scientific literature, PMS went from being the topic of a few scattered research articles and a minor clinical concern to being an official diagnostic category in the American Psychiatric Association's *Diagnostic and Statistical Manual of Mental Disorders, IIIR*, (DSM-IIIR) and the topic of scientific conferences, symposia, continuing medical education workshops, and literally hundreds of research papers.[6] In the popular media, PMS went from an unnamed status (as in a 1971 *New York Times* article headlined "Doctor Asserts Women Unfit for Top Jobs" because of "the raging hormonal influences of the menstrual cycle") to being a continuing topic of magazine and newspaper articles and a repository of shared cultural understandings expressed in television jokes, greeting cards, and cartoons.[7]

With increasing frequency, first in the upper-middle class then in most other social groups as well, women of all ages talked about PMS as something

4. A. D. Todd, *Intimate Adversaries: Cultural Conflict between Doctors and Women Patients* (Philadelphia: University of Pennsylvania Press, 1989).

5. C. K. Riessman, "Women and Medicalization: A New Perspective," *Social Policy* 14 (1983): 3–18.

6. L. M. Demers, J. L. McGuire, A. Phillips, and D. F. Rubinow, *Premenstrual, Postpartum, and Menopausal Mood Disorders* (Baltimore, Md.: Urban & Schwarzenberg, 1989); M. B. Parlee, "Psychology of Menstruation and Premenstrual Syndrome, in *The Psychology of Women: A Handbook of Issues and Theories*, ed. M. Paludi and F. L. Denmark (Westport, Conn.: Greenwood Press, 1993); R. C. Friedman, *Behavior and the Menstrual Cycle* (New York: Marcel Dekker, 1982).

7. J. C. Chrisler and K. B. Levy, "The Media Construct a Menstrual Monster: A Content Analysis of PMS Articles in the Popular Press," *Women and Health* 16 (1990): 89–104; C. A. Rittenhouse, "The Emergence of Premenstrual Syndrome as a Social Problem," *Social Problems* 38 (1991): 412–25.

they experience. Many sought medical treatment from doctors and clinics. Self-help newsletters and trade books describing PMS and its treatment proliferated and sold well.[8] Researchers (as opposed to clinicians) increasingly heard spontaneous and utterly convincing accounts from women of the misery they experienced before they were diagnosed and treated for PMS and the relief they felt afterward.

The resurgence of feminism, the challenge by the women's health movement to the medicalization of menstruation, the dramatic increase in popular and scientific writing on menstruation from a biomedical perspective, the embrace by many women of PMS as a meaningful category for their experience: how can these four developments over the past twenty years be understood and accounted for? Since the content and impact of scientific discourses were fundamentally intertwined both with the women's movement and with women's menstrual experiences, one strategy might be to begin by focusing on changes in scientific research on premenstrual syndrome during this time.

The players in research on PMS during the 1970s and 1980s are members of the social science and biomedical research communities. The contest is over what will count as the authoritative scientific description of how women experience their menstruating bodies. The context is a political struggle initiated and represented by feminism. The questions are what strategies did different groups of scientists use to contest scientific narratives of women's menstrual experiences and what were the scientific and other political-cultural effects?

In the early and mid 1970s some social scientists, mostly feminist psychologists, began focusing on menstruation as a "new" research topic, one about which academic psychology had been silent for more than twenty-five years. Their choice was in response to an antifeminist political rhetoric in the public domain which argued that gender relations in the family and workplace, at the time under attack by feminists, are justified by objective scientific facts about women's bodies and minds. Psychologists took this rhetoric at face value (as being about science and scientific truth) and sought to contest claims about women's "raging hormonal influences" with logical reasoning and empirical data.[9]

8. W. van B. Rappoport, *Premenstrual Syndrome: A Self-Help Guide* (Hollywood, Fla.: Compact Books, 1984).

9. J. Sayers, *Biological Politics* (London: Tavistock, 1982). "Women unfit for top jobs" because of their "raging hormonal influences" is actually a contemporary form of rhetorical argument from the popular media and medical literature in the late nineteenth century in

To do so, they adopted three different strategies more or less simultaneously: They marshalled scientific evidence which they claimed showed that menstruation has no impact on work-related performance;[10] they argued that women are not uniquely affected by biology, that men have hormonal rhythms too;[11] and they argued that psychological changes associated with the menstrual cycle are small to insignificant compared with other systematic changes in the moods and behaviors of both women and men (for example, changes related to the social cycle of the week).[12] While these strategies were adopted ostensibly to contest the scientific status of claims concerning the negative effects of menstruation, it is apparent in retrospect that their primary aim was to refute the antifeminist rhetorical use of science in controversies in the public domain. After all, if the menstrual cycle has no psychological effects, or none that are unique to the cycle, or none that are psychologically significant, why take it on as a topic for scientific research?

Biomedical researchers also formulated their scientific investigations around the "raging hormonal influences" rhetoric of the public domain. They asserted and defended it (or simply assumed it) as scientific fact and sought to identify the specific pathophysiological mechanisms underlying PMS. (While conventions governing scientific writing do not permit scientists to express their views on social issues directly, both the language of scientific articles and the conceptualization of research questions usually leave little doubt in the reader's mind about the social context and implied relevance of biomedical research on this illness afflicting women.)

When social scientists turned their attention to contesting biomedical researchers' claims directly (as well as continuing to pursue the three strategies mentioned above), they attempted to challenge them on intertwined methodological and conceptual grounds.[13] One strategy was to mount an implicit challenge to the biomedical conceptualization of PMS as a biologically based illness by investigating "cultural factors" (including "menstrual beliefs") that

---

the United States; then it was women's reproductive fragility that made them unfit for entry into higher education; J. Ussher, *The Psychology of the Female Body* (New York: Routledge, 1990). Both the contemporary and earlier forms of antifeminism are, of course, permeated by unspoken assumptions about gender, race, and class.

10. B. Sommer, "Menstrual Cycle Changes and Intellectual Performance," *Psychosomatic Medicine* 34 (1972): 263–69; B. Sommer, "The Effect of Menstruation on Cognitive and Perceptual-Motor Behavior: A Review," *Psychosomatic Medicine* 35 (1973): 515–34.

11. M. B. Parlee, "Mood Cycles," *Psychology Today* (April 1978).

12. S. Golub, "The Magnitude of Premenstrual Anxiety and Depression," *Psychosomatic Medicine* 38 (1976): 4–12.

13. M. B. Parlee, "Premenstrual Syndrome," *Psychological Bulletin* 80 (1973): 454–65.

influence women's menstrual experiences.[14] While some of this work resulted in the integration of questions about menstruation into research paradigms in mainstream psychology, it simultaneously had two unforeseen effects.

One was to segregate even more deeply the social scientific and biomedical research communities concerned with menstruation. (Biomedical researchers are trained to investigate the pathophysiology of diseases; for them, "cultural factors" are unrelated to the way they conceptualize their research problems. Social scientists are trained to investigate social and psychological phenomena, but they typically do not have the skills—or the license—to research human activity in the context of events occurring inside the skin of the individual.)[15]

A second unanticipated effect was to identify a simplistic culture-only explanation of PMS as a "feminist" position, both in the public controversies and in the scientific literature.[16] Given both the binary opposition between biology and culture and the equation of "real" illness with biological causation that lies at the heart of both biomedicine and the broader culture,[17] the belief that "feminists" thought PMS had only cultural "causes" (was "all in the head") further undercut the power of social scientists to contest biomedical researchers' conceptualization of PMS. Women who "had" PMS (and their doctors) were convinced that they had a "real" illness, and to them that meant precisely that it was not influenced by culture.

Social scientists also published explicit critiques of particular concepts and methods in biomedical research on PMS, and these critiques did have some of their intended impact. Biomedical investigators began consistently to use prospective research designs (daily self-reports of moods) rather than relying on

14. K. E. Paige, "Women Learn to Sing the Menstrual Blues," *Psychology Today* 4 (1973): 41–46; D. N. Ruble, "Premenstrual Symptoms: A Reinterpretation," *Science* 187 (1977): 291–92.

15. B. E. Ginsburg and B. F. Carter, *Premenstrual Syndrome: Ethical and Legal Implications in a Biomedical Perspective* (New York: Plenum Press, 1987), 405–14. In a last-ditch attempt to keep researchers holding these two perspectives in dialogue, a conference sponsored by the National Science Foundation was held in 1983 at which agreement was reached that both biological and cultural "factors" are important in PMS and that they "interact" in shaping menstrual experiences. A conclusion of this sort often results from attempts to "bring together" biomedical and social science researchers, but since it is not framed at a level of specificity that can shape scientific practice it has little effect on essentially separate research traditions and communities.

16. D. Asso, *The Real Menstrual Cycle* (New York: Wiley, 1983).

17. N. Scheper-Hughes and M. Lock, "The Mindful Body: A Prolegomenon to Future Work in Medical Anthropology," *Medical Anthropology Quarterly* 1 (1987): 6–41.

retrospective questionnaires to identify women who had PMS.[18] They accepted and advocated a distinction between PMS, a clinically significant "syndrome" in the technical medical sense, and premenstrual *symptoms* that are not medically significant or socially disabling.[19] Both changes resulted in greater conceptual clarity and empirical consistency in PMS research, and this outcome seemed equally desirable to biomedical investigators and to social scientists.

Other aspects of the methodological critiques of biomedical PMS research mounted by social scientists inadvertently consolidated rather than effectively contested biomedical researchers' perspective and claims about menstruation and PMS. For example, social scientists argued on methodological grounds that PMS needs to be carefully defined as a psychological phenomenon for research purposes and, concomitantly, that the phases of the menstrual cycle when moods and behaviors are assessed also needs to be rigorously defined and measured.

In response to pressures for rigorous and consistent definitions of PMS, a "consensus conference" was called at the National Institute of Mental Health (NIMH) in 1983 to enable researchers to discuss and agree on how PMS should be defined and measured in investigations of its correlates, causes, and treatments. The conference "was called" and participants were selected by a group of biomedically trained researchers. The participants were women and men with M.D. degrees and women with Ph.D. degrees (with some exceptions the latter were not notably secure in their institutional base). At this conference, PMS was "officially" defined for scientific purposes. (Women who thought they might have PMS were to fill out questionnaires concerning their emotions and behaviors every day for at least one complete menstrual cycle. A woman could be said to "have PMS" if her daily ratings showed increases of at least 30 percent in negative emotions in and only in the premenstrual phase.)[20]

In some ways, the research definition of PMS emerging from the NIMH consensus conference answered social scientists' critiques and calls for greater precision of definition and measurement of PMS: investigators would now be able to determine what biological correlates (markers) differentiated between

18. D. R. Rubinow, P. Roy-Byrne, M. C. Hoban, P. W. Gold, and R. M. Post, "Prospective Assessment of Menstrually-Related Mood Disorders," *American Journal of Psychiatry* 141 (1984): 163–71.

19. J. Brooks-Gunn, "Differentiating Premenstrual Symptoms and Syndromes," *Psychosomatic Medicine* 47 (1986): 363–71.

20. S. K. Severino and M. L. Moline, *Premenstrual Syndrome: A Clinician's Manual* (New York: Guilford Press, 1989).

women with and without the syndrome so defined and to accumulate information across individual studies. The consensus conference and the definition of PMS it produced did not, however, respond to more fundamental critiques of the assumptions inherent in the biomedical perspective, and the lone social scientist at the conference who voiced some of them (Randi Koeske) was ignored. It also failed to take into account the by then well-documented empirical finding that the knowledge that they are participating in research on menstruation affects women's daily mood ratings, making them more "PMS-like." The selective appropriation of some parts of social scientists' critiques but not others thus had the effect of reinscribing the dominance of a biomedical conceptualization of PMS as a physically based illness and of increasing the power of those professionally certified to diagnosis and treat "it."

Though this was not an intended outcome, biomedical researchers' consolidation of practical as well as conceptual control over research on PMS was also facilitated by social scientists' critical arguments about the importance of rigorous measurement and definition of menstrual cycle phase.[21] To define cycle phase rigorously in physiological terms, one needs to assess at least gonadal hormone levels in the blood. Given federal and most university regulations for the protection of human subjects, only physicians or medical personnel supervised by physicians (nurses, technicians) can draw blood. So the rigorous definition and measurement of menstrual cycle phase advocated in social scientists' critiques can, for all practical purposes, be done only in biomedical research settings, or by social scientists in collaboration with biomedically trained researchers. In such collaborations, the biomedical personnel almost always have more institutional power, and this translates practically into conceptual control over the formulation of research questions. (They also have greater credibility with federal funding agencies on whose grant review panels biomedical researchers increasingly predominate in times of tight research funds and concomitant scientific conservatism. This greater power with regard to funding also translates into conceptual control over what questions will and will not be asked in the research and what methods will be used.)

So the outcome of social scientists' efforts to contest biomedical researchers' claims about menstrual experiences has been to consolidate biomedical researchers' control over the formulation of scientific discourse about PMS.

21. The Society for Menstrual Cycle Research, an interdisciplinary group founded and run by feminist social scientists, was active in formulating research guidelines for defining cycle phase in a consistent way. My interpretation of some of the guideline's unintended consequences is not widely shared by these researchers.

Social scientists were able to investigate normal menstrual experiences within traditional behavioral research paradigms,[22] but they were left almost power-less to contest within biomedicine the claim that there is a biologically based illness, PMS, that negatively affects many women's work performance and family relationships.

At an international conference in 1987, attended by many of the most prominent PMS researchers, it became clear from discussions both in public sessions and in private that there was considerable agreement on the state-of-the-art evidence about PMS.[23] No known biological correlate had been reliably identified that distinguished between women with and without PMS and no biological treatment had reliably been shown to be better than placebo. It was tacitly known or explicitly agreed that placebo effects in PMS research are very high (on the order of 50 percent) and that it is difficult in practical terms to find women for research projects who meet the strict criteria operationally defin-ing PMS (women with "true PMS"). This consensus was recently confirmed, though not affirmed explicitly, by a committee of biomedical researchers and clinicians assembled under the aegis of the American Psychiatric Association (APA) to review research relevant to the diagnostic category Late Luteal Phase Dysphoric Disorder (PMS) in Appendix A of the DSM-IIIR.[24]

The APA work group on the Late Luteal Phase Dysphoric Disorder diag-nosis thoroughly reviewed the research literature on PMS, focusing primarily on studies that met clearly specified criteria for methodological adequacy. In a draft of their final report, they summarized the research articles in tabular form and in the text and presented a summary description at the end. This draft document is itself an interesting case study of the social construction of scien-tific knowledge. The summary of the section dealing with treatment of PMS, for

22. A. J. Dan and L. L. Lewis, Menstrual Health in Women's Lives (Urbana, Ill.: University of Chicago Press, 1992).

23. Demers, McGuire, Phillips, and Rubinow, Premenstrual, Postpartum, and Menopausal Mood Disorders.

24. S. J. Gallant and J. A. Hamilton, "On a Premenstrual Psychiatric Diagnosis: What's in a Name?" Professional Psychology: Research and Practice 19 (1988): 271–78. When the struggle began over whether or not PMS should be included in the American Psychiatric Association's man-ual of "official" psychiatric illnesses, it is notable that the feminist scientists most effective in questioning its inclusion were biomedically trained researchers with M.D. degrees. Perhaps because of their training and the fundamental assumptions it imparts, they were the only ones who could enter this arena of contestation with any credibility among the biomedical researchers and clinicians who controlled the discourse and set the parameters and terms of the debate within the profession. Although contested, PMS was ultimately included (under a different name, Late Luteal Phase Dysphoric Disorder) in an appendix of the DSM-IIIR, and it will also be in the revision (DSM-IV) now underway.

example, concludes that [eight treatments are named] are "superior to placebo for relief of premenstrual symptoms." By my count of the research studies *as described in the body of the report*, however, only seven of the forty-three research articles reviewed found such evidence, and it was relief of *physical* symptoms (breast tenderness, etc.) that was found, as were side effects of the treatments in several cases.[25] But since the APA definition of PMS (Late Luteal Phase Dysphoric Disorder) specifically classifies it as an *affective* (mood or emotional) disorder, treatments affecting only physical symptoms would simply not be relevant to the question of PMS treatment.

Having participated in and observed research on menstruation and PMS for the past two decades, three conclusions now seem reasonable (indeed, inescapable) to me. One is that some women genuinely experience psychological suffering and are helped by a diagnosis of Late Luteal Phase Dysphoric Disorder. A second is that, although it has not yet been identified, a pathophysiological mechanism may eventually be discovered that will lead to biological treatment more effective than placebos for distress specific to the premenstrual phase of the cycle. A third is that the overwhelming weight of scientific evidence so far suggests that further biomedical research into causes and treatments, conducted with currently available techniques and hypotheses, is not likely to be any more fruitful empirically than it has been to date. To date, there is still no sound evidence that PMS is a physiologically based illness

25. As a member of the advisory committee to the work group concerned with Late Luteal Phase Dysphoric Disorder, I pointed out this discrepancy between the text of the draft report and the summary, but I focused most of my comments on the inclusion of "changes in appetite" as one of the diagnostic criteria for Late Luteal Phase Dysphoric Disorder. I cited the large scientific literature on changes in food intake during the reproductive cycle in nonhuman animals and the rapidly increasing literature on food intake and appetite changes in human beings as well (in women with asymptomatic cycles). Why, I asked, are appetite changes that can be observed in the population of menstruating women at large included as a diagnostic criterion for a mental illness? (There is one published paper claiming appetite changes are *larger* in women with PMS than in women with asymptomatic cycles, but the data in the paper are unclear.)

When I previously raised this question with the physician in charge of the revision of DSM-IIIR, Dr. Robert Spitzer, he indicated that appetite change was included as a symptom in the diagnosis of PMS because women who show up in doctors' offices and clinics complaining of PMS report experiencing appetite changes. This is of course tautological and an error of elementary deductive logic. (Presumably the women complaining of PMS also would report, if asked, that they drank milk as infants, too, but having drunk milk as an infant does not therefore become a symptom in the diagnosis of PMS.)

One reason appetite changes have been so readily if illogically assimilated to a diagnosis of mental illness, however, may be that they represent a concretization of broader cultural issues and conflicts surrounding women's (out-of-)control appetites(s) which can be "managed" through medicalization or other disciplined productions of the "good body".

that seriously interferes with work performance and family life, or that biolog-ical treatments for PMS are more effective than placebos.

If only logic and evidence were involved, if scientific research were the disinterested, self-corrective search for truth it is often portrayed to be, I believe biomedical researchers investigating PMS would recognize that a dead end has been reached and would pursue other (or simply additional) lines of inquiry about menstrual experiences, using different paradigms, asking dif-ferent questions. They might investigate, for example, the meaning and signifi-cance of the very high cure rate of PMS using placebos, the eagerness with which some women in certain situations interpret their experiences and ac-tions as manifestations of disordered body states, the social contexts within which encounters between women and physicians result in a diagnosis of PMS, the temporal coincidence of the emergence of feminism as a social movement and PMS as a medical diagnosis of a biologically based illness afflicting women.

But science is not simply a disinterested search for truth, guided only by logic and objective data, just as biomedicine is not simply the treatment of physical diseases. Both are human activities socially organized in particular ways to produce, among other things, authoritative discourses about illnesses and how they are to be treated. One effect of these discourses is to medicalize (and thereby contain and control) deviant or potentially subversive experi-ences and actions. PMS represents women as out of control, out of role—but "safely" so. As such it simultaneously expresses and contains danger, suffering, resistance. PMS portrays a woman as not responsible for her emotions and actions and as lacking legitimate reasons for them—reasons which, if acknowl-edged, would require a morally and interpersonally serious response. Her own experience of being "out of control" leads her to seek and accept medical supervision in exchange not only for freedom from social sanctions for "inap-propriate" (unaccountable) feelings and actions but also for the subtle license a diagnosis of PMS can give her for forms of aggression and power she "nor-mally" does not accept as part of her being. ("I have PMS, so you'd better get out of my way, dammit!")

This view of science and of PMS is of course seriously at odds with that of many biomedical researchers, who rhetorically justify their activities in terms of a positivist philosophy of science and a representational theory of truth. The social power of scientists' self-justifying rhetoric comes from the fact that it expresses and reproduces assumptions and purposes broadly shared and deeply embedded in the consciousness of individuals and in a matrix of other powerful social institutions. Ironically, however, it is a view of science and truth which, if held consistently, is itself unconfirmed by empirical research over the past decade in the social studies of science and technology and in the sociology of scientific knowledge.[26]

Bruno Latour has argued, for example, that if we observe scientists in action, rather than accept their rhetoric as a description of how they operate, it is evident that disputes over knowledge claims in science (statements of fact, hypotheses) are not decided by "truth."[27] Rather, the outcome of a scientific dispute is what comes to be seen, after the fact (after the "facts" are settled), as the truth. In Latour's analysis, contestation over scientific knowledge (truth) claims is a process in which support from powerful social groups or institutions "outside" the scientific laboratory can be enlisted by linking a particular knowledge claim to interests embedded in the ongoing activities of "nonscientific" enterprises.[28] Scientific "truth," the "established facts" in a research domain, are knowledge claims that can no longer be effectively contested, that cannot be successfully challenged or countered within the conventions of scientific discourse because challengers lack requisite ties to powerful social institutions "outside" science whose support constitutes in practical terms the ability to do science in that domain. (For example, only particular people, credentialed and disciplined in particular ways, embedded in laboratories that are material monuments to "nonscientific" interests, are in a position to contest a knowledge claim in particle physics with any prospect of success.)

Latour's analysis of science in action is thus an account of scientific discourse as an arena of cultural contestation or, as a somewhat different analysis would frame it, of the social construction of scientific knowledge. It seems to me to suggest a reasonable story about the past two decades of changes in scientific research on menstruation and premenstrual syndrome.

In the course of scientific disputes over the past twenty years, it has become increasingly evident that biomedical researchers' knowledge claims about PMS have come to prevail over those of social scientists.[29] Biomedical

26. K. D. Knorr-Cetina and M. Mulkay, *Science Observed: Perspectives on the Social Study of Science* (Beverly Hills, Calif.: Sage, 1983); B. Latour and S. Woolgar, *Laboratory Life: The Construction of Scientific Facts*, 2d ed. (Princeton, N. J.: Princeton University Press, 1986); W. E. Bijker, T. P. Hughes, and T. Pinch, eds., *The Social Construction of Technological Systems: New Directions in the Sociology and History of Technology* (Cambridge, Mass.: MIT Press, 1987).

27. B. Latour, *Science in Action* (Cambridge, Mass.: Harvard University Press, 1987).

28. Ibid.; B. Latour, "Give Me a Laboratory and I Will Raise the World," in *Science Observed: Perspectives on the Social Study of Science*, ed. K. D. Knorr-Cetina and M. Mulkay (Beverly Hills, Calif.: Sage, 1983).

29. S. Laws, "The Sexual Politics of Premenstrual Tension," *Women's Studies International Forum* 6 (1983): 19–31; E. Martin, "Premenstrual Syndrome: Discipline, Work, and Anger in

researchers will no longer accept challenges to the methodology and conceptualizations that constitute PMS as a scientific fact of a particular kind. The existence of an illness called PMS is now incontestably established in the biomedical literature, and scientists in this tradition no longer take into serious account (if they refer to them at all) articles in the social scientific literature debating the status of PMS as a biomedical fact. As in the popular culture, biomedical literature now routinely and unproblematically (incontestably) refers to PMS as something some women "have." Permitted scientific disputes now concern what causes "it" and how "it" can be treated.

In hindsight and in light of Latour's analysis of science as culturally embedded practices, this outcome is not surprising. Biomedical researchers' view of PMS can be linked with and furthers the interests of powerful social institutions in this country: it is an illness whose status as scientific "fact" within a biomedical framework seems to be overdetermined as a convergence of the goals and routine activities of various enterprises "outside" the laboratory or clinical research center.

Drug companies seeking to expand the market for their products promote the idea of PMS as a physically based illness (treatable with drugs) through the kinds of activities they routinely use to expand their markets. They sponsor continuing medical education seminars on PMS to promote awareness of "it" as a physically based illness; they sponsor events for medical writers and editors of mass-circulation magazines and newspapers to promote awareness of "it" among women readers; they sponsor scientific conferences (and publication of the proceedings) to promote awareness of "it" in the community of biomedical researchers and clinicians who deal with women's reproductive functioning; they sponsor research projects on "it" by individual scientists; they commission individual clinicians to write books about "it" and its treatment. They repackage existing over-the-counter products and advertise them on

Late Industrial Societies, in *Blood Magic: The Anthropology of Menstruation*, ed. T. Buckley and A. Gottlieb (Berkeley: University of California Press, 1988), 161–81; J. N. Zita, "The Premenstrual Syndrome: 'Dis-Easing' the Female Cycle," *Hypatia* 3 (1988): 1, reprinted in *Feminism and Science*, ed. N. Tuana (Bloomington: Indiana University Press), 188–210. In brief, biomedical researchers' essential claim was and is that PMS is a physically-based illness which disrupts the work and family life of those who have it. In their most sharply contrasting claims, some social scientists have argued that PMS is one way of construing/constructing feelings and actions which could be differently interpreted, which could have different social and individual meanings. The language of feminism and collective social action, they argue, provided a more coherent understanding (and self-understanding) of women's experiences of the cultural contradictions of capitalism than does the language of PMS, illness, and medical treatment.

television and in print media to meet the increased demand for relief from this widespread and troubling illness from which many women suffer and which doctors are at last taking seriously as a "real" illness.

Physicians, seeking to maximize the size of their medically insured patient populations and minimize malpractice insurance costs, respond to changing social circumstances by incorporating PMS in their activities. In the face of skyrocketing rates for malpractice insurance for practicing obstetrics, and perhaps also in response to the changing demographics of women of childbearing age, obstetrician-gynecologists shift away from obstetrics toward exclusively gynecological practices in which a population of patients with PMS might be treated. Psychiatrists, continuing the twenty-five-year trend away from psychoanalysis and toward biological conceptions of mental illness and treatment, move to expand their practices among patient populations with biologically based mental illnesses such as PMS.[30] They included PMS in their official professional manual of diagnoses (the American Psychiatric Association's DSM-IIIR) for the first time in 1987, thus facilitating reimbursement by insurance companies for the treatment of this "disease."

Physician-researchers, seeking career advancement as scientists and often working as faculty within medical schools or in research laboratories in federal agencies, develop clinical research projects for which a physician-directed treatment program may support the costs of the research and also supply the patient population suitable for scientific investigations. Physician-researchers with large clinical practices developed through PMS clinics of various sorts are likely to be able to identify a large enough sample of women who "have" "true PMS" to conduct research that will be publishable in journals that confer scientific prestige and lead to academic advancement.

Many women and men, seeking to understand and make sense of some women's experiences of the cultural contradictions of gender under capitalism in the late twentieth century, embrace "PMS for the advantages of the sick role that accompany it. These advantages accrue not only to the individual who adopts the sick role (she is exempted from accountability for actions and

---

30. P. Brown, "The Name Game: Toward a Sociology of Diagnosis," *Journal of Mind and Behavior* 11, nos. 3 and 4 (1990): 385–406 (special issue, *Challenging the Therapeutic State: Critical Perspectives on Psychiatry and the Mental Health System*, ed. D. Cohen). This shift is partly related to status anxieties of psychiatrists vis-à-vis other more "hard nosed" specialties in medicine and to the entry of nonmedically trained therapists into the mental health field; see S. A. Kirk and H. Kutchins, *The Selling of DSM: The Rhetoric of Science in Psychiatry* (New York: Aldine de Gruyter, 1992).

feelings she would "normally" be held responsible for) but also to those in her immediate social environment and the broader society as well. In Parsons' original formulation, "The sick role is . . . a mechanism which . . . channels deviance so that the two most dangerous potentialities, namely group formation and successful establishment of the claim of legitimacy, are avoided. The sick are tied up, not with other deviants to form a 'subculture' of the sick, but each with a group of nonsick, his [sic] personal circle, and, above all, physicians. The sick thus become a statistical status and are deprived of the possibility of forming a solidary collectivity."[31]

Parsons's formulation would suggest, then, that as feminist analyses of women's dis-ease and protest declined in prominence (and shifted in meaning) in public domains over the past two decades, the analysis of women's experiences implied by PMS may serve to validate (but also to individualize, privatize, and medicalize) experiences and actions that otherwise might not have any publicly intelligible (discussable) meaning. For many women, talking about PMS (feeling angry, out of control) is better than staying silent or taking on the psychic and interpersonal consequences of feminist analysis and praxis.

It is primarily because a biomedical conception of PMS could be linked with the interests of these (and other) powerful social institutions and cultural movements that biomedical researchers were able to assert and defend against challenges their scientific statements and hypotheses about "its" nature and etiology. Drug companies, physicians (clinicians and researchers), women struggling to work double days in a cultural climate of pervasive but subtle antifeminism—all benefit in different ways from the biomedical version of PMS and do not benefit from efforts to contest it within the scientific domain.[32] So biomedical researchers were able, after some initial response to challenges by social scientists, to "up the ante" in scientific disputes about the nature, causes,

31. T. Parsons, The Social System (Glencoe, Ill.: Free Press, 1951).
32. B. Barnes, Interests and the Growth of Knowledge (London: Routledge & Kegan Paul, 1977); D. Bloor, Knowledge and Social Imagery (London: Routledge & Kegan Paul, 1976). In simplified form, the "strong program" in the social studies of science sought to demonstrate a relationship between social "interests" and the content of scientific discourses as if the former were fairly unproblematically reflected in the latter. The relationship is now widely recognized to be much more subtle and complex, however, requiring detailed empirical investigation of how, concretely and practically, interests come to be linked in various ways and to different degrees with activities in laboratories. My list of some of the social "interests" converging on and in scientific discourses about PMS is intended merely to sketch areas where such empirical investigations might fruitfully begin. Social interests in this sense should not be construed as motives and intentions of individual persons.

and treatments of PMS" by enlisting resources from these institutions and forces "outside" science.

To contest claims about PMS within the scientific domain in 1991 (that is, to publish articles about it in prestigious biomedical journals that will affect the direction of research and clinical practice and be covered in the popular media) investigators must, in practical terms, be able to draw blood, have access to a large clinical population from which women with "true PMS" can be screened, and accept without question the technology for defining and diagnosing PMS.[33] For both legal and other structural reasons, social scientists are much less likely than biomedical researchers to be able to do any of these things.

The biomedical version of PMS emerges as uncontested truth because it is incontestable, not because it is supported by an overwhelming preponderance of empirical data and reasonable arguments. Indeed, it is the very striking disjunction between the state of the current research data and the ever-increasing momentum of the biomedical version of PMS as a topic of research and focus of clinical and commercial activity that reveals the "nonscientific" forces shaping scientists' activities and scientific discourses. PMS is a gendered concept of illness that came into being in our culture in the early 1970s, when feminists were challenging gender relations and the ideologies supporting them. It furthers interests reflected in the routine activities of specific and powerful social institutions. In both the interpersonal and more broadly social domains, PMS serves to contain women's potential social protest by channeling interpretations of their suffering and actions into medical rather than political forms. These multiple cultural meanings and functions of PMS are, it seems to me, unrelated to the question of whether or not a pathophysiological mechanism for a premenstrual disease is identified in the future by biomedical researchers.

During the 1970s and 1980s, scientific discourse about PMS was an arena of cultural contestation, of struggle over what would count as the socially authoritative "scientific" meaning of some of the anger and distress some women experience. But the contest now seems to be over. One lesson feminists might draw from this case study of the cultural embeddedness of a gendered illness is

33. M. B. Parlee, "Integrating Biological and Social Scientific Research on Menopause," *Multidisciplinary Perspectives on Menopause. Annals of the New York Academy of Sciences*, ed. M. Flint, F. Kronenberg, and W. Utian, 592 (1990): 378–89. These technologies are the methods and interpretative assumptions involved in the use of self-report questionnaires about moods and the concomitant willed disregard of data and logical arguments which problematize them.

that contestation within the domain of science is not likely to be effective.[34] This may be important to keep in mind now that the same social interests (drug companies, units of the National Institutes of Health, clinicians, biomedical researchers) are lining up behind a biomedical perspective on menopause, an area with the potential for even more significant material effects on women's bodies.[35] To influence the directions of biomedical research on PMS and on menopause, more direct political pressures of the sort activist organizations successfully brought to bear on AIDS treatment research protocols are probably required.[36] Latour's analysis suggests that these and other case histories of scientific discourse as an arena for cultural contestation may yield lessons of some general significance, since this is, in practice, how scientific activity normally proceeds.

34. C. Kitzinger, "The Rhetoric of Pseudoscience," in *Deconstructing Social Psychology*, ed. I. Parker and J. Shotter (New York: Routledge, 1990), 61–75; M. B. Parlee, "On PMS and Psychiatric Abnormality," *Feminism and Psychology* 2 (1992): 105–8.

35. M. Flint, F. Kronenberg, and W. Utian, eds., "Multidiciplinary Perspectives on Menopause," *Annals of the New York Academy of Sciences* 595 (1990). Here the biomedical claim is that menopause is psychologically and socially debilitating, with physical sequelae that will require expensive medical treatment and unduly burden the health-care system unless women are prescribed and accept estrogen therapy lasting over a period of many years. (Pressure on women to take estrogen to prevent osteoporosis and hip fractures seems likely to grow as debate over health care reform further heightens the cost awareness of third-party payers.) The cultural contest in which this biomedical discourse is embedded concerns the meaning of middle-aged women's lives and bodies and the ease with which physicians will be able to administer powerful drugs whose long-term effects (including those termed and treated as "side effects") are not presently known.

36. D. Crimp, *AIDS: Cultural Analysis/Cultural Activism* 43 (Winter 1987): 3–17; reprint, Cambridge, Mass.: MIT Press, 1987); P. A. Treichler, "AIDS, Homophobia, and Biomedical Discourse: An Epidemic of Signification," *Cultural Studies* 1, no. 3 (1987): 263–305.

7

Differential Prohibition, Scientific
Discourse, and Anorexiant
Stimulants

Arthur P. Leccese

Using Anorexiant Stimulants to Obtain the "Good Body"

Although it is generally accepted that such physical attributes as height are distributed normally within the human population, those concerned with the medicalization of deviance have argued that medical concern with obesity pathologizes normal human genetic variability.[1] Concepts of health are themselves laden with sociocultural biases. Yet those who equate the "good body" with the "healthy body" might well object to the cultural hegemony of slimness and might ask why individuals and their physicians are willing to risk the potential negative consequences of acute or chronic use of anorexiant stim-

1. T. Szasz, *Ceremonial Chemistry: The Ritual Persecution of Drugs, Addicts and Pushers*, rev. ed. (Holmes Beach, Fla.: Learning Publications, 1985).

ulants[2] to achieve weight loss. Even the simple answer that obesity itself presents considerable risks of morbidity and mortality is inadequate, for there are serious problems in defining various degrees of obesity.[3] Furthermore, sophisticated statistical techniques are required to determine the relative role of obesity in diseases (such as the various cardiomyopathies) that have a host of known risk factors.[4] Even worse, there is mounting evidence that tyrannical aesthetic norms may be leading large numbers of people to reduce their weight to levels well below that which the medical community agrees is healthy. The resultant conditions of anorexia and starvation present their own risks of morbidity and mortality.[5] Even those who advocate the libertarian position that people should consider themselves obese only if they themselves feel uncomfortable with their weight cannot deny the potentially disastrous influence of aesthetic norms divorced from health concerns.[6] Perhaps, some might argue, it is time to borrow a technique from the gay rights movement, and begin the process of helping the statistically "overweight" to gain self-acceptance through a type of obesity liberation.

Regardless of whether one views obesity as a life-style choice, a statistical variation, or a medical disease, one can nonetheless insist that scientifically sound criteria be employed in evaluating the effectiveness of medical aids to weight loss. Research with animal subjects allows strict regulation and evaluation of both the quantity and the quality of food intake[7] as well as investigations

2. A class of compounds that have a stimulating effect on brain activity and suppress appetite.

3. A. H. Kissebah, D. S. Freedman, and A. N. Peiris, "Health Risks of Obesity," *Medical Clinics of North America* 73 (1989): 111–38; G. A. Bray, "Classification and Evaluation of the Obesities," and D. S. Gray, "Diagnosis and Prevalence of Obesity," *Medical Clinics of North America* 73 (1989): 161–84.

4. Kissebah, Freedman, Peiris, "Health Risks of Obesity."

5. B. F. Shaw and P. E. Garfinkel, "Research Problems in the Eating Disorders," *International Journal of Eating Disorders* 9 (1990): 545–55.

6. H. Gwirtsman, W. Kaye, M. Weintraub, and D. C. Jimerson, "Pharmacologic Treatment of Eating Disorders," *Psychiatric Clinics of North America* 7 (1984): 863–78.

7. R. W. Foltin, "Effects of Anorectic Drugs on the Topography of Feeding Behavior in Baboons," *Journal of Pharmacology and Experimental Therapeutics* 249 (1989): 101–5; M. Rosofsky and N. Geary, "Phenylpropanolamine and Amphetamine Disrupt Postprandial Satiety in Rats," *Pharmacology, Biochemistry and Behavior* 34 (1989): 797–803; D. H. Schwartz and B. G. Hoebel, "Effect of Phenylpropanolamine on Diet Selection in Rats," *Pharmacology, Biochemistry and Behavior* 31 (1989): 721–23; P. J. Wellman and R. Cockroft, "Effects of Amphetamine and Phenylpropanolamine on Latency to Feed and Cumulative Liquid Diet Intake in Rats," *Pharmacology, Biochemistry and Behavior* 32 (1989): 147–50; P. J. Wellman and A. Levy, "Inhibition of Feeding and Hoarding Behaviors by Phenylpropanolamine in the Adult Rat, *Pharmacology, Biochemistry and Behavior* 29 (1988): 79–81.

of how drug-induced variations in food consumption and food preferences influence subsequent drug effects.[8] Moreover, research with animals facilitates investigations aimed at determining the change at the level of the brain cell producing any observed anorexiant effect.[9]

Of course, ethical concerns restrict the range of research that scientists may conduct with human subjects. In addition, both subject selection and criteria for success become much more difficult in human experimentation. To define a successful anorexiant as one that lessens hunger and reduces food intake, each of these effects must be demonstrated in both normal-weight and overweight subjects. Research has shown, moreover, that compounds that induce acute reductions in hunger and food intake may not necessarily induce weight loss over long periods of time.[10] Therefore, more recent research has been aimed at answering the clinically relevant question whether putative anorexiants help obese patients to lose weight. This approach has its own difficulties, not least of which is the problem of defining qualitative and quantitative differences in human obesity.[11] If one uses a definition of obesity that is too narrow, research results may not generalize to the clinically relevant population. On the other hand, if the definition is too inclusive, research subjects may include false positives who do not actually have the clinically relevant disorder.[12]

Perhaps the most serious difficulty in evaluating the efficacy of anorexiant stimulants is determining whether these drugs will "cure" obesity (that is, ensure that weight will not be regained once the drug regimen is halted). Reviewers of the literature on drug treatment of obesity have noted that we "demand a higher standard for medications used in treating obesity than we do for treatments of any other chronic condition." These reviewers note, for example, that scientists do not consider the recurrence of ulcers after a halt in H^2 blockers as an indication of failure.[13] Further, they claim, we still regard the

8. R. Marks-Kaufman and R. B. Kanarek, "Dietary Modulation of the Anorectic Potency of Amphetamine," Pharmacology, Biochemistry and Behavior 35 (1990): 301–6; and Schwartz and Hoebel, "Effect of Phenylpropanolamine on Diet Selection in Rats."

9. S. O. Cole, "Brain Mechanisms of Amphetamine-Induced Anorexia, Locomotion and Stereotypy: A Review," Neuroscience and Biobehavioral Reviews 2 (1978): 89–100.

10. T. Silverstone, "Clinical Use of Appetite Suppressants," Drug and Alcohol Dependence 17 (1986): 151–67.

11. Bray, "Classification and Evaluation of the Obesities"; Gray, "Diagnosis and Prevalence of Obesity."

12. Shaw and Garfinkel, "Research Problems in the Eating Disorders."

13. M. Weintraub and G. A. Bray, "Drug Treatment of Obesity," Medical Clinics of North America 73 (1989): 237–49.

birth control pill as effective even though sexually active women may become pregnant when they stop taking it.

The final difficulty in evaluating the efficacy of anorexiant stimulants involves the use of a double-blind experimental design. In a double-blind experiment, neither the person giving the drug nor the one receiving it is aware of whether the drug is an experimental substance, an active placebo, or an inactive placebo. The double-blind design is commonly used to insure that the expectations, enthusiasms, and biases of the experimenters and subjects do not influence the results. At least one researcher, however, has asked, "Are there ways in which the design of studies intended to establish . . . efficacy can have a significant impact on the ultimate conclusions derived from the studies?"[14] C. Winick presented data revealing that subjects who were aware that they were part of a double-blind experiment involving placebo controls lost less weight after six weeks of phenylpropanolamine (PPA) consumption than did subjects using PPA for an equivalent time period in a real-life situation. He attributed this differential weight loss to a variety of cognitive factors, including the ambivalence about the medication displayed by those who knew they had a 50–50 chance of getting a placebo, and the superior motivation of those who chose to consume PPA in response to their individual needs rather than to the timing and needs of the experimenter. Despite the relatively diminished effect of PPA shown by studies employing a double-blind design, a variety of experiments revealed that subjects given PPA demonstrated greater weight loss than those given placebo.[15]

Conflicting conceptions of the "good body" will lead to different conclusions about the practical significance of the statistically significant experimental success of PPA. A concern for the "good body" that extends beyond culturally determined visual aesthetics to embrace a concern for health demands assessment of the safety as well as the effectiveness of the compound. Unfortunately, U.S. drug laws impose a differential prohibition upon the use of anorexiant stimulants. Attempts to reconcile the descriptive laws of behavioral pharmacology with the proscriptive laws of state legislatures introduce biases into

14. C. Winick, "Some Implications of the Double-Blind Format in Evaluating Drug Efficacy: Studies of the Appetite Suppressant Phenylpropanolamine," *Clinical Research Practices and Drug Regulatory Affairs* 6 (1988): 113–28.

15. F. Greenway, "A Double-Blind Clinical Evaluation of the Anorectic Activity of Phenylpropanolamine versus Placebo," *Clinical Therapeutics* 11 (1989): 584–89; L. Lasagna, "Efficacy of Phenylpropanolamine as an Anorectic Drug in the Treatment of Obesity," in *Phenylpropanolamine: A Review*, ed. L. Lasagna (New York: Wiley, 1988), 354–62; Silverstone, "Clinical Use of Appetite Suppressants"; Weintraub and Bray, "Drug Treatment of Obesity."

evaluations of the relative safety of PPA that confound discussions of health and chronic drug consumption, further distorting putatively scientific discourse regarding the "good body." Foucault has made it clear that putatively medical pronouncements about health and the body are a powerful means of coercing acceptance of dominant cultural values. As Mary Brown Parlee points out in her discussion of scientific discourse regarding premenstrual syndrome, the rules scientists use to communicate their research findings do not allow for the direct communication of personal views on social issues. Nonetheless, the way scientists state their research questions allows them to mask as scientific truth their culturally determined attitudes toward "the politics of the nervous system," to paraphrase the much-maligned Timothy Leary.[16]

Differential Prohibition of Anorexiant Stimulants

Amphetamine, a derivative of phenylethylamine, was the first drug widely used by modern physicians as an anorexiant. Researchers in 1937 who were investigating the efficacy of amphetamine for narcolepsy noted the weight loss that often accompanied the drug treatment. Within a year, the New England Journal of Medicine hailed amphetamine as an ideal pharmacological treatment for obesity, because "on the one hand it decreases appetite, and on the other so increases the sense of well being and of energy that physical activity is also spontaneously increased."[17] These very qualities (that is, the decrease of appetite and the sense of well-being) resulted in the overuse and misuse of amphetamine by both obese and normal-weight individuals seeking a recreational intoxication. Amphetamine is now listed as a Schedule II drug on the Drug Enforcement Administration's Schedule of Controlled Substances and cannot be legally prescribed for the purpose of inducing a pharmacologically mediated weight loss.[18]

The removal of amphetamine from the list of licit anorexiants led medicinal chemists to create a wide variety of additional phenylethylamine derivatives. It is noteworthy that the goal of their research was to create an anorexiant with little or no stimulant or pleasure-inducing potential.[19] It appears, how-

16. T. Leary, Politics of Ecstasy (Berkeley, Calif.: Ronin, 1990).
17. Silverstone, "Clinical Use of Appetite Suppressants."
18. The Drug Enforcement Administration is the governmental body that monitors the prescription of potentially addictive drugs. The drugs most rigidly controlled are listed as Schedule I or II; those less rigidly controlled, as Schedule III, IV, or IV.
19. Drug Enforcement Administration, Physician's Manual: An International Outline of the Controlled Substances Act of 1970 (Washington, D.C.: DEA, Department of Justice, 1985).

ever, that all the phenylethylamine derivatives have retained, to a greater or lesser clinically relevant degree, the stimulant and pleasure-inducing properties of amphetamine. Most of these phenylethylamine derivatives are categorized as Schedule III or IV. Apologists for differential prohibition suggest that the lesser restrictions placed upon these other substances reflect their lesser stimulant or pleasure-inducing potential.[20] A skeptical person might conclude instead that these drugs are characterized as relatively less stimulating than amphetamine simply to allow physicians, trained to loathe and fear the illicit drug amphetamine, to comfortably prescribe these "safer" agents for their patients who desire weight loss.

Despite great controversy regarding the safety of acute or chronic consumption of the phenylethylamine derivative PPA, the medicolegal establishment has so far resisted attempts to end differential prohibition by placing PPA on the Schedule of Controlled Substances. PPA is a common ingredient in a variety of widely used over-the-counter (sometimes available through the mail) nasal decongestants and diet aids, including heavily advertised products such as Acutrim and Dexatrim.[21]

Physicians who exercise independent clinical judgment and prescribe amphetamine for weight loss risk arrest and forfeiture of the right to practice medicine. Note also that most other phenylethylamines can be obtained for weight loss only with a physician's prescription. Given this differential prohibition of phenylethylamine-derived anorexiant stimulants, it is not surprising that there are those who passionately assert that PPA presents an underrecognized danger requiring restrictive legislation.[22] Advocates of PPA prohibition assert that they are merely trying to protect the obese from exploitation by unscrupulous doctors and money-grubbing pharmaceutical companies. The charge that these advocates of PPA prohibition are in fact participants in a paternalistic system aiming to coerce free individuals into compliance with dominant social values is usually met, to say the least, with great skepticism. These prohibitionists passionately assert that it is indeed the negative health consequences of PPA ingestion that justify the imposition of fines and imprisonment for those who dare to violate laws against the manufacture, sale, and possession of this drug. We can learn much about discourse regarding the

20. Weintraub and Bray, "Drug Treatment of Obesity."

21. J. E. Mitchell, C. Pomeroy, and M. Huber, "A Clinician's Guide to the Eating Disorders Medicine Cabinet," *International Journal of the Eating Disorders* 7 (1988): 211–33.

22. E. Bernstein and B. M. Diskant, "Phenylpropanolamine: A Potentially Hazardous Drug," *Annals of Emergency Medicine* 11 (1982): 311–15; A. Blum, "Phenylpropanolamine: An Over-the-Counter Amphetamine?" *Journal of the American Medical Association* 245 (1981): 1346–47.

"good body" by comparing the harshness of present and proposed antidrug laws with the comparatively mild professional and societal responses to reports of the dangers of elective plastic surgery, for example.

Prohibitionists currently enjoy powerful influence upon scientific discourse, but others assert with equal passion that the free availability of PPA accurately reflects its relative safety. These individuals are likely to deride calls for the prohibition of PPA as scientifically unsound and unjustified on the basis of "guilt by association" with other structurally related, but (putatively) pharmacologically and behaviorally distinct, phenylethylamine derivatives.[23] It will be interesting to see if future historians will one day use antiprohibitionist literature to reveal that even in the midst of a so-called War on Drugs, scientific discourse about the "good body" can (all too rarely) contest prevailing social ideologies.

Anorexiant stimulants are not the only medical intervention people have used to aid weight loss. Medical experiments have been conducted to evaluate the safety and efficacy of drugs that increase basal metabolic rate (the rate at which the body utilizes energy), drugs that modify the taste of food or the absorption from the gastrointestinal tract,[24] and even surgical techniques aimed at interfering with the normal absorption of ingested foods.[25] There are even those who seek weight reduction through the use of laxatives, diuretics, and purgatives,[26] although these techniques do not find approval in the medical community. None of these methods of weight reduction is without risk. This plethora of drugs and techniques suggests that physicians and individuals are more than willing to risk at least some potential negative consequences to attain weight loss. The willingness to take risks in the pursuit of a lower weight makes it all the more urgent that the physician and the patient have access to sound information about the relative risk-benefit ratios of the wide range of medical aids available for weight reduction. Advocates of the "good body" can rightly require that pharmacological means of countering obesity do not reduce health as they reduce weight. As noted above, however, those who seek to employ harsh punishments to prevent the use of PPA could justifiably be

23. K. S. Pruder and J. P. Morgan, "Persuading by Citation: An Analysis of the Reference of Fifty-Three Published Reports of Phenylpropanolamine's Clinical Toxicity," *Clinical Pharmacology and Therapeutics* 42 (1987): 1–9.

24. Weintraub and Bray, "Drug Treatment of Obesity."

25. Gray, "Diagnosis and Prevalence of Obesity."

26. Mitchell, Pomeroy, and Huber, "A Clinician's Guide to the Eating Disorders Medicine Cabinet."

called to task should there be noticeable disparities between assessments of the potential harm of these weight-loss techniques and the methods used to discourage their indiscriminate adoption.

Is a Body of Reduced Weight Necessarily a "Good Body"?

Different reviewers looking at the same experimental results may come to different conclusions regarding the anorexiant efficacy of PPA, perhaps because of the difficulties in evaluating the efficacy of anorexiant stimulants. The widely disparate views of scientists and others regarding the safety of anorexiant stimulants in general and of PPA in particular are of concern here. Some abhor the use of any drug as a means of aiding weight reduction, whereas others support a differential policy, in which some anorexiant stimulants are promoted while others are rigorously prohibited. Some opponents of all drugs for the treatment of obesity advocate greater tolerance for the statistically over-weight individual and a concentrated effort to elevate his or her self-esteem as well. Other opponents of all anorexiant drugs argue instead that willpower, reduced caloric intake, and increased energy expenditure must take the place of "drugs." It is not my purpose here to argue with those who advocate greater tolerance of diversity, although it may not be too much to ask that they extend their sympathies to those who are distressed with their weight for whatever reason and who seek medicinal aids to weight reduction. On the other hand, I argue against those who would deny others the benefit of all anorexiant stimulants because of their erroneous application of pseudoscientific theory and prohibitionist-motivated concerns to the acute and chronic effects of substances that may have a pleasure-producing effect on the brain. More important, the urge to justify the present differential prohibition bastardizes scientific discourse to the point where similarities among the phenylethyl-amine derivatives are downplayed as differences are exaggerated.

PPA and amphetamine, respectively, the least and most restricted of all phenylethylamine derivatives, can cause a multitude of behavioral and physical side effects at acute appetite-suppressing dosages.[27] Both drugs are similarly capable of causing a typical pattern of behavioral and physical effects at over-dose. The majority of side effects and overdose symptoms from these two equally efficacious drugs arise from excessive stimulation of the sympathetic

27. Silverstone, "Clinical Use of Appetite Suppressants."

and central nervous systems.[28] Those who would argue that the lesser potency of PPA compared to amphetamine provides a scientifically sound justification for the present differential prohibition of the two compounds must provide satisfactory answers to two related questions. First, if one asserts that the side effects of, and potential for overdose with, amphetamine are sufficiently severe to justify a blanket prohibition on its use as an anorexiant at any dose, why, then, is there no equivalent concern for the potential side effects and overdose from virtually unregulated use of the less potent but equally efficacious over-the-counter drug PPA? Once one becomes aware of distinctions between efficacy and potency, the question can and should be answered by reference to the fact that PPA-induced side effects and overdose symptoms are dose-dependent. Thus, those who advocate differential prohibition may argue correctly that in a free society consumers can be educated to take only recommended doses of PPA. Second, why cannot education also result in the clinically safe use of amphetamine as an anorexiant at low doses, relatively free of side effects and the potential for overdose? Advocates of differential prohibition must provide a scientifically sound answer.

Fortunately for the public perception of scientists' veracity, advocates of differential prohibition base their argument on differences in potency. Differential prohibition of amphetamine versus PPA, however, is usually based instead upon claims that the two compounds differ in efficacy, particularly when used chronically. A host of potential chronic drug effects might occur with amphetamine but not with PPA. These include the differential development of tolerance to target or side effects and differential development of sensitization to convulsant and adverse psychological effects.[29] The abundant literature demonstrating tolerance or sensitization to the target or side effects of both amphetamine and PPA reveals, however, that an overemphasis on the lesser potency of PPA is resulting in inaccurate suggestions of differential efficacy.[30] Similarly, advocates of differential prohibition may assert that a differential efficacy exists: chronic use of amphetamine can have toxic effects on

28. N. Weiner, "Norepinephrine, Epinephrine, and the Sympathomimetic Amines, *The Pharmacological Basis of Therapeutics*, 7th ed., ed. A. G. Gilman, L. S. Goodman, T. W. Rall, and F. Murad (New York: Macmillan, 1985), 145–80.

29. "Tolerance" means requiring increasing dosage to achieve the same effect.

30. D. S. Segal and R. Kuczenski, "Behavioral and Neurochemical Characteristics of Stimulant-Induced Augmentation," *Psychopharmacology Bulletin* 23 (1986): 417–24; W. L. Woolverton, "A Review of the Effects of Repeated Administration of Selected Phenylethylamines," *Drug and Alcohol Dependence* 17 (1986): 143–50.

the nervous system[31] and can cause a drug-induced psychosis,[32] but chronic use of PPA does not present similar risks. There are, however, persuasive studies indicating that chronic use of PPA may be associated with neurotoxicity,[33] drug-induced psychosis,[34] or a variety of other adverse psychiatric conditions.[35] It thus appears that PPA and amphetamine do not differ in their potential to induce adverse psychiatric conditions.

One can argue effectively against the proposition that "there are no camels" simply by producing an animal that all can agree is, in fact, a camel. Likewise, the mere occurrence of PPA-induced tolerance, sensitization, neurotoxicity, and adverse psychiatric effects shows that divergence from amphetamine induced effects must arise from disparities other than differences in efficacy. It is more difficult, however, to evaluate claims that amphetamine and PPA differ in their abuse potential, because it is not easy to get people to agree on what constitutes an example of drug abuse. Any difference in efficacy might be sufficient to justify a differential prohibition of amphetamine versus PPA. Yet presumptive differences in abuse liability are the primary basis upon which the Drug Enforcement Administration constructs its Schedule of Controlled Sub-

31. T. J. Crow, "Biochemical Determinants of Schizophrenic and Toxic Psychoses," *Handbook of Biological Psychiatry: Brain Mechanisms and Abnormal Behavior Chemistry*, ed. H. M. van Praag (New York: Marcel Dekker, 1981), 3–80; E. H. Ellinwood and O. D. Escalante, "Behavior and Histopathological Findings during Chronic Methadrine Intoxication," *Biological Psychiatry* 2 (1970): 27.

32. M. B. Bowers, "Acute Psychosis Induced by Psychotomimetic Drug Abuse, I. Neurochemical Findings," *Archives of General Psychiatry* 27 (1972): 440; P. H. Connell, *Amphetamine Psychosis* (London: Oxford University Press, 1958); J. M. Davis and R. F. Schlemmer, "The Amphetamine Psychosis," *Amphetamines and Related Stimulants: Chemical, Biological, Clinical and Sociological Aspects* (London: CRC Press, 1981), 161–73.

33. S. M. Mueller, "Neurologic Complications of Phenylpropanolamine Use," *Neurology* 33 (1983): 650–52; W. L. Woolverton, C. E. Johanson, R. de la Garza, S. Ellis, S. Seiden, and C. R. Schuster, "Behavioral and Neurochemical Evaluation of Phenylpropanolamine," *Journal of Pharmacology and Experimental Therapeutics* 237 (1986): 926–30; Woolverton, "Effects of Repeated Administration of Selected Phenylethylamines."

34. R. J. Harvey, "Masturbation Insanity: The History of an Idea," *Journal of Mental Science* 108 (1962): 1–25; F. J. Kane and B. Q. Green, "Psychotic Episodes Associated with the Use of Common Proprietary Decongestants," *American Journal of Psychiatry* 123 (1966): 484–87; C. B. Schaffer and M. W. Pauli, "Psychotic Reaction Caused by Proprietary Oral Diet Agents," *American Journal of Psychiatry* 137 (1980): 1256–57.

35. M. B. Achor and I. Exstein, "Diet Aids, Mania and Affective Illness," *American Journal of Psychiatry* 138 (1981): 392; J. R. Grigg and P. F. Goyer, "Phenylpropanolamine Anorexiants and Affective Disorders," *Military Medicine* 151 (1986): 387–88; B. Twerski, "Sympathomimetic-Induced Depression," *American Journal of Psychiatry* 144 (1987): 252; B. G. H. Waters and Y. D. Lapierre, "Secondary Mania Associated with Sympathomimetic Drug Use," *American Journal of Psychiatry* 138 (1991): 837–38.

stances. Governmental concern with abuse liability comes from, and influences, conceptions of the "good body."

Early in this century, a legislative and medical consensus developed, resulting in a belief that the effects of acute and chronic use of some psychoactive compounds were so personally and socially destructive that draconian penalties for the manufacture, sale, and possession of these substances were necessary to save the nation. The result was the passage of the Harrison Narcotic Act of 1914, which for the first time instituted a nationwide ban on some, but not all, substances that affect brain function.[36] While this law and others it spawned were passed ostensibly to protect the health of the American public, decisions about which drugs to ban were usually the result of a dominant group's attempts to suppress the drug-taking habits of a despised minority. Thus, the Harrison Narcotic Act copied a variety of earlier state statutes which rejected the use of cocaine because of its association with African Americans and rejected the use of opiate drugs because of their association with Asian Americans. The Harrison Act did not, however, regulate drugs presumed to be preferred by white males, particularly alcohol, nicotine, and caffeine.[37]

Actually, conceptions of the "good body" required participation in the drug-consuming habits of the majority (since these drugs were viewed as possessing quasi-medicinal properties) and rejection of involvement with the drug-consuming habits of minorities. A psychohistorian aware of the negative effects of alcohol, nicotine, and caffeine might conclude that the ferocity of legislative actions by white males against the use of cocaine, opium derivatives, and marijuana represented an attempt at self-purgation through projection.

Recent historical scholarship alerts us to search for alternative traditions of medical thought: some intelligent people questioned differential prohibition, recognizing that drug consumption did not per se violate conceptions of the "good body." People were, after all, allowed and even encouraged through advertising and government subsidies, to manufacture and consume such drugs as caffeine and nicotine. In a period of legal discrimination against minorities and women, however, it was relatively simple to promote the racist argument that certain "primitive races" needed to be protected from themselves. Moreover, the paternalistic argument that white children and women (similarly primitive people) needed to be protected from physical and psychological seductions had a special attraction. For example, California state laws

36. J. B. Bakalar and L. Grinspoon, *Drug Control in a Free Society* (Cambridge: Cambridge University Press, 1984).
37. Szasz, *Ceremonial Chemistry*

against opium first prohibited the importation of smoking opium for Asians, but not the importation of the liquid opium used in "quack" medicines and other such nostrums favored by whites in the United States.[38]

The white male physicians and legislators who advocated the use of legal sanctions to promote racist, sexist, and paternalistic conceptions of health eventually experienced the reciprocal impact of conceptions of the "good body" upon the development of differential prohibition. That is, differential prohibition itself began to influence the concept of the "good body." Some egalitarian thinkers concluded that since all humanity shares common physical characteristics, *all* humans are equally susceptible to the lure of these dangerously seductive psychoactive compounds. Then followed an extension of differential prohibitions to include all persons within the legislative control of the United States. This coincided with an intensified concern to identify which among the multitude of psychoactive compounds required precisely what kind of regulation. The changing status of the drug ethyl alcohol, through various amendments to the U.S. Constitution, reveals, for example, how differential prohibition resulted in periodic reassessments of the seductiveness of specific drugs.[39] The shifting views of state and federal governments concerning the use of peyote in the religious ceremonies of Native Americans reveals the continuing impact of racism and paternalism in the regulation of psychoactive substances.[40]

As part of the "chemical revolution in psychiatry" at midcentury, medicinal chemists created many new psychoactive compounds. Also, various factors led to the rediscovery of a host of naturally occurring psychoactive substances that were not widely known during the early phases of differential prohibition. Existing legislation could suppress anyone daring to consume substances that had previously been banned, but the lay and scientific community was becoming increasingly concerned about the misuse of those newly created or discovered, and hence unregulated, pleasure-inducing compounds.

The government justified bans against narcotics by pointing to the physical dependency that chronic use of opiate drugs caused. How could one have a "good body" if one were allowed to consume a compound that would eventually result in enslavement characterized by hideous withdrawal upon an attempt to cease drug use? Scientists were aware that a sudden halt of stimulant use did not lead to similar cessation phenomena. Yet they were equally aware

38. Ibid.
39. Bakalar and Grinspoon, *Drug Control in a Free Society.*
40. C. Vecsey, *Handbook of American Indian Religious Freedom* (New York: Crossroad, 1991).

of individuals who appeared unable to control their intake of stimulants even at great physical and psychological cost. As a result, in the early 1960s the World Health Organization created the concept of "psychological dependence" to describe the motivations of people who appeared to be excessively enamored of the pleasurable effects of stimulants.[41] The concept of the "good body" was thus extended beyond an abhorrence of consumption of drugs capable of causing physical dependency to a concern with consumption of compounds that induced pleasurable effects. In the United States this led to the creation of the Drug Enforcement Administration's Schedule of Controlled Substances, which made many stimulants and hallucinogens illegal and drew fine distinctions between the "abuse liability" of chemically similar compounds. While scientists investigating the abuse potential of various drugs may claim that they are taking part in a value-free activity, they may be no less affected by cultural prejudices about specific drug effects or popularity than PMS researchers are free of cultural prejudices toward women. It is thus legitimate to investigate the work of drug abuse researchers to determine if their actions are less a search for the truth regarding psychoactive chemicals than a search for ways to provide a pseudoscientific justification for the vagaries of the present differential prohibition.

Studies that compared the subjective effects of amphetamine and PPA in humans provide evidence that scientific discourse about the reinforcing properties of PPA has been perverted into a search for justifications for the differential prohibition of PPA versus amphetamines. Two experiments have demonstrated that PPA, when given at the appropriate doses, does indeed induce subjective effects that are decidedly amphetamine-like.[42] Surprisingly, this demonstration of equal efficacy yet differential potency did not have substantial impact on the design of a subsequent study. One group of researchers has, indeed, found evidence that acute PPA is devoid of reinforcing effects,[43] although it is at present unclear why these data conflict with the results of other research.

41. S. Peele, The Meaning of Addiction: Compulsive Experience and Its Interpretation (Lexington, Mass.: Lexington Books, 1985).

42. L. D. Chait, E. H. Uhlenhuth, and C. E. Johanson, "The Discriminative Stimulus and Subjective Effects of Phenylpropanolamine, Mazindol and D-Amphetamine in Humans," Pharmacology, Biochemistry and Behavior 24 (1986): 1665–72; F. Lee, I. Stafford, and B. G. Hoebel, "Similarities between the Stimulus Properties of Phenylpropanolamine and Amphetamine," Psychopharmacology 97 (1989): 410–12.

43. L. D. Chait, E. H. Uhlenhuth, and C. E. Johanson, "Reinforcing and Subjective Effects of Several Anorectics in Normal Human Volunteers," Psychopharmacology 242 (1987): 777–83; L. D. Chait et al., "Phenylpropanolamine: Reinforcing and Subjective Effects in Normal Human Volunteers," Psychopharmacology 96 (1988): 212–17.

The mistaken notion that the "abuse potential" of psychoactive compounds results solely from the "intrinsic reinforcing properties" of a compound arises from, and further fuels, differential prohibition. All of the studies cited above that used human subjects to investigate the subjective effects of PPA employed short-term administration of the drug, on the assumption that the cause of drug abuse could be found in the compound, rather than in the interaction of the compound with a social human being. The reinforcing effects of a compound may, however, be altered after chronic use because of the differential development of tolerance or sensitization to different aspects of the drug's effects.[44] In addition, the probability of drug consumption is increased not only by positive reinforcement but also by negative reinforcement that occurs when drug consumption removes an undesired physical condition or psychological state.[45] Scientific analysis will become valid once there is a greater understanding of factors such as chronicity of drug intake and negative reinforcement that create commonalities in the "abuse potential" of psychoactive compounds.

Mary Brown Parlee argues that the biomedical description of PMS as something a woman "has" results in the medicalization of deviant or potentially subversive experiences and action. In earlier scientific discourse about the incidence and treatment of masturbation-induced insanity,[46] paternalistic society found solitary pleasurable activity, such as that obtained from psychoactive drugs, particularly amenable to a medicalized conversion from an expressed personal choice into an irresistible urge mediated by a damaged nervous system. Parlee also notes that "my background in biology and experimental psychology equipped me very well to do research from within a biomedical perspective and failed utterly to give me concepts to analyze the social and cultural phenomena I observed and participated in as the research developed." This statement accurately reflects my own position as an individual trained to do research in behavioral pharmacology and now faced with the

---

44. Segal and Kuczenski, "Behavioral and Neurochemical Characteristics of Stimulant-Induced Augmentation"; Woolverton, "Effects of Repeated Administration of Selected Phenylethylamines."

45. A. P. Leccese, *Drugs and Society: Behavioral Medicines and Abusable Drugs* (Englewood Cliffs, N.J.: Prentice Hall, 1991).

46. E. H. Hare, "Masturbation Insanity: The History of an Idea," *Journal of Mental Science* 108 (1962): 1–25; R. McDonald, "The Frightful Consequences of Onanism: Notes on the History of a Delusion," *Journal of the History of Ideas* 28 (1967): 423–31; R. A. Spitz, "Authority and Masturbation: Some Remarks on a Biographic Investigation," *Psychoanalytic Quarterly* 21 (1952): 490–527.

need to analyze such hoary concepts as "addiction," "dependency," and "drug abuse." Parlee asserts that the hegemony of the biomedical perspective on PMS must not be allowed to justify increasing paternalistic intervention in the lives of those who have ovaries. I assert that the present hegemony of the biomedical view of addiction (to PPA or any other drug) as a disease that someone "has" must not be allowed to justify further draconian interventions in the lives of all who have human nervous systems.

The Future

Within the context of the latest so-called War(s) on Drugs, the concept of the "good body" has incorporated a "drug free" ideal.[47] Indeed, we must concede that all drugs, whether used for recreational or for therapeutic purposes, have the power to induce negative physical and psychological consequences that conflict with the ideal of the "good body." Potential consumers have the right to be told that the reinforcing effects of anorexiant stimulants present a particular hazard to the "good body," as they can contribute to the probability of chronic excessive dosage. Distortions of science and inhibition of progress in the development of therapeutic drugs occur, however, when the application of a cultural ideal results in concepts about the body that are scientifically indefensible and result in confusion about the causes of drug abuse. Data regarding great individual differences in the likelihood that one who samples stimulants will become an abuser of these drugs,[48] make it clear that there is no need to abandon a scientific perspective in order to assert that humans are autonomous creatures whose values continue to operate even in the face of powerful physiological and psychological forces that may lead to excessive drug intake.[49] Scientific discourse that overemphasizes the acute reinforcing effects of drugs, whether studied in animals or in humans, denies humans their role as agents. Furthermore, the use of fines and imprisonment to coerce adherence to a scientifically indefensible differential prohibition treats people as if they are incapable of deciding for themselves the relative risks and benefits of the consumption of psychoactive drugs for pleasure or weight loss. As noted in a

47. President's Commission on Organized Crime, *America's Habit: Drug Abuse, Drug Trafficking and Organized Crime* (Washington, D.C.: U.S. Printing Office, 1986).

48. R. K. Siegel, "Changing Patterns in Cocaine Use: Longitudinal Observations, Consequences and Treatment," *NIDA Research Monograph* 50 (1984): 92–110.

49. Peele, *The Meaning of Addiction*

different context by Judith Andre in her discussion of moral attention to bodies, the moral problem is one of injustice and a failure of respect.

Now, differential prohibition of anorexiant stimulants coexists with a more rigid prohibitionism that insists on reduction of caloric intake and increased exercise as universally preferable to pharmacological aids for weight reduction. In part the opposition to pharmacotherapy of obesity arises from a legitimate concern with the negative physical and psychological consequences of acute and chronic consumption of the anorexiant stimulants now available. There is, however, an increasing amount of research to determine the endogenous neurotransmitter and neuromodulator systems associated with naturally occurring sensations of hunger and satiety.[50] In fact, a prestigious journal of review articles recently summarized the status of this search for endogenous anorexiants, or satietins.[51] The author expressed the hope that the search for satietins would yield the discovery of effective anorexiant compounds nearly devoid of stimulant or reinforcing effects. Nonetheless, the present analysis of differential prohibition, scientific discourse, and anorexiant stimulants suggests that legitimate concern with side effects, particularly pleasurable ones, has created a bias in favor of a chimeric "drug-free" existence.[52] Even if satietins devoid of positively reinforcing properties are discovered, there will still be a tendency for individuals to increase the frequency or dosage of their satietin. By definition, pharmacologically mediated weight reduction will provide negative reinforcement that will increase the probability of satietin consumption. It would be a tragedy if this concern about possible "satietin abuse" resulted in further injustice and failures of respect, causing the obese to suffer unnecessarily increased morbidity and mortality in order to satisfy prohibitionist insistence upon the equivalency of the "good body" and the "drug-free body."

50. S. Levine, "Centrally Active Peptides: Are They Useful Agents in the Treatment of Obesity?" in Human Obesity, ed. R. J. Wurtman and J. J. Wurtman (New York: New York Academy of Sciences, 1987), 297–304; G. P. Smith and J. Gibbs, "The Effect of Gut Peptides on Hunger, Satiety and Food Intake in Humans," in Human Obesity, 132–36.

51. J. Knoll, "Endogenous Anorectic-Agents-Satietins," Annual Review of Pharmacology and Toxicology 28 (1988): 247–68.

52. President's Commission on Organized Crime, America's Habit.

Part Three

Interpretive

Narrative

and the

"Good Body"

8

Eating Disorders, Female Psychology, and Developmental Disturbances

Janet de Groot

I am so full and feel so empty. . . . The goal I try to achieve through my self-discipline is virtually unattainable. I cannot be perfect looking—not that I want this for the sake of vanity—I want it to compensate for other faults that I have not been able to rectify such as my inability to get close to people, my consistently making others angry and my fear of being completely on my own.

Introduction

These words convey the pain and frustrated efforts at self-denial experienced by a twenty-one-year-old woman with anorexia nervosa and bulimia nervosa. Women with eating disorders repudiate flesh, which to them symbolizes indulgence. This extreme attitude of denial is reminiscent of the asceticism cultivated by Gnostics, who used it to transcend and escape the world just as the anorexics' pursuit of thinness reflects the wish to need no one. The development of an eating disorder, however, is thought to be multidetermined, with biological, temperamental, developmental, cultural, and psychological factors.[1] This chapter is concerned with the psychological factors that

An expanded and altered version of this chapter will appear as "Eating Disorders, Female Psychology and the Self," in the *Journal of the American Academy of Psychoanalysis*, in press.

1. P. E. Garfinkel and D. M. Garner, *Anorexia Nervosa: A Multidimensional Perspective* (New York: Brunner/Mazel, 1982).

contribute to the development of this primarily female disorder. This has been a fertile ground for speculation by theorists and clinicians during much of this century. Yet many hypotheses about the psychology and psychodynamics of these conditions deserve reconsideration in light of recent findings regarding normal female psychology and psychological development. Further, refinements in understanding the development of subjective experience and recent theoretical contributions regarding the psychology of self may add to our understanding of the psychological disturbances associated with eating disorders.

Since Gull coined the term over a century ago, anorexia nervosa (AN) has been recognized as a distinct psychiatric syndrome.[2] The recognition of bulimia nervosa (BN) as a distinct syndrome and in association with AN is much more recent.[3] According to the *Diagnostic and Statistical Manual, IIIR*, criteria, both anorexia nervosa and bulimia nervosa are described by attitudes and behavior regarding eating and weight; they differ by parameters of actual weight, presence or absence of menses, and presence or absence of binge episodes (although a subgroup of women with AN may engage in binge episodes). Both groups share extreme concerns related to shape and weight, which may reflect a disturbance in the sense of self.

Psychological explanations have tended to focus on this most obvious psychopathological feature of women with AN and BN; indeed, many features of AN and BN have been considered secondary to a body-image disturbance.[4] Yet body image is a complex concept and includes perceptual and attitudinal components. Here, body image will be defined as a psychological representation of the size, shape, and form of the body as a whole and its component parts,[5] as well as attitudes and feelings toward the body experienced individually and in relation to others.[6] The focus on body image as a central area of

2. W. W. Gull, "The Address in Medicine Delivered before the Annual Meeting of the British Medical Association at Oxford," *Lancet* 2 (1868): 171–76; H. Bruch, *Eating Disorders* (New York: Basic Books, 1973); G. F. M. Russell, "Anorexia Nervosa: Its Identity as an Illness and Its Treatment,"in *Modern Trends in Psychological Medicine* 2, ed. J. H. Price (London: Butterworth, 1970).

3. G. Russell, "Bulimia Nervosa: An Ominous Variant of Anorexia Nervosa," *Psychological Medicine* 9 (1979): 429–48; P. E. Garfinkel, H. Moldofsky, and D. M. Garner, "The Heterogeneity of Anorexia Nervosa: Bulimia as a Distinct Subgroup," *Archives of General Psychiatry* 37 (1980): 1036–40.

4. C. G. Fairburn and D. M. Garner, "The Diagnosis of Bulimia Nervosa," *International Journal of Eating Disorders* 4 (1986): 403–19.

5. P. D. Slade, "Body Image in Anorexia Nervosa," *British Journal of Psychiatry* 153 (1988): 20–22.

6. C. Kolb, "Disturbances of Body Image," *American Handbook of Psychiatry*, vol. 4, ed. S. Arieti (New York: Basic Books, 1975).

psychological disturbance in eating disorders is supported to some extent by the empirical literature. For example, perceptual body-image distortions have been shown to be related to prognosis and treatment outcome. Marked over-estimation of body size was shown to be highly predictive of poor outcome at one-year follow-up,[7] and many workers in the field consider modification of body-image distortions to be essential to lasting recovery.[8]

Subjective experience related to the body is one aspect of the sense of self. It is only one aspect, however. George Atwood and Robert Stolorow described the self as a psychological structure through which experience acquires cohesion and continuity, whereas the sense of self refers to simple subjective awareness of the self.[9] Joseph Lichtenberg has used the term *body self* to refer to the full range of subjective experience that is centered on the body and is thus related to the attitudinal component of body image.[10] Normally, the body self is not the most predominant aspect of self-experience in adult life, although it may become so with such conditions as eating disorders, somatizing disorders, or serious physical illness. In such cases, it is essential that clinicians recognize underlying and associated psychological disturbances in the sense of self.

Women with AN or BN have in common a body-image disturbance. Because body image is a psychological construct, the underlying psychological disturbances found among women with AN and BN may be similar. This is supported by several empirical studies. Looking first to phenomenology, the syndromes overlap and bulimia may occur as a subtype in as many as 50 percent of women with AN.[11] Among women with bulimia, between 25 percent and 57 percent have a prior history of anorexia.[12] With regard to psychometric testing, the

7. D. M. Garner and P. E. Garfinkel, "Cultural Expectations of Thinness in Women," *Psychological Reports* 47 (1980): 483–91.

8. H. Bruch, "Perceptual and Conceptual Disturbances in Anorexia Nervosa," *Journal of Psychiatric Research* 2/3 (1985): 273–78; C. G. Fairburn, "Bulimia: Its Epidemiology and Management," in *Eating and Its Disorders*, ed. A. J. Stunkard and E. Stellar (New York: Raven Press, 1984); D. M. Garner and K. M. Bemis, "A Cognitive-Behavioral Approach to Anorexia Nervosa," *Cognitive Therapeutic Research* 6 (1982): 123–50; and D. M. Garner and K. M. Bemis, "Cognitive Therapy for Anorexia Nervosa," in *Handbook of Psychotherapy for Anorexia Nervosa and Bulimia*, ed. D. M. Garner and P. E. Garfinkel (New York: Guilford Press, 1985).

9. G. E. Atwood and R. D. Stolorow, *Structures of Subjectivity: Explorations in Psychoanalytic Phenomenology* (New Jersey: Lawrence Erlbaum Associates, 1984).

10. J. Lichtenberg, "The Testing of Reality from the Standpoint of the Body Self," *Journal of the American Psychoanalytic Association* 26 (1978): 357–85.

11. R. C. Casper, "On the Emergence of Bulimia Nervosa as a Syndrome: A Historical Review," *International Journal of Eating Disorders*, 2 (1983): 3–16; P. E. Garfinkel, H. Moldofsky, and D. M. Garner, "The Heterogeneity of Anorexia Nervosa."

12. C. G. Fairburn and P. J. Cooper, "The Clinical Features of Bulimia Nervosa," *British Journal of Psychiatry* 144 (1984): 238–46; Russell, "Bulimia Nervosa."

original large-scale validation of the Eating Disorders Inventory (EDI)—a self-evaluative, multiscale measure of psychological and behavioral attitudes toward eating, shape, and weight, and of the psychological traits of ineffectiveness, perfectionism, interpersonal distrust, interoceptive awareness, and maturity fears—found the similarities between women with AN alone, AN with bulimic episodes, and those with BN more striking than the differences.[13] Another study found that although women with normal-weight bulimia nervosa (NWB), anorexia nervosa–bulimic subtype (AN-B), and anorexia nervosa–restricting subtype (AN-R) have behavioral differences in that the two bulimic groups display greater impulsivity, all three groups show similarities on such measures of psychological disturbance as the EDI and a locus of control questionnaire.[14] That is, they see events as unrelated to their own behavior rather than under their personal control. Thus, the usual distinction made between women with AN and those with BN based on weight and the presence or absence of binge episodes is an oversimplification. Further, Richard Geist has suggested that the syndromes represent two variations of a defensive structure mobilized to cope with a disruption in the early parent-child relationship.[15] Thus, despite behavioral differences, women with the various types of eating disorders have a common substrate of psychological vulnerability.

Female Vulnerability to Psychiatric Illness

In the eating-disorder literature, much attention has been given to the onset of eating disorders during adolescence, particularly emphasizing the emergence of sexual conflicts, concerns about femininity, and the cultural pressures to be thin.[16] Cultural pressures regarding shape and weight and the role of women probably interact with individual psychological factors to contribute to the

13. D. M. Garner, M. P. Olmsted, and J. Polivy, "Development and Validation of a Multidimensional Eating Disorder Inventory for Anorexia Nervosa and Bulimia," *International Journal of Eating Disorders* 2 (1983): 6–13.

14. D. M. Garner, P. E. Garfinkel, and M. O'Shaughnessy, "Clinical and Psychometric Comparison between Bulimia in Anorexia Nervosa and Bulimia in Normal-Weight Women," *Understanding Anorexia Nervosa and Bulimia, Report of the Fourth Ross Conference on Medical Research* (Columbus, Ohio: Ross Laboratories, 1983), 6–13.

15. R. A. Geist, "Self Psychological Reflections on the Origins of Eating Disorders," *Journal of the American Academy of Psychoanalysis* 17 (1989): 5–27.

16. A. H. Crisp, "Premorbid Factors in Adult Disorders of Weight, with Particular Reference to Primary Anorexia Nervosa (Weight Phobia)," *Journal of Psychosomatic Research* 14 (1970): 1–22; M. Nasser, "Eating Disorders: The Cultural Dimension," *Society of Psychiatry and Psychiatric Epidemiology* 23 (1988): 184–87.

development, persistence, and recurrence of eating disorders.[17] Such interactions may also contribute to the female preponderance in other psychiatric disorders, such as major depression, phobic disorder, panic disorder, and somatization disorder. Similarly, Sara van den Berg (in a later chapter of this book) suggests that hysterical symptoms, so prevalent in the nineteenth century, are not adequately explained by the repressive bourgeois culture of that time but are also related to psychological disturbances. Among men, interactions between cultural and individual factors may result in their greater vulnerability to such conditions as alcohol abuse or dependence, drug abuse or dependence, and antisocial personality disorder.[18]

At least with depression, which may be the best-researched example, there is evidence that the twofold greater rate of depressive symptoms and treated depression among women is real and is not merely a function of gender biases in reporting,[19] in diagnosis, or in help-seeking behavior;[20] nor is it due to genetic factors.[21] Less attention has been accorded to gender influences on the development of the self, however, which may contribute to differing vulnerabilities to psychiatric disorders. We will consider here how female developmental psychology may contribute to the propensity to clinical eating disorders and perhaps to other psychiatric disorders

Female Psychology

Identity and Relationship

The literature suggests that although women with one of the three subgroups of eating disorders, may differ from others on a phenomenologic basis, they all suffer from similar psychological disturbances. It may be useful to consider

17. C. R. Hollin, J. C. Houston, and M. F. Kent, "Neuroticism, Life Stress and Concern about Eating, Body Weight and Appearance in a Non-Clinical Population," *Personality and Individual Differences* 6 (1985): 485–92;C . Steiner-Adair, "The Body Politic: Normal Female Adolescent Development and the Development of Eating Disorders," in *Making Connections*, ed. C. Gilligan, N. P. Lyons, and T. Hammer (Cambridge, Mass.: Harvard University Press, 1990), 162–68.

18. L. E. Robins and D. A. Regier, *Psychiatric Disorders in America: The Epidemiologic Catchment Area Study* (New York: Free Press, 1991).

19. W. R. Gove and M. R. Geerkin, "Response Bias in Surveys of Mental Health: An Empirical Investigation," *American Journal of Sociology* 82 (1976): 1289–1317.

20. S. Nolen-Hoeksema, "Sex Differences in Unipolar Depression: Evidence and Theory," *Psychological Bulletin* 2 (1987): 259–82.

21. K. R. Merikangas, M. M. Weissman, and D. L. Pauls, "Genetic Factors in the Sex Ratio of Major Depression, *Psychological Medicine* 15 (1985): 63–69.

normative female development to identify risk factors in women that lead to disturbances in these aspects of the processing and organizing of subjective experience.

Current research on female psychological development, such as that by Carol Gilligan and Nancy Chodorow,[22] suggests that although the currently held theory of separation-individuation[23] may apply to males, a different model is necessary for females. Freud underestimated the significance of the early mother-daughter relationship for female psychological development.[24] He continued to view the Oedipus complex as a central developmental milestone. However, more recent psychoanalytic thinking considers that the self develops in an ongoing manner with increasing cohesion and integration rather than traversing specific clinical phases, such as the Oedipus complex. Further, current research has emphasized the contribution of the infant-caregiver relationship to early development, with increasing attention given to the development of the self occurring in relation to others.[25]

Moreover, recent research indicates that female identity is more closely tied to relationships and interdependence than to issues of autonomy and separateness, which have been emphasized in male development.[26] Traditional assumptions about female development based on extrapolations from males may not be valid since gender appears to affect concepts of morality, initially learned and demonstrated in children's games and the typical role taking that occurs in resolving disputes.[27] Early developments in these spheres influence subsequent life choices and the usual manner of conflict resolution. Gilligan suggests that the typical female conception of morality is associated

22. C. Gilligan, In a Different Voice (Cambridge, Mass.: Harvard University Press, 1982); N. Chodorow, "Family Structure and Feminine Personality," in Woman, Culture and Society, ed. M. Z. Rosaldo and L. Lamphere (Stanford, Calif.: Stanford University Press, 1974); N. Chodorow, The Reproduction of Mothering (Berkeley: University of California Press, 1978).

23. E. Erikson, Childhood and Society, 2d ed. (New York: W. W. Norton, 1963); M. S. Mahler, F. Pine, and A. Bergman, The Psychological Birth of the Human Infant: Symbiosis and Individuation (New York: Basic Books, 1975).

24. S. Freud, Female Sexuality, in The Standard Edition of the Complete Psychological Works, vol. 21 (London: Hogarth Press and Institute of Psychoanalysis, 1931), 223–43.

25. H. Kohut, The Analysis of the Self (New York: International Universities Press, 1971).

26. See Gilligan, In a Different Voice; Chodorow Reproduction of Mothering; J. V. Jordan and J. L. Surrey, "The Self-in-Relation: Empathy and the Mother-Daughter Relationship," in The Psychology of Today's Woman, ed. T. Bernay and D. W. Cantor (Cambridge, Mass.: Harvard University Press, 1986).

27. J. Piaget, The Moral Judgement of the Child (New York: Free Press, 1932); L. Kohlberg, "Stage and Sequence: The Cognitive-Developmental Approach to Socialization," Handbook of Socialization Theory and Research (Chicago: Rand McNally, 1969).

with care and responsibility in relationships.[28] It may be that female identity is linked to mutual relationships throughout all stages of the life cycle. By contrast, moral thinking among males tends to focus on justice with a formal logic of fairness in rights and rules.[29] During adolescence there may be cultural pressures for young women to replace their complex relational world with one governed by the male bias toward autonomy.[30] This is the usual time of onset of an eating disorder and is seen as a time of "crisis in connection"[31] for girls. They are also confronted with pressure to aspire to an idealized conventional female expectation in which self-worth is defined and evaluated by the ability to care for and protect others.[32] Women's greater sensitivity to the well-being of others, which has been termed the "cost of caring,"[33] may contribute to their relatively greater frequency of depression and to the tendency to sacrifice their own needs and emotional experience in the service of others.

Developmental Factors

Both innate and developmental factors may contribute to women's greater orientation toward relationships. At birth, the girl is comparable in her development to a four- to six-week-old boy, and this gap in maturation widens in scope with age.[34] This greater maturity may enhance the female's capacity for relatedness.[35] Further, nonshared environmental experiences may result in even greater divergence in gender orientation to relationships. In one prospective nursery school observational study, the female infants displayed a more differentiated range of behavior toward their mothers than did the males, who played at a further distance from the mother and had more interactions with her around play objects. Female infants more frequently initiated contact, smiled, called, and waved to the mother and shared more activities and feel-

28. Gilligan, In a Different Voice.
29. L. Kohlberg, The Philosophy of Moral Development (San Francisco: Harper & Row, 1981).
30. Steiner-Adair, "Body Politic."
31. Ibid.
32. Gilligan, In a Different Voice.
33. R. C. Kessler and J. D. McLeon, "Sex Differences in Vulnerability to Undesirable Life Events," American Sociological Review 49 (1984): 620–31.
34. J. E. Garai and A. Scheinfeld, "Sex Differences in Mental and Behavioral Traits," Genetic Psychology Monographs 77 (1968): 169–299.
35. L. Sander, "Polarity, Paradox, and the Organizing Process in Development, in Frontiers of the Infant Psychology, ed. J. Call, E. Galenson, and R. Tyson (New York: Basic Books, 1983).

ings with her.[36] Daniel Stern has noted that sharing affects, intentions, and attention is the hallmark of the achievement of a subjective sense of self by the end of the first year of life.[37] Researchers found these interactions more frequently between mothers and their female infants, suggesting that females may be more in tune with their own subjective experience and that of others. These early interactions and the heightened awareness of emotional experience may enrich the emotional life of young girls but may also render them more vulnerable to the disapproving responses of others. Wendy Olesker found that girls were more upset by mother's scolding or disapproving looks than boys were and seemed to place more importance on approval than autonomy.[38] Further, it has been suggested that mothers tend to experience their daughters as more continuous with and similar to themselves. A review of case reports which reveal a history of disturbed mother-daughter relationships finds that the daughter typically has difficulty recognizing herself as a separate person. When the mother experiences depression or is unavailable for other reasons, she may not recognize the daughter as a separate person. Similarities between the mother and daughter and their greater emotional relatedness may contribute to the mother's tendency to overlook the daughter's separateness and individuality.[39]

External Confirmation

The relative importance to girls of external confirmation to consolidate the sense of identity and maintain self-esteem may heighten concern about physical appearance in females.[40] At an early age, girls are more compliant or obedient to the demands and directives of adults than boys are,[41] and this may contribute to girls' greater difficulty in identity formation. Boys appear to conform more to peer-group values, as shown in a study of ten-year-olds,[42] and this may allow them to separate their own choices from those of authorities.

36. W. Olesker, "Sex Differences during the Early Separation-Individuation Process: Implications for Gender Identity Formation," Journal of the American Psychoanalytical Association 38 (1990): 325–46.

37. D. Stern, The Interpersonal World of the Infant: A View from Psychoanalysis and Developmental Psychology (New York: Basic Books, 1985).

38. Olesker, "Sex Differences during the Early Separation-Individuation Process."

39. Chodorow, Reproduction of Mothering.

40. E. Douvan and J. Adelson, The Adolescent Experience (New York: Wiley, 1966).

41. E. E. Maccoby and C. N. Jacklin, The Psychology of Sex Differences (Stanford, Calif.: Stanford University Press, 1974).

42. E. P. Hollander and J. E. Marcia, "Parental Determinants of Peer Orientation and Self-Orientation among Preadolescents," Developmental Psychology 2 (1970): 292–302.

With respect to physical appearance, female adolescents tend to be unaccepting of bodily imperfections and, compared to boys, less satisfied with their bodies overall and more likely to want to lose weight.[43] Certainly, cultural pressures to be thin are greater for women than men. The need for external confirmation extends beyond physical appearance among women with AN, however. They tend to rely on others for confirmation of their identity.[44]

Emotions

Gender differences in emotional expression and interaction have been noted. In an observational nursery study of two- and three-year-old children, females were found to have subdued affect and to lack exuberance and excitement.[45] In contrast, the main focus of activity among the boys seemed to be shared excitement and exuberance. Eleanor Maccoby and C. Jacklin, in their 1974 review, suggest that boys have a greater tendency toward outbursts of negative emotion after the age of eighteen months. After the age of two years, this finding may be attributed to girls' tendency to decrease the frequency and intensity of their emotional reactions at a faster rate than boys.

Recent infant research[46] reveals that there are complex patterns of mutual regulation between mother and infant from an early age, rather than a unidirectional influence on development with the primary caregiver shaping the infant. Several researchers have suggested that the exploration of emotional experiences of the parent, especially the mother, is probably reinforced much more in girls than in boys.[47] Although this may allow a particular intimacy between mother and daughter, it may interfere with the girl's awareness of her own unique emotional world.

Activity

The experience of effectiveness is central to one's self-experience and may affect the nature and duration of psychiatric symptoms in adult life. Maccoby and Jacklin's extensive review of infant and child studies indicates that, al-

43. J. Wardle and L. Marsland, "Adolescent Concerns about Weight and Eating: A Social-Developmental Perspective," *Journal of Psychosomatic Research* 34 (1990): 377–91.

44. Garfinkel and Garner, *Anorexia Nervosa*.

45. W. Olesker, "Sex Differences in 2- and 3-Year Olds: Mother-Child Relations, Peer Relations, and Peer Play," *Psychoanalytic Psychology* 1 (1984): 269–88.

46. Stern, *Interpersonal World of the Infant*.

47. Jordan and Surrey, "Self-in-Relation; Chodorow, *Reproduction of Mothering*.

though males are more aggressive than females, there is only a tendency for boys to be more active than girls, particularly after age one. This was more pronounced in certain eliciting conditions, such as group situations. Aggression as found in rough and tumble play, fighting, and the readiness to respond aggressively is probably related to the effects of androgens. In fact, according to a review of animal studies and reports of girls with congenital adrenal hyperplasia, a condition that results in excessive prenatal exposure to androgens, predisposes affected girls to male-typical play, particularly initiating and becoming involved in play fights.[48]

Unlike aggression, gender differences in activity have not been linked to hormonal effects but appear to be influenced by infant-caregiver interactions. There is recent evidence that activity away from the mother tends to be more common and more often permitted and encouraged in male infants than in females. In the nursery school study reported by Olesker (1990), at nine to twelve months male infants were more attracted to toys and explored more actively at a greater distance from the mother than females. Further, there is some evidence that caregiver responses shape or maintain these activities as the mothers gave toys to the male more frequently than to the female infants. In a previous (1984) nursery study of two- and three-year-olds, Olesker found that motor activity in girls increased as they moved away from their mothers physically. Differences in activity may affect the processing of emotional experience. For example, Susan Nolen-Hoeksema has suggested that men's more active response style dampens and shortens the duration of depressive symptoms, whereas women's more ruminative style both amplifies and prolongs these symptoms.[49]

The tendency toward and the reinforcement of activity in boys may enhance experiences of mastery. This is supported by studies of locus of control—that is, whether individuals believe that events affecting them are the result of chance or luck (externality) or can be controlled through their own actions (internality). There is a trend in published studies to see college-age women as externalizers,[50] at which time their levels of achievement are sur-

48. Maccoby and Jacklin, *Psychology of Sex Differences*; M. J. Meaney, "The Sexual Differentiation of Social Play," *Psychiatric Developments* 3 (1989): 247–61.

49. Olesker, "Sex Differences during the Early Separation Individuation Process"; Olesker, "Sex Differences in 2- and 3-Year Olds"; Nolen-Hoeksema, "Sex Differences in Unipolar Depression."

50. Maccoby and Jacklin, *Psychology of Sex Differences*.

passed by men. Thus experiences contributing to the sense of agency—that is, the subjective experience of owning and voluntarily controlling one's actions which contributes to one's experience of efficacy and competence in the world—may be different for men and women.

Application to Women with Eating Disorders

As noted earlier, speculation regarding the psychological factors that may contribute to the development of eating disorders has been prominent in the eating disorder literature through out this century. With regard to psychodynamic theory, the classic drive-conflict model postulates that sexual conflicts are central in women with anorexia and explain their characteristic social inhibition or sexual withdrawal.[51] Analytic thinking focused initially on cases in which anorexia or self-starvation was seen as a defense against conflictual sexual fantasies of oral impregnation.[52] Unresolved conflicts of this kind were considered to result in compulsive eating or guilty rejection of food. Later analysts emphasized that ambivalent oral sadistic fantasies may result in similar symptoms.[53] Symptom formation, according to these formulations, arose from intrapsychic conflict, as a compromise between wishes and symptoms. Although sexual and other conflicts may be prominent in women with eating disorders, treatment that is based initially on the interpretation of unconscious conflict may be ineffective or even harmful. Indeed, when explanations are imposed on patients through interpretation and confrontation, a basic defect in their personality structure may be reinforced. They may compliantly accept interpretations without experiencing their meaning because women with eating disorders are often unaware of or confused about their subjective experience. Problems in recognizing or accurately labeling their feelings, bodily experiences, or distortions in body image were not adequately explained by these earlier formulations.

On the basis of current understanding of female psychological development, empirical observations of infants, and recent clinical and theoretical

51. Crisp, "Premorbid Factors in Adult Disorders of Weight"; P. Dally and W. Sargant, "Treatment and Outcome of Anorexia Nervosa," *British Journal* 2 (1966): 793–95.

52. J. V. Waller, M. R. Kaufman, and F. Deutsch, "Anorexia Nervosa: A Psychosomatic Entity," *Psychosomatic Medicine* 11, no. 1 (1940): 3–16.

53. J. H. Masserman, "Psychodynamics in Anorexia Nervosa and Neurotic Vomiting," *Psychoanalytic Quarterly* 10 (1941): 211–42.

advances in conceptualizing the sense of self, a new theoretical model to explain female vulnerability to eating disorders can be developed. Indeed, there is a convergence of findings and recent speculations from self psychology and female psychology, even though these literatures have largely developed separately. Both female psychology and self psychology emphasize the importance of the infant-caregiver relationship to development of the sense of self and identity. In particular, the attunement of the caregiver, typically the mother, provides an environment in which various aspects of subjective experience become integrated into a cohesive sense of self during normal development. The nature of the mother-daughter bond is such that the mother may identify more with a daughter than with a son. Therefore, the mother may be more likely to overlook the daughter's uniqueness and to confuse her daughter's experience with her own. Such a daughter may come to be less in tune with her subjective experience and more likely to require external confirmation of her experience and perceptions. In particular, there may be disturbances in the senses of affectivity and agency.

Affectivity refers to an inner sense of vitality as well as to the identification of emotions—that is, the experiencing of inner sensations of arousal and activation and the emotion-specific qualities of feeling.[54] Stern considers affectivity to be a "self invariant," contributing importantly to the development of a "core self" during the first months of life. The ability to access feelings consistently gives a familiarity to one's subjective experience and thus contributes to the sense of identity,[55] whereas agency refers to the sense of authorship of one's actions and non-authorship of the actions of others, including the experience of volition, the sense of control over self-generated action, and the expectation of consequences resulting from one's actions.[56] Disturbances in the subjective experience of affectivity and agency are common among women with eating disorders. Although the drive for thinness in young women with eating disorders may reflect the current cultural emphasis on thinness for women, it may also reflect a distorted attempt to achieve a sense of mastery and to ward off disturbing affects. In the following discussion, I will present observational and empirical evidence from the literature that supports a psychopathological model of disturbances in normal female development and the sense of self among women who develop eating disorders.

54. Stern, Interpersonal World of the Infant.
55. R. N. Emde, "The Prerepresentational Self and Its Affective Core," Psychoanalytic Studies of the Child 38 (1983): 165–92.
56. Stern, Interpersonal World of the Infant.

Sense of Self

I feel completely empty. . . . I know not what is at my core that issues my actions. I am only aware of the multiple people that continually dictate conflicting thoughts into my head. . . . When I look in the mirror I see a shadow of a person who no longer exists. For I have no identity, unless it can be found in my illness. . . . But how do I cast off that identity, when I have lost sight of any other? I could abandon it if I knew what would replace it.[57]

This young woman speaks of the distress of having an eating disorder, yet it provides her with an identity, albeit a precarious one. She feels like a "shadow of a person who no longer exists." Thus she clings to skinniness as her identity. Many clinicians who have written of this central preoccupation with a "fear of fatness" in anorexics agree that it is related to preexisting underlying psychological disturbances, as evidenced by this young woman's anguish. That is, anorexia has been conceived of as a disturbance in the sense of self, a self that these young women believe must be concealed in all circumstances.[58].

Empirical evidence of disturbances in the sense of self comes from self-concept studies among adolescents with anorexia. Using the Offer Self-Image Questionnaire, Regina Casper and colleagues and William Swift and colleagues have documented significant disturbances in the self-images of adolescent females with AN-R and AN-B as compared to the normal adolescent population.[59] Those with AN reported disturbances in emotional tone, body- and self-image, impulse control, and social relationships. Despite their subjective insecurities, they scored within the normal range on the "superior adjustment" subscale, which measures interpersonal empathy, capacity to anticipate, and achievement orientation. This reflects the clinical impression of a good superficial

57. J. M. de Groot and G. Rodin, "Eating Disorders, Female Psychology and the Self," *Journal of the American Academy of Psychoanalysis*, in press.

58. Bruch, *Eating Disorders*; Russell, "Anorexia Nervosa"; M. P. Palazzoli Selvina, *Anorexia Nervosa* (London: Chaucer Press, 1974); H. Bruch, *Conversations with Anorexics*, ed. D. Czyzewski and M. A. Suhr (New York: Basic Books, 1989); A. M. Rizzuto, R. K. Peterson, M. Reed, "The Pathological Sense of Self in Anorexia Nervosa," *Psychiatric Clinics of North America* 4 (1981): 471–87; A. Goodsitt, "Self Psychology and the Treatment of Anorexia Nervosa and Bulimia," in *Handbook of Psychotherapy for Anorexia and Bulimia*, ed. D. M. Garner and P. E. Garfinkel (New York: Guilford Press, 1985), 55–82.

59. R. C. Casper, D. Offer, and E. Ostrov, "Self-Image of Adolescents with Acute Anorexia Nervosa," *Journal of Pediatrics* 98 (1981): 656–61; W. J. Swift, N. J. Bushnell, P. Hanson, and T. Logemann, "Self-Concept in Adolescent Anorexics," *American Academy of Child Psychiatry* 25 (1986): 826–35.

adjustment based on the expectations of others, despite underlying self-doubts and uncertainty. Researchers have characterized the premorbid personality structure of anorexia as typified by dutiful achievement, excellent perfor-mances, and obedient submission, a version of what Winnicott referred to as a "false self."[60] Similarly, women with bulimia experience disturbances in the sense of self, but, unlike the perfectionistic "false-self" anorexic, bulimic women are described as undifferentiated.[61]

Of the various aspects of the self, disturbances in the senses of affectivity and agency appear to be most central to women with AN and BN. Indeed, the triad of disturbances that Bruch saw as fundamental to women with anorexia are profound feelings of ineffectiveness, difficulty in identifying emotions, as well as the pursuit of thinness.[62]

Affectivity

In the descriptive literature, it is suggested that women with anorexia are alexithymic. Alexithymia is a term derived from the Greek meaning absence of words for emotions. It refers to a difficulty in describing subjective feelings, an impoverished fantasy life, and a cognitive style that is literal, utilitarian, and externally oriented.[63] This appears to apply to anorexic women who are ob-served to be vague and evasive in reporting feelings and excessively preoc-cupied with such external details as bodily appearance, fear of fatness, and dietary habits.[64] They are also reported to have difficulty in recognizing and identifying internal bodily stimuli, a capacity that David Garner and others have referred to as interoceptive awareness. This is most notable in patients with eating disorders in their difficulty in recognizing hunger.[65] However, they may

60. D. W. Winnicott, "Ego Distortions in Terms of Time and False Self," *Maturational Pro-cess and the Facilitating Environment* (New York: International Universities Press, 1960). See also Garfinkel and Garner, *Anorexia Nervosa*.

61. C. Steiner-Adair, "New Maps of Development, New Models of Therapy, the Psy-chology of Women and the Treatment of Eating Disorders," in *Psychodynamic Treatment of Anorexia Nervosa and Bulimia*, ed. C. Johnson (New York: Guilford Press, 1991).

62. Bruch, "Perceptual and Conceptual Disturbances in Anorexia Nervosa."

63. H. H. Wolff, "The Concept of Alexithymia and the Future of Psychosomatic Re-search," *Psychotherapy and Psychosomatics* 28 (1977): 376–88; P. E. Sifneos, *Short-Term Psychotherapy and Emotional Crisis* (Cambridge, Mass: Harvard University Press, 1972); G. J. Taylor, R. M. Bagby, and J. D. A. Parker, "The Alexithymia Construct: A Potential for Psychosomatic Medi-cine," *Psyshosomatics* 32 (1991): 153–64.

64. Bruch, *Eating Disorders*.

65. Garner, Olmsted, and Polivy, "Development and Validation of a Multidimensional Eating Disorder Inventory for Anorexia and Bulimia"; Bruch, *Eating Disorders*.

also have difficulty in identifying inner states such as fatigue, in differentiating emotional states from physical ones such as hunger, and in recognizing and acting spontaneously on a feeling state.[66] Empirical studies have confirmed these descriptions. Women with AN were found to have deficits in affective expression and in the elaboration of their fantasy life. With the Toronto Alexithymia Scale (TAS), 67 percent of an AN sample were found to be alexithymic compared to 6.7 percent of normal controls; this disturbance was not related to level of depression or duration of illness.[67]

Like women with AN, women with BN are found to be alexithymic, but at times they appear to be overwhelmed by their affect state. They may be unable to identify their feelings at those times, and typically are unable to link them with specific situations, memories, or fantasies. Deficits in emotional awareness were documented in a comparative study, which found that women with BN had significantly higher scores on the TAS than control women.[68] The TAS scores were significantly correlated with depression ratings, suggesting that, at least in the BN group, the affect disturbance may be correlated with mood. Further studies of affect identification find that BN women show greater disturbance in the interoceptive awareness subscale of the EDI than non-bulimic restrained and nonrestrained eaters.[69]

Evidence of greater emotional fluctuation among women with BN than among normal controls comes from several studies. Binge-vomit episodes may be used for emotional regulation. For instance, women with NWB experience significantly more dysphoric and fluctuating moods throughout the day[70] and this is not significantly correlated with depression. Binging and vomiting episodes have been found to be preceded by high levels of anxiety or a significant drop in mood,[71] and although they may be followed by increased

66. Bruch, *Eating Disorders*; S. H. Sands, "Eating Disorders and Female Development: A Self-Psychological Perspective," in *Dimensions of Self Experiences: Progress in Self Psychology*, vol. 5, ed. A. Goldberg (Hillsdale, N.J.: Analytic Press, 1989).

67. G. J. Taylor, M. P. Bourke, J. D. Parker, and M. R. Bagby, "Alexithymia and Neuroticism in Anorexia Nervosa" (Paper presented at the annual meeting of the American Psychiatric Association, New Orleans, 1991).

68. D. C. Jimmerson, P. E. Sifneos, D. L. Franks, and N. A. Covino, "Alexithymia and Affect-Deficit Symptoms in Bulimia" (Paper presented at the annual meeting of the America Psychiatric Association, New Orleans, 1991).

69. E. M. Rossiter, G. T. Wilson, and L. Goldstein, "Bulimia Nervosa and Dietary Restraint," *Behaviour Research and Therapy* 27 (1989): 465–68.

70. C. Johnson and R. Larson, "Bulimia: An Analysis of Moods and Behaviour," *Psychosomatic Medicine* 44 (1982): 341–51; A. K. Lehman and J. Rodin, "Styles of Self-Nurturance and Disordered Eating," *Journal of Consulting Clinical Psychology* 57 (1989): 117–22.

71. D. K. Elmore and J. M. de Castro, "Self-Rated Moods and Hunger in Relation to Spontaneous Eating Behaviour in Bulimics, Recovered Bulimics and Normals," *International*

depression, anxiety is diminished. Thus the binge-purge episode may act as a physiological mechanism for temporarily relieving intolerable tension states.[72]

These findings support a disturbance in affectivity, in that both anorexic and bulimic women are deficient in emotional awareness and regulation. Women may use such behaviors as starvation, hyperactivity, binging, and purging to subdue, distract from, or explain affects.[73] This suggests a link between the senses of affectivity and agency, and disturbances in both areas have been noted. Women with eating disorders have little awareness of their emotional experience and feel unable to regulate affects, which contributes to their sense of ineffectiveness.

Disturbance in Agency

> I relish the feeling of my bones pressing against the sheets.... My pain is manifested by my body, for then it becomes tangible. My bones, my profile, become constant reminders to me of the control I possess. I feel my bones and feel one with my body, as though I can control it, ... I want to lose more so my body can be mine—it has never been mine, it will never be enough.[74]

The experience of self-control among women with eating disorders is extremely fragile, as conveyed by this young woman, who fears that she can never even own her body. Hilde Bruch emphasized that a sense of ineffectiveness was central to the psychological picture of women with anorexia. This sense of ineffectiveness, which can be regarded as a disturbance in the sense of agency, pervades all areas of their lives including thought and activity.[75] It is postulated that the deficiency in her sense of agency is due to the woman's early experience of impotence in her attempts to get her parents to see her beyond the appearance of her body. That is, the child's profound helplessness

---

Journal of Eating Disorders 9 (1990): 179–90; W. H. Kaye, H. E. Givertsman, D. T. George, and D. C. Jimerson, "Relationship of Mood Alterations to Bingeing Behaviour in Bulimia," British Journal of Psychiatry 149 (1986): 479–85; R. Davis, R. Freeman, and L. Solyom, "Mood and Food: An Analysis of Bulimic Episodes," Journal of Psychiatric Research 19 (1985): 331–35.

72. Elmore and de Castro, "Self-Rated Moods and Hunger"; Kaye, Givertsman, George, and Jimerson, "Relationship of Mood Alterations to Bingeing Behaviour in Bulimia."

73. A. Goodsitt, "Self-Regulatory Disturbances in Eating Disorders," International Journal of Eating Disorders 2 (1983): 51–60.

74. de Groot and Rodin, "Eating Disorders, Female Psychology and the Self."

75. Bruch, "Perceptual and Conceptual Disturbances in Anorexia Nervosa"; Bruch, Eating Disorders.

originates in her realistic inability to change her mother's fixed way of seeing her.[76] The constant activity and exercise typical of women with anorexia may be attempts to feel whole and cohesive particularly when the integrity or cohesion of the self is threatened—for example, when they feel overwhelmed with affect. These young women are also dependent on external contingencies for their well-being[77] and frequently experience their actions as being externally influenced.

Evidence for this disturbance in agency is found in the empirical literature as women with anorexia or bulimia have been found to report higher levels of ineffectiveness on the EDI than a control group of female college students.[78] On a locus of control measure, women with bulimia scored lower than normal-weight controls in their sense of internal control.[79] This is reflected by the significantly higher rates of impulsive behavior (for example, drug and alcohol use, stealing, and sexual intercourse) among women with NWB and AN-B than among normal controls and women with AN-R.[80] The impulsive behavior of women with bulimia is symptomatic of a disturbance in the subjective experience of feeling in control of their actions. By contrast, women with anorexia are so fearful of losing control that they maintain a rigid stance of overcontrol—for example, counting calories, engaging in constant activity. Although they are behaviorally different, women with anorexia and bulimia experience disturbances in the subjective experience of agency, which is closely tied to the disturbance in affectivity.

Conclusions

Recent studies of infancy and of female psychological development and recent conceptualizations regarding the sense of self make it possible to develop a new theoretical model of female vulnerability to eating disorders. Both female psychology and self psychology emphasize the importance of the infant-caregiver relationship to the development of the sense of self and identity. That is, the attunement of the caregiver, typically the mother, provides an environ-

76. Rizzuto, Peterson, Reed, "Pathological Sense of Self in Anorexia Nervosa."

77. Goodsitt, "Self-Psychology and the Treatment of Anorexia Nervosa."

78. Garner, Olmstead, and Polivy, "Development and Validation of a Multidimensional Eating Disorder Inventory for Anorexia and Bulimia."

79. S. R. Weiss and M. H. Ebert, "Psychological and Behavioral Characteristics of Normal-Weight Bulimics and Normal-Weight Controls," *Psychosomatic Medicine* 45 (1983): 293–303.

80. Garfinkel, Moldofsky, and Garner, "Heterogeneity of Anorexia Nervosa."

ment in which various aspects of the subjective sense of self become reinforced and integrated during normal development. A mother with limited empathic ability may be less able to provide the mirroring necessary for the infant's development of a cohesive sense of self. Further, the mother may identify more with a daughter than a son, and thus be even less able to recognize her daughter's uniqueness. Her daughter may come to be less in tune with her own subjective experience and more likely in adult life to require external confirmation to retain a stable sense of self. In particular, her sense of agency and affectivity may be defective, disturbances typical of women with eating disorders. Although the drive for thinness in young women with eating disorders may be related to the cultural emphasis on thinness for women, it may also reflect an attempt to achieve a sense of mastery over physical and emotional states.

Adolescence may be a time of "crisis in connection" for girls. They are confronted with pressure to conform to an idealized conventional female expectation, in which self-worth is defined and evaluated by the ability to care for and protect others. At the same time, there may be cultural pressures for the young woman to replace her complex relational world with one in which there is a bias toward autonomy.[81] For a young woman whose sense of self is disturbed, particularly the senses of agency and affectivity, this conflict may seem overwhelming, and she may then attempt to control her body in an effort to receive external validation.

81. Gilligan, In a Different Voice; Steiner-Adair, "Body Politic."

Textual Bodies: Narratives
of Denial and Desire
in *Studies on Hysteria*

Sara van den Berg

Studies on Hysteria (1895) began as a collaboration between Sigmund Freud and Josef Breuer.[1] Breuer, however, contributed only parts of the introduction, the initial case report on Anna O., and one segment of the "theoretical" section. Most of the book was written by Freud, whose real collaborators are his patients. By listening, he enables his patients to discard the indirect language of symptom and to speak directly of desire and its cost. What they say supports his theory that hysteria is a contorted language of desire and denial. He frequently quotes his patients, appropriating their language to enunciate his theory, and he repeatedly expresses his gratitude for their formulations of the hysterical conflict between knowing and refusing to know, between desire and

1. Sigmund Freud and Josef Breuer, *Studies on Hysteria*, in *The Standard Edition of the Complete Psychological Works of Sigmund Freud*, vol. 2, ed. and trans. James Strachey (London: Hogarth Press, 1893–1895). All quotations cited are from this edition.

the denial of desire. He arranges their stories in a sequence that supports his theory, but the apparent clarity of his presentation is belied by layers of revisionary comments and corrective footnotes. His text, its line of argument initially distorted by evasion and clarified by recursive commentary, mimics the disorder and recovery he traces in his patients. He and they become fellow speakers of a new language that acknowledges rather than conceals painful memories and that would become the basis of psychoanalysis.

Freud's distinctive theory of hysteria and his new therapeutic emerge gradually through the narratives of his patients. At first he is as puzzled as they, bewildered by their disorder and its plethora of unpleasant, disabling symptoms. They present bodies that cannot move or cannot keep still; that cannot eat or cannot stop eating; that cannot speak or cannot keep silent, uttering obscenities, clacking sounds, formulas, or foreign tongues; that discharge blood, mucus, or vaginal fluids; that are tormented by facial pain or tingling sensations in fingers and toes. Their posture is at once seductive and threatening, displaying intense engagement and la belle indifférence. If the hysterical body is a book, its narrative seems written in an undecipherable code designed to repel rather than entice a reader.

However real the suffering of the hysteric, none of her symptoms coincide with organic disease. To quote Monique David-Ménard, "Hysteria is not acquainted with the anatomy of the nervous system."[2] As Freud notes in "Some Points for a Comparative Study of Organic and Hysterical Motor Paralysis" (1893 [1888–1893]), part of the puzzle lies in the linkage between the hysteric's body and everyday language: "It takes the organs in the ordinary, popular sense of the names they bear: the leg is the leg as far as its insertion into the hip: the arm is the upper limb as it is visible under the clothing" (I.169). To a medical reader of the body, the purported linkage between the hysteric's language and her disease is nonsensical. By privileging his patients' everyday language over his own professional discourse, Freud revises his understanding of the relation between pain and neurosis. Pain neither causes nor is caused by neurosis but is "merely used, increased, and maintained by it" (II.174). Freud's chosen task is not to categorize the symptoms of hysteria but to read the problematic language of the hysterical body, a language that links mental and physical pain, past and present life, experience and fantasy, denial and desire.

Freud describes twenty cases of hysteria. His accounts range from four

2. Monique David-Ménard, Hysteria from Freud to Lacan: Body and Language in Psychoanalysis, trans. Catherine Porter (Ithaca, N.Y.: Cornell University Press, 1989), 2.

thorough presentations to brief vignettes to footnotes, and even include his own experience of a hysterical state. He has designed this series of case histories to define hysteria and justify his new therapeutic method.[3] After initially endorsing Breuer's reliance on hypnotism, Freud demonstrates how "concentration" alone can stimulate in the patient revelations that make sense of her puzzling symptoms. The organization of the book is linear: questions posed by one case are answered by the next. The organization is also recursive, both in the main text and in the footnotes he added as late as 1924. This second pattern of presentation enables Freud to rewrite his narrative, not only to indicate the development of his understanding but also to disentangle what might be termed his own complicity in hysteria, as he reveals secrets that he, like his patients, initially felt compelled to conceal. He finally discards narrative in favor of an alternative mode of representation in order to avoid the literary expectations of suspense and completion that narrative stirs up in its readers. The last segment of the book, divided into theory and drama, addresses the problem of symbolic utterance, both theorizing and enacting how the body of language can translate, and ultimately heal, the painful language of the hysteric's body.

Breuer does not seem to share Freud's concern with the problem of language or with the theoretical difficulties in the writing of clinical narratives. Freud's segment of *Studies on Hysteria*, while deferential to Breuer, betrays a certain tension between the two men. As the younger man seeking to establish himself professionally, Freud eagerly sought publication of the book, but the two men were already beginning to pull away from each other.[4] Freud even uses the speech of one of his patients to imply that he finds it a bit uncomfortable to be closely identified with his colleague. Freud's final case study, the narrative of Elisabeth von R., ends with a footnote relating her punning hallucination about the two men:

> Her two doctors—Breuer and I—were hanging on two trees next each other in the garden. The hallucination disappeared after the analysis had brought out the following explanation. The evening before, Breuer had refused to give her a drug she had asked for. She

3. Kathryn Hunter, *Doctors' Stories: The Narrative Structure of Medical Knowledge* (Princeton, N.J.: Princeton University Press, 1991).

4. Albert Hirschmüller, *The Life and Work of Josef Breuer* (New York and London: New York University Press, 1989).

had then set her hopes on me but had found me equally hard-hearted. She was furious with us over this, and in her anger she thought to herself: "There's nothing to choose between the two of them; one's the *pendant* [match] of the other." (II.181n)

Since this footnote seems no more than a supernumerary example to amplify Freud's argument, one wonders at his decision to end the clinical section of his book in this way. In part this dream is a rueful joke at the patient's expense, for neither physician was willing to service her drug addiction. The placement of the passage in Freud's narrative lends it additional force as a typically Freudian joke at the expense of the two physicians, for by 1924 there was certainly a good deal to choose between Freud and Breuer. Breuer affirms the utility of hypnosis as a therapeutic tool; Freud rejects it. Breuer is content to describe hysteria; Freud struggles to interpret its language and etiology. Although both men show a respect for hysterical patients that is rare for their time, Breuer—like his patients—chooses to minimize or erase the sexual etiology of the disease.

Freud's remarks on Anna O. implicitly criticize Breuer for disregarding the issue of sexuality: "Breuer's patient, Anna O., seems to contradict my opinion and to be an example of a pure hysterical disorder. This case, however, which has been so fruitful for our knowledge of hysteria, was not considered at all by its observer from the point of view of a sexual neurosis, and is now quite useless for this purpose" (II.259). Moreover, in breaking off the treatment of Anna O., Breuer denies himself the discovery of transference—perhaps because its erotic component seems threatening or improper. Freud suggests as much in a 1932 letter to Stephan Zweig describing Breuer's purported flight when Anna claimed she was pregnant with his child in a dramatic episode of hysterical childbirth.[5]

Freud's comments on Anna O. introduce a review of his own case reports in *Studies on Hysteria*. Of Emmy von N., for example, Freud writes that he emulated Breuer not only in using hypnosis but also in neglecting the role of sexual neurosis in her hysteria: "I regarded the linking of hysteria with the topic of sexuality as a sort of insult—just as the women patients themselves do" (II.260). He then reviews the cases of Lucy R., Katharina, and Elizabeth von R.,

5. See Dianne Hunter, "Hysteria, Psychoanalysis and Feminism: The Case of Anna O," 9, no. 3 (Fall 1991): 465–88. Breuer's biographer, however, has called that claim into question; see Hirshmüller, *The Life and Work of Josef Breuer*. Whatever the truth, nothing in Breuer's narrative suggests his sensitivity to the therapeutic importance of the doctor-patient relationship.

women differing in age and marital status, and concludes that he was remiss in not considering the role of sexual neurosis in all of them (II.260). He criticizes his own "reticence," but stops short of debunking the existence of a "pure hysteria" without a "neurotic sexual foundation" (II.260). He struggles to defer to Breuer, suppressing his own beliefs in deference to those of his senior colleague: "an elucidation of these sexual neuroses would overstep the bounds of the present joint publication" (II.261).

Despite his attempt at deference, Freud's text qualifies and finally rejects Breuer's assumptions as well as his methods. Freud recognizes that his patients' narratives of denial mask a variety of narratives of (forbidden) desire: of woman for man, of woman for woman, of parent for child, of child for parent, of patient for analyst, of analyst for patient. His narratives unmask their denials, and his own as well. Near the end of his first narrative, the case study of Emmy von N., Freud admits that "what I was allowed to hear was no doubt an *editio in usum delphini* [a bowdlerized edition] of her life-story" (II.103). His own work with her and other early patients is also marked by a detectable self-censorship. His narratives become more thorough and more explicit, culminating in the footnotes of 1924, which identify the molesters of Katharina and Rosalia and critique his narrative of Emmy von N. The direction of his main text, however, shifts from identifying the traumatic cause of hysteria to analyzing the relationship between hysteria and language as symbolic expression. Freud speculates that "hysteria and linguistic usage alike draw their material from a common source" (II.181).

Most of the political critics who discuss hysteria focus on the hysteric's disorderly body rather than on her language. Carroll Smith-Rosenberg, discussing the epidemic of hysteria in nineteenth-century America, contends that the body of the hysteric, in its exaggerated posturing of assertion and withdrawal, mimed the dilemma of woman, and in that display challenged as impossible, as unlivable, the cultural ideal of perfect femininity. Peter Stallybrass and Allon White, building on Bakhtin's formulations of "the classical body" and "the grotesque body," describe the hysterical body as struggling to maintain or attain the classical ideal (pure, closed, smooth, disciplined, still, harmonious, clothed, graceful, upright, fragrant) while unwillingly manifesting the grotesque (impure, open, rough, disorderly, noisy, naked, awkward, inverted, smelly).[6] That struggle was made more difficult, White argues, because

6. Carroll Smith-Rosenberg, "The Hysterical Woman: Sex Roles and Role Conflict in Nineteenth Century America,"in her *Disorderly Conduct: Visions of Gender in Victorian America* (New York: Alfred A. Knopf, 1985); Peter Stallybrass and Allon White, *The Politics and Poetics of Transgression* (Ithaca, N.Y.: Cornell University Press, 1986).

nineteenth-century industrial society had severely curtailed the holidays that offered cultural license to indulge the grotesque body. The curtailment was exacerbated for bourgeois women because their lives were designed to be private, their pleasures restrained by the ascetic ideals of decorum and propriety. Noting that several of Freud's patients were deeply troubled by fantasies of circus animals or carnivalesque disorder, White suggests that they futilely attempted to repress in themselves the festive need denied them by their world.[7] Adapting the feminist psychoanalytic rhetoric of "carnival" developed by Juliet Mitchell, Julia Kristeva, and Luce Irigaray, he emphasizes the carnivalesque excess of the hysterical body but locates its cause in the hysteric's conflict with society.

Bourgeois culture of the nineteenth century may have been repressive and may have made the hysteric more visible, but the long history and worldwide occurrence of the disease preclude any narrow explanatory schema of external cultural causation. Moreover, the culture inhabited by Freud, Breuer, and their patients not only fostered the occurrence of hysteria but also provided the ground for discovering its etiology and cure.[8] As Freud learned how to read the language of the hysteric's body, he discovered how to write his own book and cure his own hysterical thinking. His narratives move from contradictions, reticence, and lies to consistency, revelation, and truth telling.

Critics unsympathetic to Freud have argued that he was trapped, like his patients, in a language of denial and repression. Mary Jacobus, developing a suggestion made by Juliet Mitchell, argues that Freud's narratives, in their controlled process of revelation, resemble "hysterical utterance."[9] Jacobus is not claiming for Freud traits associated with the female hysteric—fragility, hypersensitivity, and social inhibition—which male writers like Gustave Flaubert frequently claimed for themselves.[10] Rather, she argues that Freud as writer does deliberately what his patients do unconsciously: he withholds what he knows. His clinical narratives, then, are the counterparts of his pa-

7. Allon White, "Hysteria at the End of Carnival: Festivity and Bourgeois Neurosis," in *The Violence of Representation*, ed. Nancy Armstrong and Leonard Tennenhouse (London and New York: Routledge, 1989).

8. See Ilza Veith, *Hysteria: The History of a Disease* (Chicago: University of Chicago Press, 1965); Phillip R. Slavney, *Perspectives on "Hysteria"* (Baltimore and London: Johns Hopkins University Press, 1990).

9. Mary Jacobus, *Reading Woman: Essays in Feminist Criticism* (New York: Columbia University Press, 1986), 197. See also Juliet Mitchell, "Femininity, Narrative, and Psychoanalysis," in her *Women: The Longest Revolution* (New York: Pantheon Books, 1984).

10. Jan Goldstein, "The Uses of Male Hysteria: Medicine and Literary Discourse in Nineteenth Century France," *Representations* 34 Spring (1991): 156–57.

tients' stories. Jacobus implies that he withholds knowledge not only from his reader but from his patient as well, so that patient and physician are accomplices in a fiction of reticence and revelation. The hysteric knows she is the sexual being she both fears and desires to be, despite her attempts to conceal and deny her desire. The analyst also conceals that he knows, thereby assuming the role of authority as well as ally. Both patient and analyst would seem to be trapped in contradiction. Freud's narratives represent the undoing of the hysterical knot, both his patients' and his own. His initial diffidence gives way to increasingly explicit acknowledgment of the sexual etiology of hysteria. But more is revealed, and more is at stake, than the seduction theory. In the process of presenting this series of case reports, Freud raises other issues as well: the insufficiency of hypnosis, the analyst's role in analysis, the linkage of hysteria and language, and the problem of narrative as a mode of representation. Freud's text, a palimpsest of recursive additions, commentaries, and footnotes, dramatizes his own escape, albeit partial, from the cultural reticence and denial that initially entangles him as well as his patients. That escape, as we shall see, is manifest in his rejection of narrative at the end of his book. Undoing the narrative of hysteria finally requires him to discard the narrative mode. He frustrates his readers' literary expectations and offers them instead the intellectual austerity of analytic theory and the dramatic intensity of clinical dialogue.

Hysteria, as Freud and Breuer show, is a disorder of memory. "Hysterics," Breuer declares, "suffer mainly from reminiscences" (II.7). The hysteric cannot remember, nor can she forget. When Freud sets out his first account of his work with a hysteric, Emmy von N., he, too, is overwhelmed by memories, by a sense of failure, and by the problems of representation:

> I did not carry the analysis of the symptoms far enough, nor pursue it systematically enough. I shall perhaps be able best to give a picture of the patient's condition and my medical procedure by reproducing the notes which I made each evening during the first three weeks of the treatment. Wherever later experience has brought me a better understanding, I shall embody it in footnotes and interpolated comments. (II.48)

Because Freud begins his account by proclaiming his lack of understanding, he takes refuge in the apparent certainty of chronology, detailing his notes on the first three weeks of the treatment. That chronology, however, does not suffice as a narrative device. Even James Strachey, Freud's translator, labels the chronology "self-contradictory as it stands" (II.48n) and finds it necessary to append a corrected version (II.307–9).

The inadequacy of chronology as a technique for presenting his findings emerges as Freud describes the way hysterics like Emmy von N. interpret their experience and the way therapeutic insight is achieved. He compares his patient to an "ascetic medieval monk who sees the finger of God or a temptation of the Devil in every trivial event of his life and who is incapable of picturing the world even for a brief moment or in its smallest corner as being without reference to himself" (II.65–66). Her analytic narratives, so often dismissed by other physicians as mere babble, Freud comes to regard as a complex set of "false connections" (II.67). Moreover, in the narratives of the hysteric, "communications are given in a reverse chronological order"—from the most recent and least important to the "primary impression, which is in all probability the most important one causally" (II.75n). Time's arrow runs in two directions at once during psychoanalysis: the patient moves forward in insight by moving back into memory. Even a double-directed arrow does not suffice; the process of insight can also be figured as a gyre, at once widening and narrowing as it circles about the patient's pain. The multiple directions of psychoanalytic treatment offer a special challenge to representation, which Freud tries to address by creating a text that can qualify, adumbrate, and even countermand chronology. Chronology must be overlaid by the discontinuous process of understanding, resulting in a palimpsest of footnotes and interpolated commentary.

Chronology is not the only model of narrative that Freud finds problematic in presenting the narrative of hysteria. His desire to interpret the disorder to his patient and to formulate a theory of interpretation for his readers causes him additional confusion. Like Cäcilie M., whose emotional outbursts are ill-suited to present circumstance but often anticipate the subsequent breakthrough of an unconscious memory, Freud faces the problem of prolepsis. He wants to display a theory, building up a convincing array of cases—yet a clinical example may seem better suited to a subsequent argument than to its apparent use. The case of Cäcilie M., for example, the only one to migrate from the footnotes to the main text, is discussed near the beginning and again near the end of the clinical section. Freud's presentation of this case, which he describes as the richest and most instructive he knows, mimics the gaps Cäcilie M. experienced in her own memory—"as though her life was chopped in pieces" (II.70n).

Another type of difficulty results from his initial understanding of interpretation as a mode of instruction. As Freud disentangles Emmy von N.'s "confusion" (II.172–73) he often tries to give her "lessons" that she does "not take in"—for example, "that there is a whole multitude of indifferent, small things lying between what is good and what is evil—things about which no one need reproach himself" (II.65). The linkage between principle and practice so central to the ideology of Western culture overwhelms Emmy von N. Freud begins treatment with the aim of "wiping away" the horrifying fantasies (of rats, of her aunt in a coffin, etc.) that torment his patient into crying out, "Keep still!—Don't say anything!—Don't touch me!" (II.51–52). Slowly he begins to see that just as the binary instructional model of principle and practice has no effect, so also the other binary model of cause and effect, which implicitly constitutes the treatment, is inadequate. Freud comes to regard hysterical symptoms as a "maze of sign-reading" and concludes, "It is difficult to attribute too much sense to them" (II.93n). Phenomena that seem ascetic (like Emmy von N.'s anorexia) turn out to be an overflowing cornucopia of meaning. The hysteric who seems so ascetic proves quite the opposite, appropriating disparate materials from every aspect of her life to figure, ever more indirectly, her original trauma. This psychological procedure at once narrows reality and totalizes it. The technique of cathartic erasure is useless unless Freud and the patient first read the many texts written on the "bad" body that is trying so hard to be "good."

The language of morality, so prominent in the reference to the "ascetic medieval monk," pervades Freud's account of Emmy von N. Freud knew that hysteria was often regarded as a disease of moral and sexual degeneracy, and he ends his account by expressing his admiration for her asceticism:

> It has also struck me that amongst all the intimate information given me by the patient there was a complete absence of the sexual element, which is, after all, more liable than any other to provide occasion for traumas. . . . The patient behaved with the greatest and to all appearances with the most unforced sense of propriety, without a trace of prudishness. . . . I cannot help suspecting that this woman who was so passionate and so capable of strong feelings had not won her victory over her sexual needs without severe struggles, and that at times her attempts at suppressing this most powerful of all instincts had exposed her to severe mental exhaustion. . . . Frau Emmy von N. gave us an example of how hysteria is compatible with an unblemished character and a well-governed mode of life. The woman we

[Freud and Breuer] came to know was an admirable one. The moral seriousness with which she viewed her duties, her intelligence and energy, which were no less than a man's, and her high degree of education and love of truth impressed both of us greatly: while her benevolent care for the welfare of all her dependents, her humility of mind and the refinement of her manners revealed her qualities as a true lady as well. To describe such a woman as a "degenerate" would be to distort the meaning of that word out of all recognition. (II.103–4)

As far as Freud is concerned, Emmy von N. may seem a "grotesque body" to a casual viewer, but her life exemplifies the classical ideals of purity and virtue, reticence and denial. On the one hand, he wants Emmy von N. to speak her suffering, so that she can erase the pictures that torment her. On the other hand, he praises her reticence and her self-denial.

If Freud's narrative describes the tragic results of Emmy von N.'s attempt to be the admirable lady he celebrates, it also records the analogous conflict between his own desire and denial. Freud draws the analogy between himself and his hysterical patient rather early in the case study. The passage occurs in a footnote that Strachey describes as Freud's first "tentative approach" to the interpretation of dreams. As he struggles to clarify the "false connections" hysterics often make between a new symptom and its possible cause, Freud recalls his own attempt to understand the "vivid dreams" that came to him when he was obliged to sleep in a new, harder bed:

I succeeded in tracing all these dreams back to two factors: (1) to the necessity for working out any ideas which I had only dwelt upon cursorily during the day . . . and (2) to the compulsion to link together any ideas that might be present in the same state of consciousness. The senseless and contradictory character of the dreams could be traced back to the uncontrolled ascendancy of this latter factor. (II.69n)

His "senseless and contradictory" dreams, like the narratives and symptoms of his patients, spring from a compulsion to bring order out of disorder, an uncontrollable urge to control the uncontrolled. Freud the dreamer is, then, a type of hysteric.

Freud the writer is also in some sense implicated in hysterical thinking.

The passage just quoted is part of a very long footnote which interrupts Emmy von N.'s admission that she fears her menstrual period will interfere with the therapeutic massage she receives from Freud every day. The footnote begins by offering a version of the events that led up to the statement but quickly moves on to describe another researcher, Bernheim, and then to discuss "false connections." That concept is illustrated by a long discussion of Emmy von N.'s "mistrust" of Freud and her unwillingness to take the cool baths he prescribes because she superstitiously and fearfully links her memory of such baths in San Domingo to a revolution which had just broken out there and which might occasion harm to her brother, who was living there. Freud then identifies as the characteristic modus operandi of hysterics a "compulsion to associate," and at that point he identifies that same trait in himself as a dreamer. Then he introduces the case of another hysteric, Cäcilie M., whose moods are often inappropriate to her current circumstances but proleptic of a subsequent hysterical "reminiscence."[11] On the one hand, this footnote constitutes a narrative of desire: Freud struggles to conceptualize how hysterics make "false connections" of different kinds, bringing to bear on this problem additional information from several sources (the case of Emmy von N., his own dreams, and Cäcilie M.). On the other hand, this footnote can also be read as a narrative of denial: Freud never, in his written text, gives any indication that he replied to Emmy von N.'s concern that her menstrual period would interfere with her therapeutic massage. His reticence on this point implicates him in his culture, of course: one wonders what he could have said to his patient, and what he could have put in print. Finally, the associations that Freud here labels "false connections" would before too long be recuperated as the primary activity to be analyzed. It is not difficult for a modern reader to link Emmy von N's fear of change to the revolution, for example, or Freud's work to his new, harder bed.

There are other errors of commission and omission in Freud's treatment of Emmy von R. At one point he tells her a "white lie" and on another occasion "jokes" at her expense by manipulating her behavior after hypnosis (II.80). He never investigates certain fantasies, although they recur in his written record of the case. Most prominent among these is her fear of toads: she once imagines finding a toad under a rock (II.55), later remembers with horror a dream of toads crossing a road (II.62), and on yet another occasion cannot speak the

11. Peter J. Swales, "Freud, His Teacher and the Birth of Psychoanalysis," in Freud, Appraisals and Reappraisals: Contribution to Freud Studies, vol. 1, ed. Paul E. Stepansky (Hillsdale, N.J.: Analytic Press, 1986), 3–82.

word, indeed can scarcely spell "t - o - a - d" (II.79). On the first of these occasions, Freud remarks in a footnote that it was a mistake not to inquire into her fantasy (II.55n), but nothing in the case report links these recurrent images. These errors spring from Freud's laudable concerns: to describe the single psychological process at work in hysteria, and to argue a single therapeutic for undoing the many disparate symptoms manifest in hysteria. In the case of Emmy von N., the undoing of hysterical symptoms seems no more than erasure: "you will not . . ."; "it will no longer . . ." Freud, like his patient, at this point seems unable to distinguish major and minor symptoms; he is still preoccupied with each symptom, each syllable written on the body. The effect is an undifferentiated excess of response not all that different from that of the "ascetic medieval monk."

The preoccupation with individual symptoms at the expense of a discrimination among them is explicit and, to a modern reader's eyes, blameworthy in a narrative of denial that occurs in a footnote late in Freud's narrative of Emmy von N. This footnote sets up a remarkable, implicit connection between Emmy von N.'s reticence and Freud's. Just before Freud praises her discretion about sexuality, he inserts a rather lengthy footnote describing a "lively and gifted girl" who came to him complaining of difficulty in walking and a rapid tremor in her hands. Her father was present during her hypnoses. At a critical moment, "she gave way to the extent of letting fall a significant phrase; but she had hardly said a word before she stopped, and her old father, who was sitting behind her, began to sob bitterly. Naturally, I pressed my investigation no further; but I never saw the patient again" (II.101n). It is not hard to guess what the girl was on the verge of saying about her "old father." More troublesome is Freud's declaration, "*Naturally* I pressed my investigation no further." His rhetoric implies a kind of sympathy for the father. Freud does not ban the father from the room and defends his own reticence to inquire further. Yet he regards his discretion as ineffectual, even damaging. Despite his tact, "I never saw the patient again."

The case of Emmy von N. ends by endorsing the reticence of both patient and physician. Both compose "bowdlerized" narratives of desire and shame contained—narratives of denial. Yet Freud knew that the original therapeutic of cathartic erasure gave only temporary relief, and he knew as well that denial is an erasure that fails. In subsequent case studies, using a progressive overlay of footnotes and revisions, Freud undoes the hysterical thinking that he shared with his patients, replacing the contradictory desire to speak and keep silent with a new desire to tell the plain truth.

The case of Lucy R. marks an advance on several fronts. Treating a young governess tormented first by the inability to smell, then by the smell of burnt pudding, finally by the smell of a cigar, Freud for the first time gives up the technique of hypnosis in favor of a new method. He asks the patient to tell him whatever she thinks or sees when he places his hand on her forehead. His motive for undertaking this change has little to do with an advanced understanding of hysteria, and more to do with his own frustration when a patient proved recalcitrant to hypnosis. He finds the effort "an embarrassing situation" and thinks it "wise to avoid both the word and the embarrassment" (II.109).

Far more important than this change in method is Freud's new basis of treatment. He decides "to start from the assumption that my patients [know] everything" (II.110). After first relating a typical patient's reply to his interpretations—"I hoped that would not be it" (II.111), Freud records his suggestion to Lucy R. that she loved her young charges' father and quotes her reply: "I didn't know—or rather I didn't want to know. I wanted to drive it out of my head and not think of it again; and I believe latterly I have succeeded" (101.117). Freud untangles a set of linked desires and rebukes that embarrassed Lucy R., each an experience of guilt converted into a different olfactory torment. She has not, in fact, "succeeded" in driving her knowledge out of her head, but experiences it as a series of symbolic symptoms. Freud's interpretations all center on Lucy R.'s futile desire for her employer and different stages in her hopes and disappointment. By the end of the narrative, he can quote with some admiration and puzzlement her rationale for continuing as the children's governess: "I can have thoughts and feelings to myself" (II.121). This statement rests on her earlier denial: "We're not responsible for our feelings, anyhow" (II.117). That denial, in turn, rests on her trust in the power of external class status to limit relationships: "It was distressing to me only because he is my employer and I am in his service and live in his house. I don't feel the same complete independence towards him that I could towards anyone else. And then I am only a poor girl and he is such a rich man of good family. People would laugh at me if they had any idea of it" (II.117). Because she relies on these socioeconomic barriers, and because Freud does not laugh at her, Lucy R. can go on to speak with "no resistance" of the love she feels for her employer.

Discussing the chain of Lucy R.'s olfactory symptoms, Freud suggests that "the symptoms that had arisen later masked the earlier ones, and the key to the whole situation lay only in the last symptom to be reached" (II.124). To a modern reader, the event that precipitates her hysterical symptoms is just as significant and suggests a rather different account of the desire that so disturbs her. This other desire she cannot so easily admit. Her discomfort begins when she receives a letter from her own mother (II.115). Lucy R.'s wish to take the place of her young charges' mother may be at odds with another forbidden desire to reunite with her own mother, to be once again a child, or even her own erotic desires for the children. The mnemonic smell of burnt pudding arises when she is rebuked for allowing a woman to kiss the children on the mouth, an image that can be linked to Lucy R.'s fantasy about her mother kissing her, as well as to her fantasy of becoming the children's stepmother. The tertiary symptom, the odor of cigar smoke, she traces to a later event, when her employer yells at an elderly male guest, "Don't kiss the children" (II.123). This rebukes both of her desires, to kiss and to be kissed. These elements in the case of Lucy R. support Freud's subsequent, very late suggestion that hysteria is linked to pre-Oedipal issues of mother-daughter desire and subsequent homosexuality, although at this point Freud's advance is confined to making explicit the heterosexual desire never even addressed in the preceding case of Emmy von N.

Just as Freud's empathic identification with Emmy von N. is suggested by the way he interpolates his own experience into the narrative of her case, here also his references to himself suggest an important analogy between Freud and Lucy R. Like her, he fears embarrassment, and his narrative, like hers, is designed to defeat that fear. Of special importance in this regard is the personal footnote that Freud inserts after Lucy R. is quoted as not knowing, or not wanting to know, what she subsequently admitted knowing full well. He begins by expressing his admiration for Lucy R.'s account of her mode of knowing:

> I have never managed to give a better description than this of the strange state of mind in which one knows and does not know a thing at the same time. It is clearly impossible to understand it unless one has been in such a state oneself. I myself have had a very remarkable experience of this sort, which is still clearly before me. If I try to recollect what went on in my mind at the time I can get hold of very little. What happened was that I saw something which did not fit in at all with my expectation; yet I did not allow what I saw to disturb my fixed plan in the least, though the perception should have put a stop to it. I was unconscious of any contradiction in this: nor was I aware of my feelings of repulsion, which must nevertheless undoubtedly have been responsible for the perception producing no psychical effect. I

was afflicted by that blindness of the seeing eye which is so astonishing in the attitude of mothers to their daughters, husbands to their
wives and rulers to their favorites. (II.117n)

Like Lucy R., Freud both tells and does not tell, wants to talk and not to talk,
remembers and forgets. The footnote tells little of external events but sets up a
complex conflict of recollection, expectation, perception, and contradictory
feelings. What is most provocative, however, is the way Freud situates himself
in an imaginary version of the three relationships that were interwoven in the
fantasy life of Lucy R.: mother and daughter, husband and wife, ruler and
favorite. The first, I would argue, Freud never reaches in his work with Lucy R.
The second and third are the two kinds of relationships she imagined having
with her employer. It is only later in his book that Freud postulates a simple
concept of transference, but this footnote at once asserts and denies transference relationships, formulating what Freud "knows and does not know." In
that present moment as a physician, as in the past he describes, he is "afflicted
by [a] blindness of the seeing eye."

Despite that blindness, Freud uses the case of Lucy R. to make his first
proposal concerning the hysterical process that his therapeutic method attempts to undo. In the process he names "conversion," the person wants "to
do away with an idea, but all he succeeds in doing is to isolate it psychically"
(II.123). Later, Freud argues, other affects and symptoms collect around that
unacceptable idea, forming a kind of poisoned pearl. The person's attempt to
split that idea off from consciousness instead contaminates the whole, taking
new experiences into its own distorting sphere. Symptoms multiply, but there
remains a single cause and a single mode of symptom formation. Repression
begets repression, in layers of conversions and displacements. The idea of
conversion clarifies not only the process of hysterical thinking but also the
reversal of Freud's own conflicted mode of interpretation and writing. Ultimately, his analytic interpretations can be read as the reverse of hysterical
conversions.

Freud's implication in hysterical thinking and its slow reversal is most
dramatically displayed in the brief report of Katharina, daughter of Freud's
summer landlady. In a narrative that Peter Gay somehow manages to describe
as "charming,"[12] Freud presents a harrowing tale of incest, rape, and pregnancy. According to his main text, the villain of the piece is Katharina's "uncle,"

12. Peter Gay, Freud: A Life for Our Time (New York and London: W. W. Norton, 1988), 73.

who assaults her and later her cousin, whom he impregnates. Unlike Lucy R., the "virginal" fourteen-year-old Katharina had no role as a desiring subject; she is rather the object of another's unsought desire. What Freud offers her is the chance to reclaim control over her own body by voicing her forbidden knowledge of the male body. After twice urging Katharina to tell him "just one thing more," he stops short:

> But she gave me no more definite answer. She smiled in an embarrassed way, as though she had been found out, like someone who is obliged to admit that a fundamental position [Grund der Dinge] has been reached where there is not much more to be said. I could imagine what the tactile sensation was which she had later learnt to interpret. . . . But I could not penetrate further [aber ich kann nicht weiter in sie dringen], and in any case I owed her a debt of gratitude for having made it so much easier for me to talk to her than to the prudish ladies of my city practice, who regard whatever is natural as shameful [turpia]. (II.132)

This passage blends reticence and assertion of several kinds. Freud urges Katharina to speak but accepts and shares her meaningful silence. Yet he contrasts what they share to his conversations with "prudish ladies" who are quick to find obscene meaning in anything physical. Despite setting up that contrast, Freud writes as a kind of hysteric, his language blending reticence and cultural reserve, on the one hand, and sexual innuendo on the other. He reports the meaningful silence he shared with Katharina in a language saturated with connotations.[13] Moreover, while he reports her silence he also reports her willingness to speak, and there are secrets they share that he chooses not to reveal in his main text.

Freud's use of obvious sexual innuendos misleads his readers, who may not think there is any need to "penetrate" further to understand his text. Yet, like Katharina, he offers an indirect hint of an additional meaning. In a footnote contemporaneous with the main narrative, Freud compares Katharina to another hysterical girl who says her symptoms began when "I saw my father get into bed with my mother" (II.134n). In another footnote, added in 1924, Freud identifies Katharina's "uncle" as her father (II.134n). These two footnotes mark the development of Freud's text from concealment to indirection to candor, a

13. Patrick J. Mahony, On Defining Freud's Discourse (New Haven: Yale University Press, 1989), 25–28.

process of undoing the desire to deny that he all too often shares with his patients. In the 1924 footnote, Freud not only lifts "the veil of discretion" but labels it a deceit that damages his whole enterprise: "Distortions like the one which I introduced in the present instance should be altogether avoided in reporting a case history. From the point of view of understanding the case, a distortion of this kind is not, of course, a matter of such indifference as would be shifting the scene from one mountain to another" (II.143n).

Deceit, distortion, la belle indifférence—the traits of the hysteric are finally abandoned by the physician and chronicler. Because of that candor, later interpreters have been able to suggest that Katharina's victimization involved "her mother's and father's mutual victimization of each other, the mother's possible collusion in the family incest, and Katharina's identification with Franziska and possibly with the Oedipal mother as the father's sexual victims."[14]

Freud's reticence to and about Katharina is usually read in Oedipal terms. Strachey's translation, "But I could not penetrate any further,"[15] because it preserves the sexual connotation of the German text, suggests an analogy between Freud and Katharina's father. Mahony, noting the sexually charged repetition of penetration (dringen) and thing (Dinge), as well as references to copulation and birth, scopophilia, and the play of deictics, argues that Freud's narrative of her original experience blurs into his narrative of his encounter with her, and that Freud had a "very deep sexual reaction to Katharina."[16] However, the male organ he surreptitiously alludes to several times in his narrative he does not name to Katharina, nor does he force her to name it. Perhaps Freud's reticence to name the male body in his conversation with her can be read as a silent gift that counters her father's importunity.

Freud's silence about the truth of Katharina's situation in his report of the case suggests an unconscious linkage between Freud and Katharina's mother as well. Long before confiding in Freud, Katharina had told her mother ("aunt") about the sexual attacks "when there was already talk of a divorce." Her mother replied, "We'll keep that in reserve. If he causes trouble in the Court, we'll say that too" (II.132). Katharina's state then "ceased to interest" her mother, "who was entirely occupied with the dispute" (II.132–33). In much the same way, Freud holds in reserve the identity of Katharina's assailant, perhaps because he

14. Ibid., 32.
15. Sigmund Freud and Josef Breuer, Studien über Hysteria, in Sigmund Freud, Gesammelte Werke, vol. 1 (London: Imago Publishing Co., 1952), 192.
16. Mahony, On Defining Freud's Discourse, 36–37.

is "entirely occupied" with his own theoretical and therapeutic project. Despite our admiration for Freud's growing candor, the reader cannot but be haunted by the image of the vomiting child, herself haunted by the hallucination of her father's enraged face and abandoned not only by her mother but by Freud as well: "I hope this girl, whose sexual sensibility had been injured at such an early age, derived some benefit from our conversation. I have not seen her since" (II.133). Freud is not always so abrupt. In the case of Rosalia, a young singer, Freud works with his patient in the protected world of therapy to "abreact" the experience of sexual abuse: "I made her abuse her uncle, lecture him, tell him the unvarnished truth, and so on, and this treatment did her good" [II.171]. In another footnote of 1924, Freud reveals "In this instance, too, [the abuser] was in fact the girl's father, not her uncle" (II.170n).

At this point in his chronicle of hysteria, Freud insists on the sexual propriety of Emmy von N. and the sexual "ignorance" of Katharina, who "was not yet capable of coping with sexual experiences" (II.133). He explicitly labels Katharina's disease a hysteria that originates not from fantasy or desire but from "sexual trauma." The delay between her father's assault on her and the outbreak of her hysterical symptoms (which Freud traces to the assault on her cousin) results not from a splitting of the consciousness, Freud argues, but from the time lapse between the event and the girl's understanding of it (II.133). However, Freud edges toward claiming otherwise: "I should like at this point to express a doubt . . . whether even adolescents do not possess sexual knowledge" (II.134). This remark is the kind of wry joke at his own expense found elsewhere in his book—when, for example, he is given undeserved credit for curing Mathilde H. by hypnotism (II.163).

Freud's fourth and final thorough case study traces his treatment of Elizabeth von R., a twenty-four-year-old hysteric whose original physician thought "there was no trace of the usual indications of that [sexual] neurosis" in her history (II.135). Freud slowly learns otherwise, untangling a history of desire and denial that so torments his young patient that she can scarcely walk, stand, or even lie down. Her difficulty in walking Freud traces to her erotic response first to her unrequited love for her brother-in-law, with whom she walked in the park prior to her sister's sudden death, and ultimately to the touch of her father's leg while she nursed him through his fatal illness. Her difficulty in lying down Freud traces to the nighttime train journey she endured when she first learned of her sister's heart disease. Freud describes the undoing of her symptoms and shares the great pleasure he felt when he finally saw his once-hobbled patient at a Viennese ball: "I did not allow the opportunity to escape me of seeing my former patient whirl past in a lively dance" (II.160).

Despite his clinical success, his "human sympathy" for her travails, and his delight in her cure, Freud's clinical narrative seems almost an afterthought. His real interest, and that of his readers, has moved from understanding the motive of hysteria to understanding its mechanism. He rejects different models of causation: heredity, predisposition, and such specific external events as nursing the sick. As evidence against the latter, he introduces a vignette of a healthy woman who remained free from hysteria despite a set of experiences even more daunting than those of Elizabeth von R. (II.162–64). This vignette is of great interest because the woman's behavior stands in such sharp contrast to that of the hysterical women Freud struggles to help. Instead of trying to "forget" painful events, this woman keeps her painful memories alive in annual "festivals of remembrance" (II.163), private rituals that hold meaning only for her. No feelings of moral shame drive her to isolate certain events from the rest of her consciousness; she integrates her experiences and her feelings.

The hysteric, on the other hand, is unable to sustain that integration. Instead, "ideas of an erotic kind . . . conflict with all her moral ideas" (II.164). Hysteria, moreover, denotes a "special psychical state" in which the patient is not aware of the conflict between desire and denial. The patient struggles to maintain this lack of awareness, splitting an ever-larger group of feelings from the rest of the "ideational content" of her mind (II.165). The question for Freud becomes not how to alleviate physical or mental pain, but rather why the hysteric feels physical pain when one might expect her to feel great mental pain (II.166). He no longer wants to describe the conflict between denial and desire, but rather to discover how the hysteric can bridge the apparent gap between body and mind that has so long been taken for granted in the Cartesian world.

Freud's answer is to posit an intermediate symbolic world. The hysteric, he declares, has taken the circumstance of actual physical pain and converted it to symbolic use. Thus, the choice of physical pain is in some way predetermined by the actual circumstance of the body, but the neurosis can appropriate, increase, and maintain that pain for its own symbolic purpose (II.174). The hysteric experiences pain in a kind of aesthetic state that is neither physical nor mental but a substitutive realm between those two. Since hysteria seems to develop in the realm of the symbolic, Freud devises a treatment in a dramatic version of that realm, the transitional space of psychoanalytic dialogue. He uses expression to counter repression. The hysteric cannot use the symbolic world of language, but seeks refuge in the presymbolic body. Yet that body is itself an obstacle to her, blocking her attempt to live in the world. If hysterical symptoms can be read as in some sense a retreat into the nonverbal phase of the pre-Oedipal body, the psychoanalyst urges the patient back into the consciously symbolic realm of language. For example, when Cäcilie M. can describe insults that felt like "a slap in the face" her overt language rescues her from the silent speech of atypical facial neuralgia (11.178). Freud learns to read hysteria in relation to language, but he recognizes that the mechanism of symbolization is not operative in the same way in both realms. "It may be," he writes, that hysteria "does not take linguistic usage as its model at all, but that both hysteria and linguistic usage alike draw their material from a common source" (II.181). In the clinical vignettes presented near the end of Studies on Hysteria, Freud decodes the puzzling language of several patients. These women derive their private language of pain and desire from "edifying" or "occult" books they read, from stories they are told, or even from single words (II.273–78). Language provides the material for their own formation of symbols, but they flee from verbal language and its communally derived meanings to use instead an idiosyncratic language of physical symptoms. By summoning up their textual and linguistic memories, Freud is able to restore them to the world of language, and therefore to the human community, in which they can use words rather than their bodies to tell their truth.

The puzzle of the symbol underlies both Freud's subject matter and the linguistic nature of his book. His text, like the body of the hysteric, twists and turns as his pattern of assertion and evasion is slowly untangled. Each story is more direct, less reliant on the withholding of secrets. Yet there is no escaping the pattern of desire and denial. At the end of the body of his text, Freud himself is still caught by the claims of reticence and denial. His last reference to Cäcilie M., for example, still draws back from any explicit account of the "painful sight" that aroused in her feelings of "conflict and defense" (II.79). Describing her attacks of facial pain as "associative reverberations," he writes only in general terms: "She had a whole quantity of sensations and ideas running parallel with each other" (II.180). Like the body of the hysteric, the body of Freud's text has a whole quantity of clinical materials and ideas running parallel with each other. He seems to resolve the conflict between his own desire and denial in favor of full revelation when he adds the footnotes of 1924. Yet other molesters go unidentified, and other reports remain incomplete. Freud's "associative reverberations" continue, however, and the full palimpsest of his work on hysteria can be surveyed only by attending to his subsequent series of letters, lectures, and essays on the problem of conversion.

This reading of *Studies on Hysteria* may make some contribution to the controversy about Freud's formulation and abandonment of the "seduction theory."[17] Within the main body of his text, Freud clearly moves away from defining hysteria in causal terms and comes to focus on the operational problem of how the hysteric experiences pain. In the final chapter Freud swerves in a new direction. He presents fewer specific details about symptoms, causes, and specific circumstances and instead emphasizes the patient's mental operations of uncertainty, conflict, and contradiction. Ultimately he scarcely bothers to give clinical "facts" but describes only the mechanism of conversion or his own clinical technique (cf. II.275–77).

The progressive lack of narrative concern in Freud's final clinical vignettes correlates with the incomplete or incoherent stories told by his patients. These vignettes seem to be cases of child abuse, illicit heterosexual and homosexual desire, autoeroticism, and transference love, but the sexual element of these cases is rarely named and never completely discussed. Freud is concerned only to demonstrate the effectiveness of his therapeutic technique in a wide range of cases.

In the first vignette, he describes a woman tormented for six years with a hysterical cough. By placing his hand on her head and asking her to describe what comes to mind, Freud traces the origin of her cough to the death of her aunt's dog, which "became attached to her, followed her about everywhere, and so on." He discovers that the cough recurred upon the death of her uncle, "the only member of the family who had loved her. . . . But there was something attached to the idea of 'love' which there was a strong resistance to her telling me" (II.273). Rather than speculate about her uncle, Freud moves at once to a second vignette, this time of an elderly woman, troubled since girlhood by severe anxiety attacks which she attributes to thyroid medication. Her rigid piety and distrust of Freud seem to make her an unsuitable candidate for his therapeutic method, but he is able to help her remember early experiences of sexual fear (stirred up by a "pious" book she read) and sexual attraction to her brothers' tutor (II.274). Once again, the vignette slights the clinical details and outcome of the case in order to focus on Freud's therapeutic method and its utility for even a "recalcitrant" patient (II.273–74).

In the third example, Freud describes a "happily married" young woman

17. Jeffrey Masson, *The Assault on Truth: Freud's Suppression of the Seduction Theory* (New York: Farrar, Strauss, Giroux, 1984).

whose anxiety attacks he traces to the seductive behavior of a governess "of whom she had been very fond." When the governess's behavior was discovered, she was dismissed, and the children were told that she had left "in order to get married" (II.274–75). Freud makes no attempt to link the purported marriage of the governess and the actual marriage of his patient, nor does he discuss the complex feelings that marriage might occasion in his patient. Another woman is of interest because of the "remarkable form" of her memories. Like Emmy von N., under hypnosis she does not summon up clear images but only "what seemed to be a meaningless series of words" (II.276). On examination, those words prove to be the abstract of a harrowing narrative. She and her sister were sexually assaulted by "a certain man," and her sister was later taken "raving mad" to an asylum (II.276). Freud's wording leaves it unclear whether he is left in the dark about the man's identity or chooses to keep his patient's secret. He seems indifferent to the reader's curiosity and instead emphasizes the importance of his therapeutic decoding of her apparently disconnected words. His final vignette, of a young woman suffering abdominal pain, gives virtually no information about her history, or indeed about the outcome of her case. Freud focuses entirely on his attempt to understand her associations to visual images, which seem at first no more than a physiological response to the pressure of his fingers on her closed eyes, but then can be read as generalized allegories, and finally stand revealed as associations to the title pages of occult books she has recently read.

At this point Freud breaks off his narrative. Although there is much in the narrative to suggest that this "very intelligent and apparently happy young married woman" may have been troubled by masturbation ("when I am agitated in certain ways") and also to suggest that she fantasized that Freud was both "God the primeval force" and a "gigantic lizard which regarded her inquiringly but not alarmingly" (II.277), Freud's only concern is his triumphant decoding of the puzzling images which "initiated [him] into her mental struggles and her self-reproaches" (II.278). She becomes for Freud a kind of occult book, her language analogous to the mysterious Sanskrit of the texts she reads. He in turn offers her a new language, a different kind of text in which to write rather than read herself.

These vignettes do not emphasize the sexual etiology of hysteria but rather seem to assume it and go on to celebrate a new therapeutic method. The footnotes about Katharina and Rosalia that Freud added in 1924 support the "seduction theory" of causation, but the function of these footnotes should be regarded less as the capstone of a conceptual argument than as the undoing of his own methodological "hysteria." The swerve toward analysis of thought rather than cathartic erasure of memory remains primary. It is noteworthy in this regard that Freud left other seducers unidentified, such as the "certain man" in the vignette cited above. Freud's minimizing of the "seduction theory" may be read by some as a reversion to a hysterical language of denial and evasion, but it may also be read as a confirmation of what the structure of *Studies on Hysteria* implies—that psychoanalysis alters not events but their interpretation. Freud no longer struggles to discover and erase the origin of hysteria but to understand and describe the operation of repression and memory in different patients.

There is, however, something else to consider about the issue of causation. Later in his career, in his account of the Dora case and elsewhere, Freud ties the origin of hysteria to a disruption of the bond between mother and child. The case histories he presents in *Studies on Hysteria* at least hint at such disruptions. Emmy von N.'s mother had been in an asylum, which Emmy knew about only from her nursemaid's terrifying tales. At the age of fifteen, she found her mother lying on the floor after a stroke; four years later she "came home one day and found her mother dead, with a distorted face" (II.55). (That same year she was terrified by her discovery of a toad under a stone.) Katharina was emotionally abandoned by her mother; Lucy's symptoms began when she received a letter from her mother; Elizabeth von R.'s symptoms were linked to her mother's departure from her father's sickroom. Elizabeth's mother, moreover, is a significant informant during her treatment; it is from her, presumably, that Freud learned of Elizabeth's "excessive demand for love" (II.159–61). Similarly, the case of Mathilde H. emphasizes her mother's decisive role in breaking off her engagement (II.163n). In both cases, the emotional bond between mother and daughter seems especially intense; the mother presumes to know the daughter's feelings and dictates her actions. Human life, like Freud's text, is a palimpsest, each phase of development overlaid on the rest. The Oedipal abuses and desires Freud describes would have been decisively shaped by the pre-Oedipal experiences of his patients.

The recovery of that palimpsest becomes Freud's major therapeutic goal. Moving ever further from case histories, Freud focuses on the different forms resistance may take in the patient (II.278–82) and describes how the physician can counteract that resistance. First, he declares, the physician must arouse the patient's "intellectual interest" so that the patient will become a "collaborator . . . with the objective interest of an investigator" (II.282). Second, "We must endeavor, after we have discovered the motives for his defence, to deprive them of their value or even to replace them by more powerful ones" (II.282). Finally, Freud insists on the important role of the physician as elucidator, teacher, and even father confessor, "who gives absolution, as it were, by a continuance of his sympathy and respect after the confession has been made" (II.282). The first of these claims pushes Freud and the reader toward objectivity and theory, the third toward subjectivity and drama. The second is at once the core problem, the goal, and the major action of any psychoanalysis. Freud describes the drama of discovery and replacement as a struggle to escape: "The patient only gets free from the hysterical symptom by reproducing the pathogenic impressions that caused it and by giving utterance to them with an expression of affect" (II.283). The struggle occurs in the symbolic, fictive world of the analysis. The replacement is an aesthetic reconstruction, yet the patient can use that substitutive reconstruction to make possible a new construction of being.

At the end of his book, Freud tries to resolve the real question of his work: how to tell his patients' tales and his own. As he tries to bring forward their "file of memories," his great problem remains how to represent and interpret their experience. He recognizes the competing claims to order: linear chronology, concentric stratification, and a third, most difficult to describe:

> What I have in mind is an arrangement according to thought-content, the linkage made by a logical thread which reaches as far as the nucleus and tends to take an irregular and twisting path, different in every case. This arrangement has a dynamic character, in contrast to the morphological one of the two stratifications mentioned previously. While these two would be represented in a spatial diagram by a continuous line, curved or straight, the course of the logical chain would have to be indicated by a broken line which would pass along the most roundabout paths from the surface to the deepest layers and back, and yet would in general advance from the periphery to the central nucleus, touching at every intermediate halting-place—a line resembling the zig-zag line in the solution of a Knight's Move problem, which cuts across the squares in the diagram of the chess-board. (II.289)

As Freud struggles to describe a visual, verbal symbol of the way symptoms are "overdetermined" (II.290), he turns to yet another game, a "Chinese puzzle" (II.291). What comes to mind for a modern reader is the theory of psychoanalytic play formulated by D. W. Winnicott, who argued for the importance of play with a "transitional object"—the originative symbol of the "me" and the "not-me" so crucial to a child's development.[18] If the body of the hysteric can be read in some sense as a failed transitional object, a mode of symbolization that fled from the utility of language, Freud's text offers a linguistic body that can undo the conversion disorder of hysteria. His book is a kind of successful transitional object, at once a symbol of the "me" and "not-me" of its author, as he struggles in the body of his text to honor both the painful experiences of his patients and his own claim to understand the nature and remedy of their suffering.

If desire and denial are the intertwined motives of hysteria, they are the nature of all tale-telling as well. By the end of his book, Freud recognizes that the new "more powerful" motives that replace the motives of hysterical defense will be a new version of desire and denial. These motives are enacted in the drama of the psychoanalytic dialogue, the transitional space or play world of the temporary therapeutic relationship.[19] In the last few pages of his book, Freud turns from the austere abstractions of theory to the intense drama of psychoanalytic practice. He admits that he was initially "annoyed" by the new material created by the relationship of analyst and patient, "till I came to see that the whole process followed a law" (II.304). Instead of a dichotomy of law and drama, Freud posits an order common to both realms. It matters not, therefore, whether the patient reenacts her past directly or in the indirect mode of her transference relationship with her physician. Real life and symbolic reenactments operate according to the same laws.

In the final paragraph of Studies on Hysteria, the relationship between the worlds of history and therapy is presented neither in narrative nor in theoretical terms, but in dramatic dialogue. The reader becomes a privileged listener, as Freud quotes what he says to a typical patient who poignantly protests that no treatment can alter "my circumstances and the events of my life." Freud quotes himself in reply: "You will be able to convince yourself that much will be gained if we succeed in transforming your hysterical misery into common unhappiness. With a mental life that has been restored to health you will be better armed against that unhappiness" (II.305). In most of this book, the

18. D. W. Winnicott, "Transitional Objects and Transitional Phenomena" (1951), in his *Playing and Reality* (London: Tavistock, 1971).
19. See Roy Schafer, *The Analytic Attitude* (New York: Basic Books, 1983); "Narration in Psychoanalytic Dialogue," *Critical Inquiry* 7 (1980): 169–90; *Narrative Actions in Psychoanalysis*, Heinz Werner Lecture Series, 14 (Worcester, Mass.: Clark University Press, 1981).

reader has been invited to identify with Freud the narrator and theorist. Now, through self-quotation, Freud presents himself as a character in a dramatic scene. The interpreter's bond with his reader yields to the therapist's bond with his patient. The turn to drama breaks down the dichotomies of reader and narrator, of reader and patient, even of patient and physician, as Freud posits a human bond of "common unhappiness" and hope. The narrative mode that privileged the interpreter, that objectified the hysteric and mimicked the twists and turns of her suffering body, is replaced by a moment of intimacy and promise. The asceticism of the psychoanalytic dialogue subsumes the timeless abstractions of law and the symbolic narratives of history in a dramatic exchange pointed toward not the past but the future. Narrative and theory recede, and as we enter Freud's consulting room the book disappears.

10

Flannery O'Connor and the
Celebration of Embodiment

William F. Monroe

To a newcomer, Flannery O'Connor's world will seem an unlikely place for the celebration of embodiment. In *Wise Blood* (1952), her first novel, she subjects us to a surreal sequence of grotesque and degenerate characters marked by bestial features. The cheeks of Asa Hawks are streaked with lines that give him "the expression of a grinning mandrill" (20).[1] Mrs. Watts, whose bed, according to bathroom graffiti, is the friendliest in town, has teeth that are "small and pointed and speckled with green" (18). Behind the windshield of Hazel Motes's "high rat-colored car" his face is "sour and frog-like" (46, 48). On the train he eats "something spotted with eggs and livers" (8). And the physical repugnance has its moral analog. Mrs. Flood knows that "the government not only sent [her tax money] to foreign niggers and a-rabs, but wasted it at

1. All page numbers in parentheses are from Flannery O'Connor, *Collected Works*, ed. Sally Fitzgerald (New York: The Library of America, 1988).

home . . . on every idiot who could sign his name on a card" (120). Sabbath Lily Hawks is a more willing and even younger Lolita, who admits to being "filthy right down to the guts." "I like being that way," she says, "and I can teach you how to like it" (95). Many readers have noted the scarcity of admirable characters in O'Connor, and *Wise Blood*, to be sure, is peopled by Boschian, nightmarish figures whose mundane patterns of duplicity and intolerance are punctuated only by gratuitous hurt.

Many readers rightly focus on O'Connor's preoccupation with matters spiritual, but O'Connor also has an abiding concern with corporeality and embodiment: tastes, colors, sensations. Her fiction often explores the question raised by Judith Andre in "Respect for Bodies": What is a morally desirable attitude toward the body? It is not, safe to say, the animal lust of Enoch Emery for the frightening creature emerging from the waters of Forest Park—a municipal swimming facility situated, appropriately, next to the Taulkinham zoo:

> First her face appeared, long and cadaverous, with a bandage-like bathing cap coming down almost to her eyes, and sharp teeth protruding from her mouth. Then she rose on her hands until a large foot and leg came up from behind her and another on the other side and she was out, squatting there, panting. She stood up loosely and shook herself, and stamped in the water dripping off her . . . she padded over to a spot of sun almost directly under where [Enoch and Haze] were sitting. (47)

In a moment the woman is "raising her knees[,] settling her backbone down against the concrete" and pulling "the bathing suit straps off her shoulders" (48). Enoch, a creature with "a fox-shaped face" and "wise blood like his daddy," is transfixed by this provocative display and can only whisper "King Jesus!" with a libidinous and blasphemous hunger (20, 44, 48). Throughout her first novel, in fact, O'Connor satirizes carnal knowledge as a trap for the unenlightened or unreflective: "wise blood" is for her a humorous oxymoron. Like Othello, she is tempted to cry out in revulsion and contempt, "Goats and monkeys!" And like Hazel Motes, another young misfit, O'Connor is tempted to turn to purification and ascetic denial as a means of escaping the world's "poisonous looks" and "evil smiles." Yet by the time she comes to write "Parker's Back" in 1964, O'Connor has turned unmistakably toward a motif of embodiment, a celebration of physicality and even carnality. Though she was always tempted by mystical otherworldliness, in her fiction she abandons the penitential way, the gnostic way of negation, dualism, and renunciation.[2] O'Connor's artistic journey—her exploration of the modes and motives of abnegating the body—may perhaps offer clues to the varieties of asceticism now permeating late twentieth-century culture.

In her influential study of medieval asceticism, Caroline Walker Bynum argues that women's food asceticism was not, as others have assumed, a passive "internalizing of the church's negative views of flesh and female." Asceticism was, rather, an active "rebellion against the moderation of the high medieval church, which was moving toward a more positive sense of the body." According to Bynum, the church's expansiveness, inclusiveness, and worldliness threatened to coopt those who preferred isolation and independence.[3] Medieval food asceticism was therefore not an internalized acceptance but a personalized rejection of dominant cultural values. By extension, then, anorexia, bulimia, celibacy, and other manifestations of asceticism may be seen as a postmodern reappearance of gnostic isolation—a mode of alienation from the enculturated world motivated not by a desire for acceptance or esteem but by a recurrent need for isolation and control.

Gnosticism and the Denigration of the Body

Kenneth Burke reminds us that our twentieth-century culture is by no means the first to engender remarkable and influential strategies of asceticism and alienation. Perhaps all historical epochs have fostered marginalized or alienated individuals and groups who have expressed estrangement from their cultures by means of fasting, self-mutilation, and other forms of asceticism. In *Attitudes toward History*, Burke describes the attempt to renounce "corporate" or group associations entirely, to escape all political and communal identifications. He explains the dilemma faced by the "enlightened"—the "wised-up" intellectuals, poets, and philosophers—at the end of the Greco-Roman era: "As Hellenism drew to a close, and the disorders of the state made it impossible for the earnest man to identify himself with the emperor . . . many of the 'enlightened' were enfeebled by the attempt to avoid all identification what-

---

2. By using a capital G I mean to indicate the historical Gnostic movements of the first centuries of the Common Era. Gnosticism with a small g is meant as a heuristic term for an attitude or strategy that can be used to explain the motives of fictional characters and authors as well as flesh-and-blood human beings.

3. Caroline Walker Bynum, *Holy Feast and Holy Fast: The Religious Significance of Food to Medieval Women* (Berkeley: University of California Press, 1988), 218.

ever. And in thus attempting to reject any corporate identity, they automatically despoiled themselves (with inanition, emptying [purging], boredom, alienation as the result)."[4] In their obsession to avoid impure identifications, some of the most conscientious and circumspect men and women of Latinity abandoned Roman public life.

Hans Jonas describes the Gnostic movement as the most potent of these renunciations. Jonas did much as a scholar to potentiate our modern fascination with the late Hellenistic religion known as Gnosticism, a syncretic dualism that influenced many Greek and Jewish sects as well as pre-Christian and early Christian religious thought.[5] Ihab Hassan, Harold Bloom, Paul Zweig, Cleanth Brooks, and John Desmond, as well as Jonas, have discerned the heuristic value of Gnostic traditions.[6] Elaine Pagels and Rosemary Radford Ruether are notable feminists and scholars of comparative religion who have found in historical Gnosticism a powerful countervailing theology, a perennial religious impulse beneficially subversive of the masculine, monotheistic orthodoxies of the West.[7] There is also a proto-feminist gnostic axis associated with Elizabeth Cady Stanton's revision of scripture and some of the work of Gertrude Stein. But Jonas was the first to see the similarities between ancient Gnosticism and modern strategies of alienation. The Gnostic Religion, Pagels says, "remains, even today, the classic introduction" to Gnosticism.[8]

Jonas's comparison suggests the possibility of using gnosticism as a generic term signifying an aversion to worldly communities and their cultural demands and expectations—an aversion that is perennial, if usually peripheral, in the West.[9] Central to all versions of historical Gnosticism is a radical distinction

4. Kenneth Burke, Attitudes toward History, rev. 2d ed. (Los Altos, Calif.: Hermes, 1959), 264.

5. See, for example, Hans Jonas's definitive The Gnostic Religion: the Message of the Alien God and the Beginnings of Christianity, 2d ed. (Boston: Beacon Press, 1972).

6. See James M. Robinson, ed., The Nag Hammadi Library in English, 3d rev. ed. (San Francisco: Harper & Row, 1988); Cleanth Brooks, "Walker Percy and Modern Gnosticism," Southern Review 13 (1977): 667–87; John F. Desmond, "The Scriptural Tradition and Faulkner's Gnostic Style," Southern Review 25 (1989): 563–68.

7. Rosemary Radford Ruether, Sexism and God-Talk: Toward a Feminist Theology (Boston: Beacon, 1983); Elaine Pagels, The Gnostic Gospels (New York: Random House, 1979).

8. Pagels, Gnostic Gospels, xxxi.

9. If we view the historical Gnostics as fabricators of responses to the flux and confusion of a dubious world, then we would expect versions of the Gnostic strategy to appear at other times in history as well, and certainly in our own "age of anxiety." In an article entitled "Gnosticism and Modern Nihilism" (Social Research 19 [1952]: 430–52) published about a decade before The Gnostic Religion, Jonas's express purpose is explaining the correspondences between first- and second-century Gnosticism and similar twentieth-century attitudes; in

between the material and the spiritual, between the world and God. The customs and preferences of a physical world are utterly foreign to the knowing ones. Basic to Gnosticism, Jonas says, "is the feeling of an absolute rift" between the enlightened remnant and the world.[10]

Gnostic cosmogony ingeniously posits an unseeing and ignorant Demiurge as the creator of the world, for "the true God cannot be the creator of that to which selfhood feels so utterly a stranger." The possession of knowledge (*gnosis*) sanctions a "privative mood": the gnostic of whatever age is the knowing one in the midst of the unknowing, the light in the midst of darkness, and thus the gnostic's "divine spark," or *pneuma*, is the efficient cause of his or her alienation. The true gnostic will therefore be forever at war with the world, and in fact this conflict is seen as "the assertion of the authentic freedom of the self."[11]

If Gnostic cosmogony asserted a radical dualism between God and the Demiurge, Gnostic theology drew a sharp distinction between the saved, who were not "of this world," and the damned, who were. If their alienation gave rise to notions of an antiworldly God and pneuma, it also engendered a derisive attitude toward those who seemed at home in the world. Centuries later, some Calvinistic Christians would see the earmarks of "election" in worldly success; the Gnostics, conversely, cultivated their estrangement, for the sign of their superiority was a failure to thrive.[12] The Gnostic vision, in sum, sees the fruits of this world as categorically impure, and flourishing within it remains undesirable and indeed impossible for the privative knowing ones. Summarizing Jonas's conclusion, Pagels says that the gnostic worldview has been understood to combine "a philosophy of pessimism about the world . . . with an attempt at self-transcendence."[13] Paul Zweig, who traces the reappearance of gnosticisms in the West, connects what he calls "subversive individualism" with our recurrent fascination with Narcissus, especially during moments of turmoil and uncertainty.[14] For Zweig, individualistic narcissism,

---

this vein he reminds us that Spengler declared our world to be "contemporaneous" with the Greco-Roman world of the first Christian centuries.

10. Jonas, *Gnostic Religion*, 435.

11. Ibid., 436, 444.

12. This individualistic soteriology had its hermetic "ecclesiastical" counterpart. The "movement" was widespread but ill-defined; it amounted, really, to a diffuse but ubiquitous adversary culture.

13. Pagels, *Gnostic Gospels*, xxx.

14. Paul Zweig, *The Heresy of Self-Love: A Study of Subversive Individualism* (Princeton, N.J.: Princeton University Press, 1980), 3–21.

somewhat paradoxically, often features an ascetic denigration of the body. This denial of things physical functions as part of a subversive pattern, a means of resisting the metaphors of embodiment posited by the dominant culture. *Wise Blood*, completed by a sleep-deprived writer who was experiencing an acute, mysterious, and life-threatening illness, may be profitably read as depicting in Hazel Motes just such a strategy.

Wise Blood

A sharp division between good and evil, spirit and flesh, a tradition of mystical apotheosis beyond the prison of ignorance or stultifying conformity, and a history of antinomian attempts to "exhaust the flesh" constitute a powerful legacy for modern writers, including O'Connor. Especially since 1945, realistic fiction in the United States has depicted a world that is consistently "sick, hostile, or treacherous," a "world of horror mingled with a strong sense of the ridiculous." The modern fictional hero, according to James E. Miller, reflects "some mixture of horror, bewilderment, and sardonic humor—or, to use the popular term, alienation." The typical pattern of action in such fiction is the quest, "the quest absurd in a world gone insane or turned opaque and inexplicable, or become meaningless."[15] The action of *Wise Blood* manifests the recurrent gnostic strategy of pessimism-cum-transcendence and hence corresponds to the typical "novel of the absurd" described by Miller.[16] The absurd quest in question is that of Hazel Motes and consists of his gnostic attempts to overcome or escape an inhospitable and treacherous world. Hazel fluctuates between antinomian excess, the attempt to prove that he is already "clean" and in no need of redemption, and ascetic mortification to purify himself. During his adolescence, he has seen "something white" at a carnival, "squirming a little, in a box lined with black cloth" (35). The squirming white thing is a naked woman, and to expiate "the nameless unplaced guilt that was in him," he puts stones and small rocks in his shoes and walks "through the woods for what he knew to be a mile." He thinks, "That ought to satisfy Him," and waits. But

15. James E. Miller, *Quests Surd and Absurd* (Chicago: University of Chicago Press, 1967), 5.
16. Ibid., 12. Miller cites four earmarks of the absurd novel: first, an inverted or nightmarish world; second, a disoriented, disaffected, alienated hero suffering from spiritual nausea; third, a quest for a self that is lost or nonexistent; fourth, a hodgepodge of events "compounded indiscriminately of horror and humor, a bizarre and even sick comedy that repels at the same time that it evokes guilty and perhaps sinister laughter."

"Nothing happened. If a leaf had fallen he would have taken it as a sign" (36). His ascetic mortification of the flesh has been ineffectual.

By the time Haze arrives in Taulkinham, he has already settled on bestial license as an alternative way to renounce and "exhaust" the flesh. Both dissoluteness and indulgence, like ascetic denial, are gnostic strategies of transcendence and escape. Libertinism repudiates loyalty to nature through excess and abuse, Jonas explains, while asceticism asserts the absolute freedom of the purely spiritual subject through abstention and nonuse. Ready to try the mode of excess, Haze intends to gorge himself on Mrs. Leora Watts. He finds her cutting her toenails in a white iron bed, wearing "a pink nightgown that would better have fit a smaller figure." Her white skin "glisten[s] with a greasy preparation," and Haze's "senses [are] stirred to the limit." Haze goes quickly to sit on the edge of her bed and draws "a long draught of air through one side of his nose." After the "pink tip of Mrs. Watts's tongue" appears, Haze picks up her foot, "which was heavy but not cold, and move[s] it about an inch to one side." Mrs. Watts knows when she has been propositioned, and her mouth splits "in a wide full grin" to show those pointed, speckled teeth:

> "You huntin' something?" she drawled.
> "Something on your mind?" Mrs. Watts asked, pulling his rigid figure a little closer.
> "Listen," he said, keeping his voice tightly under control, "I come for the usual business."
> Mrs. Watts's mouth became more round, as if she were perplexed by this waste of words. "Make yourself at home," she said simply. (17–18)

But Haze is not at home. He was a stranger on the train, using aggression to hide his inept terror, and he feels no more at home with Mrs. Watts: "If she had not had him so firmly by the arm, he might have leaped out the window" (18).

Haze, however, has not given up on the physical world yet. After his congress with Mrs. Watts, marked not by pleasure but by terror, Haze makes a fresh attempt to lose himself in matter and materialism. He follows a venerable American script and purchases an automobile. But the ancient Essex sounds "as if the motor were dragging out the back," and it leaks water, gas, and oil—all the "vital fluids" (46). Despite the car's questionable status, Haze becomes a preacher of the gospel of the "Church Without Christ," insisting from the nose of the Essex that "Where you come from is gone, where you thought you were going to never was there" (93). The "new jesus" Haze accidentally calls for is a version of relativism: "there's only one truth and that is that there's no truth" (93). He wants the certainty that the things of this world are not revelations of the spirit. When his attempt to preach a new materialist gospel fails, Haze commits a desperate crime, killing his "double," Solace Layfield. He would have liked the car to become a special place of respite; instead it becomes a murder weapon.

The night after he runs down his rival, Haze tries to escape Taulkinham to begin preaching his Church Without Christ in a new city. But the Essex is pushed over an embankment by a policeman who tells Haze "I just don't like your face" (117). At about the same time, he finds himself with a girl much younger and presumably more innocent than Mrs. Watts. But in Sabbath Lily Hawks, whose innocence he intends to debauch, Haze discovers a feral female who is, in her own words, "just pure filthy right down to the guts" and who calls him to her bed with, "Take off your hat, king of the beasts" (95, 96).

At this point, Haze apparently realizes that using bestial excess to confirm that he is already "clean" has been an ill-conceived strategy. While libertinism, according to Jonas, is "the most insolent expression of metaphysical revolt," asceticism "acknowledges the world's corrupting power" and "is animated more by fear than contempt."[17] Whether we call it materialism, bestialism, or libertinism, the effort to debauch and thereby exhaust the flesh has been a trying, tedious, and altogether unhappy process for O'Connor's hero. So Haze, feeling lost and fearful, switches from bestial excess to self-immolation. He methodically mixes a solution of quicklime and rubs it into his open eyes, thereby returning to a strategy of denial and disembodiment. Sabbath Lily, furious that her charms have not enticed Haze to embrace her "filthy" world, abandons him to Mrs. Flood, their avaricious and exploitive landlady.

In a pattern reminiscent of bulimia's gorging and purging, Haze returns to an even more extreme asceticism. Mrs. Flood has noticed that the now-blind Haze walks "as if his feet hurt him." One day she picks up his extra pair of shoes to find them "lined with gravel and broken glass and pieces of small stone" (125). Eventually Haze stops eating the food Mrs. Flood prepares; he claims to be taking his meals elsewhere and begins a long period of fasting and physical decline. She warns that he will "pick up an infection," that the first wind will "blow a virus" into him (126). Weakened by his refusal to eat, Haze does catch the flu and cannot get out of bed to take his long walks. One morning Mrs.

17. Pagels, *Gnostic Gospels*, 275.

Flood brings in his breakfast only to find that "the old shirt he wore to sleep in was open down the front and showed three strands of barbed wire, wrapped around his chest." She insists that "these things" are not "natural," or at least not "normal." But it is from the natural and the normal, of course, that Haze desires liberation. "It's like one of them gory stories," Mrs. Flood says; "it's something that people have quit doing—like boiling in oil or being a saint or walling up cats." But, Haze says, "They ain't quit doing it as long as I'm doing it" (126–27).

Haze's new ascetic regimen strikes us too as unnatural and strange—"something that people have quit doing." Yet is not Mr. Motes, as Mrs. Flood calls him, but another manifestation of Kafka's twentieth-century hunger artist? O'Connor got the idea for Haze's self-blinding after reading Robert Fitzgerald's translation of the Oedipus cycle. Her solution to the artistic problem of how to end the novel was making Haze a sightless exile from carnal and sensuous humanity. And indeed, Haze's ascetic actions speak, as it were, the words of Oedipus after his self-blinding: "Drive me out of this country as quickly as may be / to a place where no human voice can ever greet me."[18] He intends to shut out the world by shutting down his senses. It is appropriate, then, that Hazel Motes's last journey, the fatal one, is begun when Mrs. Flood says, "I see there's only one thing for you and me to do. Get married" (128). Haze, fearing the human contact and cohabitation offered by Mrs. Flood, puts on "his shoes that were still lined with rocks" and rushes out "on one of the coldest days of the year," "so weak from the influenza that he tottered when he walked" (128, 127). Mrs. Flood says, "Nobody ought to be without a place of their own to be . . . and I'm willing to give you a home here with me, a place where you can always stay, Mr. Motes" (129). Yet a home here, in a world of Mrs. Floods, is exactly what Mr. Motes wants to escape.

Like the true gnostic, Hazel Motes is driven by the pneuma, the divine spark. Pagels quotes the Gnostic Gospel of Philip: "You saw the spirit, you became spirit. You saw Christ, you became Christ."[19] Like the medieval ascetics discussed by Caroline Bynum, a now pietistic Hazel Motes wants, "without compromise or moderation, to imitate Christ" (218). Like the fasting women who feared co-optation by an encompassing church, Haze struggles to avoid being engulfed by Mrs. Flood. Though he maintains his residence in her dilapidated boardinghouse, he does not want a home with her or, indeed, a home anywhere. Haze's asceticism, an ever more pernicious regimen of self-flagellation

18. Sophocles, The Oedipus Cycle, trans. Dudley Fitts and Robert Fitzgerald (New York: Harvest/HBJ, 1977), 73.

19. Pagels, Gnostic Gospels, 134.

and denial, is a strategy of control allowing him to transcend both Mrs. Flood and the world.

The physical and moral ugliness of O'Connor's world has led some critics to list her with a group of gnostic or otherwise dualistic writers that would include William Blake, Herman Melville, T. S. Eliot, Hermann Hesse, Laurence Durrell, Jack Kerouac, Allen Ginsberg, and C. J. Jung.[20] Certainly the world of *Wise Blood* is a cruel one, a predatory, often bestial wasteland that would seem to call for an ascetic renunciation and escape. Frequently, for instance, there is the banal evil of racism. When Haze pleads with the barker at the carnival to let him into the "SINsational" tent, the man initially thinks he is too young to see the show. But when Haze, trying to figure out what the mysterious attraction might be, asks, "Is it a nigger? . . . Are they doing something to a nigger," the barker realizes that he is old enough to know the ways of the world: "Gimme that fifteen cents," the man says, "and get in there" (61).

O'Connor uses the grotesque animality of her characters to convey the brutish morality of their world. Three "youngish" women on the train are "dressed like parrots" and have hands that are "red-speared at the tips"; the one who blows cigarette smoke in Haze's face has "a bold game-hen expression and small eyes pointed directly at him" (15–16). The steward on the train is "a white man with greased black hair and a greased black look to his suit," who "moves like a crow, darting from table to table." O'Connor uses such Boschian descriptions to suggest the baseness of her grotesque menagerie.

Often these carnal characters say or do something to confirm the bestial nature suggested by their appearances. The potato peeler man, who wears "a shirt patterned with bunches of upside-down pheasants and quail and bronze turkeys," tries to entertain a street crowd and sell a few worthless utensils by humiliating Enoch:

> "What's yer name?" the peeler man asked.
> "Name Enoch Emery," the boy said and snuffled.
> "Boy with a pretty name like that ought to have one of these," the man said, rolling his eyes, trying to warm up the others. Nobody laughed but the boy. (38)

20. See Richard Smith's "Afterword: The Modern Relevance of Gnosticism," in *The Nag Hammadi Library in English*, 3d rev. ed., ed. James M. Robinson (San Francisco: Harper & Row, 1988); Frederick Asals, *Flannery O'Connor: The Imagination of Extremity* (Athens: University of Georgia Press, 1982); William F. Monroe, "T. S. Eliot's Gnostic Impulse," *Literature and Theology* 6, no. 2 (June 1992): 191–206.

Similarly, the crow-like steward befools Haze in order to aggrandize himself in the eyes of the parrot-women. First he embarrasses Haze by pushing him back out of the dining car; then, when Haze tries to place an order orally, the steward says sharply, "Write it down, sonny," and winks at one of the women. After Haze eats the speckled food, the steward, now passive-aggressive, refuses to total the bill. "Every time he passed the table, he would wink at the women and stare at Haze" (17). The point is that O'Connor associates her characters with "upside-down" birds, cormorants, predators, and scavengers in order to portray the hateful brutishness and moral ugliness of the world. Here, at least, we find no celebration of creation and embodiment. The natural world would indeed seem a place to be transcended.

Flannery's Sickness and "Parker's Back"

Many readers mistakenly identify Hazel Motes with Flannery O'Connor, assuming that the author of Wise Blood is advocating a life of mortification and ascesis. For Frederick Asals, Hazel Motes is an absurd hero who turns away from the world, denying the physical and sensible in blindness, asceticism, and the pursuit of death.[21] Asals disagrees with those who discover O'Connor's characteristic Christian humanism in Wise Blood; for him, this is a novel that expresses a deeply "Manichean" or "Gnostic" vision (58). If O'Connor did not take sufficient care to distance herself from Haze's mode of penitence and self-inflicted suffering, perhaps the lapse can be explained by her own medical condition as she was completing the manuscript. By August of 1949 several of the chapters had seen or would soon see print, and Robert Giroux had forwarded a contract from Harcourt for the publication of the entire novel. Fourteen months later, Flannery was still with her friends the Fitzgeralds in exurban Connecticut trying to finish the book. In December 1950, when Sally Fitzgerald put her on a train for Georgia, Flannery seemed tired and her gait a bit stiff. By the time she arrived in Atlanta, she looked, her uncle later said, "like a shriveled old woman."[22]

Flannery's mother, Regina, to whom Wise Blood is dedicated, called to tell the Fitzgeralds that Flannery was dying of lupus. Systemic Lupus Erythemato-

21. Frederick Asals, Flannery O'Connor, 58.
22. Flannery O'Connor, The Habit of Being: Letters of Flannery O'Connor, ed. Sally Fitzgerald (New York: Vintage, 1980), 22.

sus, or SLE, is an autoimmune disorder in which the patient's antibodies run amok, attacking the tissues and organs of the body. The name lupus comes from a telltale butterfly rash that gives a bestial, wolfish look to the patient's face. As John Stone writes, "The [disease] process amounts to a kind of immunological betrayal of its owner by the body, an absolute autoimmune revolution."[23] Though Flannery's father died of the disease, Stone notes that 90 percent of those afflicted are women. The disease strikes most frequently during the childbearing years, and, true to form, Flannery's first attack came at age twenty-five, effectively ending any possibility of her bearing children. The disease did not actually take her until almost fourteen years later, but she became a chronic invalid, bound to Andalusia, her mother's ancestral farm. With injections of ACTH and cortisone, she was able to survive the first life-threatening crisis, during the winter of 1950–51, but for several weeks she was debilitated by high fevers and, as she indicated in a letter several years later, suffered from intractable insomnia, a side effect of the steroids. She actually finished Wise Blood during what she called "the cortisone period," a time of sleeplessness and steroid-induced psychosis.[24] In a letter written during this hospitalization, she tells a friend and classmate, "I don't believe in time no more." Perhaps for Flannery the world had come to seem what the Gnostics always said it was: a persistent evil dream.

Yet despite the ravages of her disease,[25] I cannot agree with those who think O'Connor is offering us a gnostic deliverance from embodiment at the end of Wise Blood. O'Connor's purpose is not to condemn this world of corruption and perversion but to give it life and death and meaning. It does seem clear, though, that in this first major work, more than in her subsequent fiction, O'Connor combines a pessimism about the world with at least a yearning for a private, spiritual transcendence. She had written almost all of her first novel at

23. John Stone, "The Wolf Is at the Door," New York Times Magazine (April 3, 1988), Sec. 6: 40–41;

24. O'Connor, Habit of Being, 23.

25. Andrew Boyles, "Toxic Oil Syndrome," Biomedical Inquiry 3, no. 1 (Spring 1991): 8–10. In an article on toxic oil syndrome, Andrew Boyle offers a particularly graphic description of the symptoms of SLE and other autoimmune disorders: "The illness typically began with a cough, fever, headache, rashes of various kinds, nausea and pains in the muscles and abdomen. . . . [After] two or three months . . . [n]ervous tissues degenerated, and muscles deteriorated painfully. Blood pressure in the lungs rose as a sign of progressive lung disease and a prologue to heart failure. . . . In many cases, antibodies to the patients' tissues appear in the blood, while resistance to commonplace infections is feeble. The skin thickens and stiffens, the arms wither, and the hands twist into stiff claws. Similar effects on the connective tissues give form, flexibility, and strength to the vital organs eventually kill the victim."

the School for Writers in Iowa, at Yaddo in Sarasota Springs, New York, and while staying with the Fitzgeralds in Connecticut. Had she been able to remain in such artistic enclaves she might well have become one of the "knowing ones" and persisted with the pessimism-cum-transcendence theme. But her illness forced her back to the South, back to Georgia, Milledgeville, Andalusia, and the tender mercies of Regina Cline O'Connor. For me, her extraordinary courage is proven by her affirmation of the hideously ordinary, the grotesquely carnal existence of the contorted "freaks" and fanatic "cripples" who populate her stories. And this affirmation of the body as good is all the more astounding when we consider the betrayal of Flannery's own body, her "freakish" appearance and grotesque disability.

Perhaps the best way to demonstrate O'Connor's affirmation of embodiment, her renunciation of asceticism, is to examine the last story she worked on. In a letter dated just twelve days before renal failure caused her to lapse into a coma, Flannery writes, "I'm still puttering on my story ['Parker's Back'] that I thought I'd finished—but not long at a time. I go across the room & I'm exhausted" (594). Despite its author's physical morbidity, "Parker's Back" reveals none of the fascination with asceticism and suspicion of the body that can be discerned in Wise Blood. Even though O'Connor's body had betrayed her, even though, like Yeats, she must have felt that her soul was "fastened to a dying animal," she never yielded to the gnostic impulse to denigrate the body.[26] O'Connor the author continued to celebrate incarnation even as O'Connor the patient, overcome with exhaustion and sickness, crawled toward death.

Sarah Ruth Parker, on the other hand, systematically denies the claims of the body and cultivates a fanatic, iconoclastic Christianity. Her suspicion of earthly things, what the Gnostics called hylic or "wooden stuff," intensifies when the material is enhanced by the artifices of fallen humanity. Hence her disdain for—and perhaps repressed fascination with—her husband's tattoos and her insistence that they be married in the "County Ordinary's office because Sarah Ruth thought churches were idolatrous" (663). O'Connor describes her as "plain, plain. The skin on her face was thin and drawn as tight as the skin on an onion and her eyes were grey and sharp like the points of two

---

26. Smith, "Afterword," 536. The phrase comes from Yeats's "Sailing to Byzantium" (1928), a poem that Smith specifically associates with Gnostic transcendence ("Afterword," 536). In the same poem, the speaker seems to long for an otherworldly existence where "Once out of nature I shall never take / My bodily form from any natural thing" (The Collected Poems of W. B. Yeats [New York: Macmillan, 1956], 191–92).

ice picks" (665). "In addition to her other bad qualities," Parker thinks, "she was always sniffing up sin. She did not smoke or dip, drink whiskey, use bad language or paint her face, and God knew some paint would have improved it, Parker thought" (665).

Yet there is in Sarah Ruth a hunger for the physical and the iconic. When Parker's truck breaks down in front of her mother's shack, she watches him furtively from "beyond a clump of honeysuckle" or through a window in the house. She drops Parker's hand when her eyes discover that his arm is covered with tattoos—"as if she had accidentally grabbed a poisonous snake"—but not before she has "peered at the back of the stubby reddish [tattooed] hand" and "gazed at [the loud design] with an almost stupefied smile of shock" (657). Parker associates the tattoos with sexuality, for he had "found that the tattoos were attractive to the kind of girls he liked but who had never liked him before," and "he had never yet met a woman who was not attracted to them" (658, 657). And in fact, when Parker suggests to Sarah Ruth that "you ought to see the ones that you can't see," "two circles of red appeared like apples in the girl's cheeks and softened her appearance" (657).[27]

There is something else Parker has that Sarah Ruth, in the words of Eudora Welty,[28] has "a gnawing and a craving for": food. Half-starved, Sarah takes one of Parker's apples "quickly as if the basket might disappear if she didn't make haste" and then chews it "slowly but with a kind of relish of concentration" (660, 661). Parker has clearly played the serpent—a serpent is prominently displayed on the arm that Sarah Ruth drops "like a poisonous snake"—and even Eve to Sarah Ruth's tall, rawboned mannishness.

Yet Sarah Ruth clings tenaciously to her food asceticism. After the marriage Parker begins "losing flesh" because Sarah Ruth "just threw food in the pot and let it boil" (664). Parker's dissatisfaction grows, and "there was no containing it outside of a tattoo." O'Connor thus contrasts Parker's multicolored, tattooed body with Sarah Ruth's astringent spirituality. Whereas Hazel Motes in *Wise Blood* is clearly superior to the greedy and xenophobic Mrs. Flood, in "Parker's Back" O'Connor wants us to sympathize, not with the ascetic, who in this story is a woman, but with the self-indulgent illustrated man. Caroline Gordon, who

27. *USA Today* (March 1991). If we can trust Madison Avenue to know what excites desire, then tattoos surely have some kind of erotic power. When the first television Marlboro man died in March 1991, his son remembered one of his father's favorite stories. To get the horseman ready for a shoot, the makeup artist spent three minutes on his face but devoted three hours to inscribing a small, anchor-shaped tattoo on the back of his hand.

28. Miss Welty expresses her savor for this overheard Southern locution in *Eudora Welty*, the Public Broadcasting System television production.

read an early draft of the manuscript, suggested that Flannery had "succeeded in dramatizing a heresy" (593). Flannery's friend "A." apparently misunderstood Gordon's observation, assuming that the degenerate Parker, who eventually has a terrifying, Byzantine Christ tattooed on his back, is the heretic. But Flannery corrects her: "No, Caroline didn't mean the tattoos were the heresy. Sarah Ruth was the heretic—the notion that you can worship in pure spirit" (594). Sarah Ruth remains staunchly gnostic, unmoved by her husband's gesture. Parker's back, now covered with a "still, straight, all-demanding" Christ, is soon wounded by his ascetic wife.

Unlike Sarah Ruth, Parker himself is now in spiritual and physical motion: for the first time his body is put in the service of another. He has always seen his physical nature as something flawed and imperfect, an object in need of repair. Tattoos, an analog of cosmetic surgery, have been his means of changing, remodeling, and transforming himself. For Parker, as perhaps for other obsessive "body sculptors," remodeling his body has been a mode not of cultural conformity but of self-absorption and control. Despite Parker's compulsive alterations of his physical appearance, O'Connor describes him as "heavy and earnest, as ordinary as a loaf of bread"; but, as Sally Fitzgerald suggests, he is a loaf of bread that has been consecrated by the end of the story.[29] As he whispers his given name to Sarah Ruth, he feels a "light pouring through him, turning his spider web soul into a perfect arabesque of colors, a garden of trees and birds and beasts" (673). No longer are the birds and beasts of this world images of imperfection, stupidity, or predation. Creation is transmogrified. No longer are the turkeys and pheasants "upside-down." A fox-shaped face, for a writer whose own has been made wolf-like by lupus, is no longer a straightforward sign of bestialism or degradation. O. E. is no longer egocentric and self-absorbed, and his very flesh, embedded with worldly images and icons, becomes radiant as he grudgingly whispers his given names, "Obadiah Elihue."

Sarah Ruth, however, does not participate in the transfiguration. She flies into an abusing, battering rage when she sees the face of Christ tattooed on her husband's flesh: " 'Idolatry!' Sarah Ruth screamed. 'Idolatry! Enflaming yourself with idols under every green tree! I can put up with lies and vanity but I don't want no idolator in this house!' and she grabbed up the broom and began to thrash him across the shoulders with it" (674). She continues beating Parker

29. Brian Abel Ragen, *A Wreck on the Road to Damascus: Innocence, Guilt and Conversion in Flannery O'Connor* (Chicago: Loyola University Press, 1989), 11–54. Ragan mentions Sally Fitzgerald's interpretation and examines the theological implications of "Parker's Back" in detail. I wish to acknowledge my debt to his useful book.

until "she had nearly knocked him senseless and large welts had formed on the face of the tattooed Christ" (674). "He's a spirit," Sarah Ruth shouts. "No man shall see his face." Sarah Ruth's violence against Parker mirrors the self-inflicted violence of Hazel Motes, and the underlying theology that motivates her is not different from Haze's gnostic dualism. She smashes the Byzantine icon by wounding Parker's tattooed back and thereby rejects the orthodox tradition of incarnation, spirit made flesh. For Sarah Ruth and Haze, the body can only be a site of evil and sin, an abomination before the Lord. For Parker and for the sickly Flannery O'Connor, the body—even though diseased and disfigured, like hers, or botched, like his—can become an arabesque of goodness, a multicolored incarnation of spirit.

Diseased Embodiment

A month before she died, Flannery wrote of her lupus that "the wolf, I'm afraid, is inside tearing up the place" (591). She was also coping with cystitis and a kidney infection that she had contracted after abdominal surgery. The massive doses of prednisone and ACTH that she took to alleviate the effects of the antibodies on her body's vital organs left her, and them, susceptible. To give her "good" antibodies a chance to combat the kidney infection, and because the nitrogen in her blood had increased by a third, her doctor was forced to drastically reduce the doses of prednisone. Without the steroids, though, the "bad" antibodies were free to do their worst: the wolf inside was loose. "So far as I can see," Flannery wrote to her friend Maryat Lee, "the medicine and the disease run neck & neck to kill you" (590).

Yet the illness in 1964 did not seem as severe to Flannery as the first onset in 1950–51: "This time is not as bad as the last—because I know what's wrong with me" (578). She jokes about her body having declared a "moratorium on making blood," something that apparently happens in lupus, and about "hearing the celestial chorus—'Clementine' is what it renders when I am weak enough to hear it. Over & over. 'Wooden boxes without topses, They were shoes for Clementine.'" "The transfusion cut that out," she writes, "must come from not enough blood getting to the head" (578). Two weeks later, feeling somewhat better, she writes, "No more 'Clementine' or 'Coming for to Carry Me Home'" (590).

In fact, throughout her last months of decline she uses her sense of humor to maintain her courage in the face of her body's revolt against itself. She writes to Robert Fitzgerald about the "successful" surgery that resulted in the kidney infection and cystitis as well as a reoccurrence of the lupus symptoms: "Me, I just got out of the hospital where I had my middle entered by the surgeons. It was all a howling success from their point of view and one of them is going to write it up for a doctor magazine as you usually don't cut folks with lupus. . . . Nothing turned out malignant and I will soon be restored on turnip green potlicker" (568).

She also writes to her friend "A." about a nurse whose tales about the "low life in Wilkinson County" and "it were" sentence constructions compelled Flannery to laugh aloud while recovering from the abdominal surgery. She says, "I reckon [that nurse] increased my pain about 100%," but suggests that the laughter and revelation of human character were worth the physical discomfort (569). The LPN, Flannery says, "was a dead ringer for Mrs. Turpin," a vain, bigoted, and self-righteous character in her recently published "Revelation." She told Flannery "all the time what a good nurse she was. . . . She said she treated everybody alike whether it were a person with money or a black nigger" (569). Perhaps her illness had taught her a greater tolerance for human foibles and complacence. In any case, she seems more amused than enraged by the unstudied characters of Milledgeville and hopes she will not get so sick that she ends up in Piedmont, an antiseptic, big-city hospital in Atlanta. She likes hearing "the groans being groaned in the other rooms" of the little country hospital in Baldwin County. There was, she wrote, a lady across the hall who, whenever they touched her, "roared LORD LORD LORD in the voice of a stevedore. At night when she coughed a nurse came in also in a voice you could hear anywhere [and] said 'Pit that old stuff out, Sugar. Pit it out. Pit that old stuff out. Pit it out, Sugar,' etc." (571). This odd delight in the excretory functions of the body, even as morbidity overwhelmed her own, is worth remarking. Flannery's humorous letters let us know that, even in extremis, she is still taking surprising joy in a grotesquely embodied world.

As a recipient of long-term cortisone therapy, Flannery would have suffered the characteristic disfigurements of Cushing's Syndrome: excessive facial hair, moon face, buffalo hump, osteoporosis. On 1 July 1964, as she was still "puttering with 'Parker's Back,'" she notes in a letter that she had "been in the hospital 50 days already this year" (591). Her resilient humor notwithstanding, Flannery did know the anguish and isolation of illness. Once in a 1956 letter she dropped her characteristic irony to reveal the loneliness of her chronic condition: "In a sense sickness is a place . . . where there's no company, where nobody can follow" (163). Making her ascetic, monastic cell of sickness exemplary was doubtless a powerful temptation. So much of what we read contains the urgent, egotistical subtext: This is the way I am or must be; it is an ideal that you should emulate.

Her lupus kept Flannery O'Connor *at home* in many senses of that phrase: her chronic illness kept her embedded in the hylic stuff of Andalusia, Milledgeville, and Baldwin County. But she did not make confinement, disability, or asceticism into a model for others. In her fiction characters are, as she was, frankly disabled, disfigured, and, yes, crippled in the full connotation of the word. But her genius is the ability to see value, even surpassing goodness, in the physically damaged or diseased, the morally reprobate and vainglorious, in the meanest human form—an idiot child, a mentally retarded girl, a fiercely ugly woman with a wooden leg. Flannery O'Connor's own body turned against itself and in a superficial sense was anything but good. Nonetheless, sickness and success taught her, as she said, "the hard way," that nothing of importance "could be worked out on the surface." In her last story, O'Connor rejects gnostic asceticism as too simplistic, superficial, and formulaic; instead she affirms the more complex and profound goodness of the body, not as a locus of desire and gratification, a site of political contestation and negotiation, or a commodity for consumption—but as an embodied symbol, a fleshy and bloody icon, an incarnation of suffering and redemption.

Part Four

Cultural

Ideals

and the

"Good Body"

11

The Beauty of the Beast:
Male Body Imagery
in Anthropological
Perspective

David D. Gilmore

"El hombre como el oso: lo mas feo lo mas hermoso"
(Men are like bears: the uglier, the more handsome)

The pithy refrain above, part of Spanish folklore and wisdom, can be heard in any pueblo in Spain whenever the subject of sex or gender difference arises. I heard it often in my own field site, a farming community near Seville City, fairly typical of towns throughout the region.[1] Like most other peasants, Spanish villagers have deeply held philosophies about human physical beauty and ugliness. These are discrete for male and female. In fact, the sexes are contrasted with such gleeful vehemence that male and female ideals are virtually

1. David D. Gilmore, *The People of the Plain* (New York: Columbia University Press, 1980); David D. Gilmore, *Aggression and Community* (New Haven: Yale University Press, 1987). Research in Spain took place in 1972–73, 1980, 1984, and 1991. Fieldwork was supported by grants from the National Science Foundation, the Wenner-Gren Foundation, the American Philosophical Society, the National Endowment for the Humanities, the H. F. Guggenheim Foundation, and the Program for Cultural Cooperation. All translations from the Spanish in text are my own. More information on Andalusian rural culture and sexual mores may be found in my books on the subject.

opposite in formal and thematic terms—as are expectations about comportment and role. For Spanish peasants used to dealing with coarse realities, the human male, like other animals, has an important corporeal presence; like all other things in nature, the male body is valorized by invidious comparison. The criteria of male worth, as of woman's loveliness, are grounded in flesh, in visual properties symbolizing hierarchies of value.

The man who turns heads—the *hermoso* man—is not necessarily visually striking: rather, they say he is powerful, strong, dominant. Like Don Juan, he inspires fear and respect rather than love. Throughout the Mediterranean region, excellent men are likened metaphorically to savage animals such as brave bulls, fierce bears, virile rams—all admired for their courage, force, and, especially, their potential for violence when threatened.[2] The operative element can be summarized as "fierceness." As a visual representation, it encapsulates the essential masculine virtues, not just crude power, but also honor, activity, stamina, competitiveness, and of course, dominance—"Alpha male" qualities, a primatologist might say. Following Claude Lévi-Strauss, one may speak of homologies, not just external analogies that link human and natural categories, but also parallel internal homologies between active and passive, the animal world, and the valorization of the sexes as physical beings.[3]

When pressed, people in Spain explained their ugly bear: women should be passive and fecund ("beautiful"), but it is the function of the male to be assertive and active ("powerful"). This entails the capability of inspiring dread in others, thereby fending off predators. Hence the bear's ugliness, by analogy, makes it more terrible and thus more worthy of respect; consequently "beautiful" (*hermoso*) in the trope inverts the northerner's contrasting aesthetic models. Ideals about male morphology, then, being based on arbitrary symbols of power and magnetism, are particularly germane to the epistemological questions raised in this volume about the body as a reification of moral abstractions. For the human body in Spain, as in most cultures, provides a visual metaphor for deepest moral as well as aesthetic values. These are always informed by what Sandra Bem has called "gender schema" but can vary to an astonishing extent.[4] To what extent are these "cultural" contrasts shared by both sexes? To paraphrase Sigmund Freud, what do women *see* (in males)?

2. Anton Blok, "Rams and Billy Goats: A Key to the Mediterranean Code of Honour," *Man* 16 (1981): 427–40.

3. Claude Lévi-Strauss, *Le Totemisme Aujourd'hui* (Paris: Presses Universitaires Françaises, 1962).

4. Sandra Bem, "Gender Schema Theory and Its Implications for Child Development," *Signs* 8 (1983): 598–616.

Beauty: Power as Female; Male?

For men everywhere, not just in Mediterranean countries, physical attractiveness is often organically conflated with character, with social dominance or
action: "Men are attractive by activity."[5] Yet anthropological research has
shown that this linkage is often a masculine *assumption* not necessarily shared by
women—a kind of genderized self-definition. Questions of male "beauty" are
much more complex than a simple equation linking men to power and
women to beauty would imply. My intention here is to explore cultural metaphors for conceptualizing attitudes toward the male body as both object and
instrument. We start with some tribal peoples and then return to the West,
looking for contrasts and parallels.

Anthropologists have noted that the way the body is socially construed
constitutes at once an icon and a discriminant of gender dimorphism, of
tertiary sexual characteristics (those socially ascribed).[6] As we can see from the
Spanish case above, the good male body, at least in one corner of the Mediterranean world, engages some curious paradoxes in which "beauty" and behavior are juxtaposed in ways inappropriate or supererogatory for females, so
what is visually ugly in the male can be ethically beautiful. These paradoxes are
revealing if compared to images of the ideal male body in other cultures,
including our own. Taking a classic ethnographic example from an African
popular verse (the Yoruba of Nigeria), we see a common thread in cultural
emphasis on male ethical qualities over the visual.[7]

> A man may be very, very handsome,
> Handsome as a fish within the water,
> But if he has no character,
> He is no more than a wooden doll.

5. Robin T. Lakoff and Raquel L. Scherr, *Face Value: The Politics of Beauty* (Boston: Routledge & Kegan Paul, 1984), 213.

6. Some of the best works by anthropologists using a comparative approach toward
beauty, aesthetics, and body imagery in preindustrial societies are the following: Richard L.
Anderson, *Art in Small-Scale Societies*, 2d ed. (Englewood Cliffs, N.J.: Prentice-Hall, 1989);
Richard L. Anderson, *Calliope's Sisters: A Comparative Study of Philosophies of Art* (Englewood Cliffs,
N.J.: Prentice-Hall, 1990); John Blacking, *The Anthropology of the Body* (New York: Academic
Press, 1977); Warren d'Azevedo, ed., *The Traditional Artist in African Societies* (Bloomingdale: Indi-
ana University Press, 1973); Evelyn P. Hatcher, *Art as Culture: Introduction to the Anthropology of Art*
(Lanham, Md.: University Press of America, 1985); Edmund Leach, "Aesthetics," in *The Institu-
tions of Primitive Society*, ed. E. E. Evans-Pritchard (Glencoe, Ill.: Free Press, 1954), 25–38.

7. Robert F. Thompson, "Yoruba Artistic Criticism," in *The Artist in Traditional African Societies*, ed. Warren d'Azevedo (Bloomington: Indiana University Press, 1973), 19–61.

A suggestive parallel is our own English use of the term *handsome* for physically attractive men. The word actually derives from the Anglo-Saxon "handy," meaning not physically appealing at all but rather useful or serviceable.[8] Webster defines handsome as convenient or easily handled: also generous, considerable, or imposing—that is, something that performs well, that works. But unlike the dictionary glosses for beautiful, handsome connotes neither delicacy nor grace, which are confined to the feminine beautiful.[9] We also have in English the expression "handsome is as handsome does," suggesting that beauty for males is bound up with character and achievement rather than purely visual criteria. This active/passive distinction underlies Western conceptions of human formal attractiveness. Female beauty, as Freud noted long ago,[10] "has no obvious use" apart from decorative pleasure excited in the (presumably male) viewer.[11] We do not say "beauty is as beauty does." Male comeliness, then, is more than skin deep. Or is it?

Aesthetics and Gender: Western Paradigms

A formal distinction between male and female beauty has a venerable pedigree in Western discourse. Such dichotomous aesthetic schemes contain "the bases of the whole world picture of a people."[12]. Early Enlightenment studies of aesthetics emphasized sexual differences not only as a matter of outward appearance but as Platonic dualism for contrasting "naturally" opposed pairs. A prime exemplar is Edmund Burke's *Philosophical Enquiry into the Origin of Our Ideas of the Sublime and the Beautiful.* Crystallizing the thought of his time, Burke defines beauty as deriving from passive qualities such as fragility, smoothness, and

8. Arthur Marwick, *Beauty in History* (London: Thames and Hudson, 1988), 24–25.

9. Elaine Hatfield and Susan Sprecher, *Mirror, Mirror . . .: The Importance of Looks in Everyday Life* (Albany: State University of New York Press, 1986), 3.

10. Sigmund Freud, *Civilization and Its Discontents*, trans. James Strachey (New York: W. W. Norton, 1930), 50. For Freud, human beauty, by which he seems to mean exclusively female beauty, becomes an "aim-inhibited impulse," a sublimation of sexuality.

11. Sigmund Freud, *Three Essays on the Theory of Sexuality*, trans. James Strachey, in *Standard Edition*, vol. 7 (London: Hogarth Press, 1949 [1905]), 35. The erotic impulse in males, triggered by visual cues, is transformed by means of repression into a visual gratification. "There is to my mind no doubt that the concept of 'beautiful' has its roots in sexual stimulation and its original meaning was 'sexually stimulating.' " Reflecting the beliefs of his time to a greater extent here than elsewhere in his works, Freud has little to say about female sexual response and male appearance, viewing female arousal as triggered by nonvisual stimuli.

12. Vytantas Kavolis, "The Value-Orienting Theory of Artistic Styles," in *Art and Aesthetics in Primitive Societies*, ed. Carol F. Joppling (New York: Dutton, 1971), 251.

delicacy, arguing that beauty entails helplessness, nonassertiveness, and small-ness. Beauty, so defined, is essentially feminine, and, indeed, for Burke the "fair sex" is obviously capable of the greatest physical beauty.[13] Burke, the father of modern conservatism, takes this an irreducible given. But, although Burke finds that men are also capable of beauty, he is very careful to distinguish between the Sublime and the Beautiful and thereby to polarize male and female principles on both moral and aesthetic grounds.

The Sublime takes on certain mystical qualities; by imperceptible degrees these generate epistemological assumptions linking power to core values such as sacredness and nobility and, finally, to masculinity. For Burke, sublimity has to do with greatness, large size, strength, magnificence, and impressiveness. Far more majestic than mere beauty, sublimity is exalted power, exemplified most concretely by the majesty of God. Rather than inspiring "love" and protective feelings in the viewer, sublimity instead inspires awe, even fear or "terror."[14] The Sublime overwhelms rather than charms; sublimity is awesome, minatory, dreadful. Unsettling the observer, this quality has something of the aggressive about it, something definitely phallic. As in the Spanish aphorism about the ugly bear, ideal manliness is not conventionally beautiful but rather fearsome, awe-inspiring. As Robert Graves put it, "Men do; women are."[15] Such ideas have come in for a drubbing recently at the hands of feminists who condemn the "beauty trap" that supposedly ensnares only women, leaving power to men.[16] But how salient are such dualistic notions worldwide? Are men everywhere so obsessed with their own powerfulness and so contemptu-ous of their own comeliness? What does male "beauty" consist of in non-Western (exotic) cultures?

Human Physical Beauty: A Survey

Early studies of body imagery and ideals of physical comeliness in different cultures mirrored the standard Western views discussed above. Charles Dar-

13. Edmund Burke, *A Philosophical Enquiry into the Origin of Our Ideas of the Sublime and the Beautiful*, ed. with Introduction by J. T. Boulton (London: Routledge & Kegan Paul, 1958 [1757]),98.

14. Ibid., 116.

15. Graves cited in Peter Schwenger, *Phallic Critiques: Masculinity and Twentieth-Century Litera-ture* (London: Routledge & Kegan Paul, 1984), 118.

16. Susan Brownmiller, *Femininity* (New York: Fawcett Columbine, 1984); Naomi Wolf, *The Beauty Myth* (New York: William Morrow, 1990).

win was the first to compare ideals of beauty and of sexual appeal.[17] He found that a bewildering variety of criteria exist, but that the allure of beauty was largely a female trait—the result of eons of natural selection. This is the sociobiological view still espoused by many.[18] In a classic study of cross-cultural ideals of beauty, Clellan Ford and Frank Beach reached pretty much the same conclusion. More recently, psychologists Ellen Berscheid and Elaine Walster speak of the "dazzling variety" of characteristics associated with physical attractiveness in different cultures, although Donald Symons, Arthur Marwick, and Linda Jackson argue that cultural variability has been somewhat overemphasized, especially concerning the criteria for female attractiveness.[19]

Regardless of their conclusions on variability, virtually all observers stress that physical beauty, defined as the capacity to attract, is largely a female trait. According to these early observers, men seem to be judged by other, mainly behavioral, standards. For example, Ford and Beach write: "One very interesting generalization is that in most societies the physical beauty of the female receives more explicit consideration than does the handsomeness of the male. The attractiveness of the man usually depends predominantly upon his skill and prowess rather than upon his physical appearance." In a recent cross-cultural survey, Suzanne Frayser concurs: "Social and physical skill seem to have a more marked influence on defining a man's appeal to a woman than vice versa." Furthermore, it is striking to what degree criteria of female facial beauty are consistent from culture to culture. Citing the published accounts of the Victorian explorer and libertine Richard Francis Burton, Darwin wrote that "a woman whom we consider beautiful is admired throughout the world." Thus we have some scholarly support for the "men do/women are" paradigm of conventional Western wisdom.[20]

17. Charles Darwin, "The Origin of Species by Means of Natural Selection," from *The Descent of Man and Selection in Relation to Sex*, in *Great Books of the Western World*, vol. 49, ed. R. M. Hutchins (Chicago: Encyclopedia Britannica, 1952 [1871]).

18. Donald Symons, *The Evolution of Human Sexuality* (New York: Oxford University Press, 1979), 185; Camille Paglia, *Sexual Personae* (New Haven: Yale University Press, 1990); Helen E. Fisher, *The Anatomy of Sex* (New York: W. W. Norton, 1992).

19. Clellan S. Ford and Frank A. Beach, *Patterns of Sexual Behavior* (New York: Harper Colophon, 1972 [1951]); Ellen Berscheid and Elaine Walster, "Physical Attractiveness," in *Advances in Experimental Social Psychology*, vol. 7, ed. Leonard Berkowitz (New York: Academic Press, 1974), 186; Symons, *evolution of Human Sexuality*, 185; Marwick, *Beauty in History*, 31; Linda Jackson, *Physical Appearance and Gender: Sociobiological and Sociocultural Perspectives* (Albany: State University of New York Press, 1992), 60–61.

20. Ford and Beach, *Patterns of Sexual Behavior*, 94; Suzanne Frayser, *Varieties of Sexual Experience* (New Haven: HRAF Press, 1985), 186; Darwin, "Origin of Species," 573.

To be sure, much recent scholarly research has provided empirical backing for the Darwinian notion. This work suggests "a relative universal"[21] of female pulchritude and a greater variability for men because of the linkage of male beauty with accomplishment.[22] In a synoptic study of thirty-seven cultures, David Buss reaches the same conclusion as Darwin about the supposed commonalities of beauty criteria for women.[23] Again, men seem more closely tied to culture, to the vaulting human spirit, to achievement, while women are mired in morphology, in biology, as in Sherry Ortner's gender scheme: man:woman::culture:nature.[24]

What is most interesting about all this is how we have managed to overlook consistent evidence that in many cultures, the appearance of the male is as important as that of the female, although perhaps in different ways. The evidence is there; it has simply never been systematically studied. The stress on male looks, not performance, varies from culture to culture. In some this stress on male appearance reaches an apogee actually surpassing emphasis on female beauty. A striking example comes from northern Africa among numerous tribes forming a broad continuous band from Mauritania in the west to Kenya in the east (the Sahel region consisting of semidesert areas on the southern fringes of the Sahara). These Sahelian cultures constitute what might be called a "Narcissus band" or "Male beauty belt." In these cultures, men are vitally concerned about their physical beauty. In a few apex societies, they are even more concerned than the women. One such tribe, the Wodaabe, part of the larger Fulani group, actually regard men as more beautiful than women and even stage male beauty contests with women judges! In this society, it is the men, not the women, who are the pretty sex objects, using makeup and other body adornments to lure female attention. Yet men in this society are strong warriors and political leaders.

Male beauty in these cultures and others discussed below seems to have at least two social meanings. As one might expect, one of these is erotic. In many

21. Marwick, *Beauty in History*, 31.

22. John Liggett, *The Human Face* (New York: Stein and Day, 1974); Judith H. Langlois and Lori A. Roggman, "Attractive Faces Are Only Average, *Psychological Review* 1 (1990): 115–21.

23. David M. Buss, "Sex Differences in Human Mate Selection Criteria: An Evolutionary Perspective, in *Sociobiology and Psychology: Ideas, Issues, and Applications*, ed. Charles Crawford, Martin Smith, and Dennis Krebs (Hillsdale, N.J.: Erlbaum, 1987).

24. Sherry Ortner, "Is Female to Male as Nature Is to Culture?" in *Women, Culture, and Society*, ed. Michelle Rosaldo and Louise Lamphere (Stanford, Calif.: Stanford University Press, 1974).

disparate cultures, men are considered heterosexual sex objects and so stimulate interest in the opposite sex with cosmetics, as do women in most other
cultures. So, like women in the West, the African Adonises primp and preen
and fret over their imperfections and wrinkles. The other meaning is more
complex and needs additional anthropological treatment. This meaning concerns the identification of male physical beauty with certain ethical and moral
principles in which masculinity itself comes to "stand for" a tribal or ethnocentric self-image, hence assuming symbolic centrality as a visual representation of group identity. In this more abstract sense, male beauty partakes of the
emphasis on power and majesty, but as an apotheosis of national identity. Such
a meaning creates special ethical and normative pressures on men. What is true
of Sahelian Africa is, I believe, true of virtually all cultures to some degree. The
psychological pressures on males to measure up to such iconic images have
never been adequately examined by anthropologists or by social psychologists
working in Western contexts.

The African Adonis Complex

West Africa is the home of numerous agricultural peoples with highly developed art forms depicting the human form.[25] Many of these tribal peoples are
connoisseurs of physical beauty, with varying emphasis upon male or female
attractiveness. Like Westerners, some West Africans put a premium on the
physical appearance of the female over the male. A prime example of this
exclusive concern with female beauty is the Mende tribe of Sierra Leone,[26] as
described by Sylvia Boone.[27] The Mende are a patrilineal, polygamous people
living in small towns and villages and practicing rice cultivation for market sale.
The status of women is relatively high, especially since women control much
of the marketing and are economically independent.

The Mende believe that of all things in the world, people are the most
beautiful, and woman is the most gorgeous creation of God. Beauty itself in
Mende thought is said to be exclusively a feminine trait. The Mende describe
all beautiful objects as "fine like a woman." A handsome man, if recognized as
such, is said to be "like a woman." There is literally no conceptual or linguistic

25. d'Azevedo, ed., *The Traditional Artist in African Societies*.
26. The use of the term *tribe* is simply for convenience sake and does not imply an acceptance of a taxonomic category as found in structural-functional usage.
27. Sylvia A. Boone, *Radiance from the Waters: Ideals of Feminine Beauty in Mende Art* (New
Haven: Yale University Press, 1986).

equivalent to formulate expressions of male handsomeness.[28] Not only is beauty always feminine, but *all* women, and in fact all female creatures, are beautiful simply by being female. The Mende have a proverb to the effect that "Nothing that has a vagina can be called ugly." Glorifying feminine pulchritude as nearly divine, the Mende simply do not recognize parallel physical attributes or qualities in men. So for example, while woman's hair is always beautiful, "the blacker the better," the Mende say that "men don't have hair." Recalling the ugly-handsome bear in Spanish usage, the Mende say that men cannot be beautiful, but instead should "look aggressive and fierce."[29] The beauty and the beast again! The Mende stand at one extreme of the continuum of cultures that localize physical beauty in women. The pressures on women to measure up are of course enormous. The Mende say it is the moral obligation of all woman to make themselves beautiful; failure to be beautiful is a moral flaw.

A striking contrast is found not far away, among the Fulani tribes of northern Nigeria. Here is where the Adonis complex, as I like to call it, reigns supreme. Like the Mende, the Fulani people are patrilineal, patrilocal, and polygamous. But like some other pastoralist northern African peoples, the Fulani regard men, not women, as the most beautiful creatures on earth. The reasons for this are unclear but have to do with tribal ideals linking masculinity with tribal identity. A salient example of this aesthetic can be found among the Wodaabe tribe, a branch of the Fulani living in the Bornu Emirate of north-eastern Nigeria. The Wodaabe are a Muslim people who herd goats, cattle, and camels and have been excellently rendered in Derek Stenning's classic study and in Robert Brain's lively book on human beauty.[30] Interestingly, the status of women among the Wodaabe is somewhat lower than among the Mende, so that any correlation between women's political position and beauty ideals seems to fall by the wayside. Women do not inherit property in this society, men control the herds, and marriages are arranged by fathers. In other respects, the Wodaabe follow the moral and sexual standards of Sudanese Islam, which is not especially favorable to women, pace Naomi Wolf.[31] Yet among the Wodaabe, it is the men, not the women, who are the passive objects of erotic desire.

28. Ibid., 82.
29. Ibid., 138.
30. Derek J. Stenning, *Savannah Nomads: A Study of the Wodaabe Pastoral Fulani of Western Bornu Province, Northern Region, Nigeria* (London: Oxford University Press, 1959); Robert Brain, *The Decorated Body* (New York: Harper & Row, 1979).
31. Wolf, *Beauty Myth*, 24.

Wodaabe men spend much time in beautifying themselves. They carry pocket mirrors and combs at all times. They lavish great amounts of time and energy in painting their faces and arranging their precious hairdos, which they smear with ointments. The ideals of Wodaabe male beauty are very specific: clear and light-colored skin; a taut body, slender and graceful; a high forehead (which the men assiduously pluck); smooth, thick, glossy hair; a long, straight neck; big, flashing eyes with pronounced lashes; white teeth; and, in particular, a fine, straight, long, and prominent nose.[32] The stress on the nose is critical to Wodaabe notions of human beauty; it bears a brief digression. "The nose is, for Wodaabe and pastoral Fulani in general, one of the chief criteria of beauty. . . . It figures importantly in metaphor." Indeed, the Wodaabe regard their straight noses as their most distinguishing feature and their most beautiful attribute— the detail that differentiates them from, and makes them aesthetically superior to, despised neighboring peoples.[33] So important is the characteristic Wodaabe nose as a point of pride that men, who normally have bigger noses than women, are thus considered more beautiful—one of the curious twists of Wodaabe human aesthetics, not found in many other cultures.

The culmination of this tribal celebration of masculine pulchritude is the famous *gerewol* ceremony. Essentially this is a male beauty contest (captured in glorious technicolor by German filmmaker Werner Herzog in the ethnographic movie "Herdsmen of the Sun"). In the gerewol ritual, the eligible young men are on public display as sex objects for the girls in a reversal of the Western (or Mende) pattern. One of the goals of this festival is for the youths to entice a girl into marriage, which also reverses the active-passive roles of Western culture. Brain describes the gerewol:

> The Fulani girls watch their men. They are themselves loaded with bracelets, necklaces and brass rings. . . . The youths, oiled, ornamented and painted, line up before the women like red and indigo gods, their hair decorated with cowries [shells] and surmounted by long ostrich feathers. At each side of the face hang fringes of red stripes, delicately bordered with indigo, and the same indigo paint is used to darken the lips. At the corners of the mouth are dark triangular patterns, while other designs are painted on the nose and cheeks. The basic complexion colour is ochre, and the upper half of the body,

32. Brain, *Decorated Body*, 133.
33. Ibid., 56–57.

the chest and the neck, is polished like mahogany. Each youth also carries a ceremonial axe, the crest of which represents a man's coiffure while the patterns of the body painting are worked on it.[34]

The gerewol, with its florid displays of male beauty and sexual allure, lasts for a solid week. The youths decorate themselves for hours beforehand as the anointed future stud bulls of this pastoral community. When it is time to go on stage, the young men line up in front of the women judges; they sing and dance, drawing themselves up to their full height, arching their backs and looking expectantly at the women. They bare their gleaming teeth and blink their flashing eyes. The crowd of women makes loud comments, critiquing each entrant, the old women ridiculing and shaming the ugly and the graceless. The boys go into contortions, tiptoeing to look taller, thrusting back their shoulders, undulating, rolling their eyes, and grimacing as the girls draw nearer to get a better look. As girls leave their group and approach the boys individually, the excited youths start to preen frantically and make faces in an attempt to seduce the young maidens to choose them. With a slight movement of her hand, the female judge indicates the dancer she has chosen as the most handsome.[35] The lucky one who is chosen gets to spend the night with the girl who has selected him. The Wodaabe are an Adonis culture where physical beauty is the main measure of a man's social worth.

Woman's position as the judge of masculine comeliness is accepted and woven into the very sinews of the social order. A woman is thereby granted an unusually degree of sexual, if not political, freedom. Frequently, a Wodaabe wife will spot a gorgeous young swain from among the multitudes that pass her door. Overwhelmed by his physical charms, she may simply seduce him and run away with her new lover, abandoning her husband and family. Her husband protests, but there is nothing he can do: in a reversal of the typical Western pattern, he has lost out to a younger, more beautiful rival. A common occurrence among the Wodaabe, this scenario is called deetuki, or love match. In anthropological terminology, it is called Cicisbean marriage—that is, the socially accepted union of a married woman and her unmarried lover. Rare in the West, and highly disreputable in most other places, it is an everyday affair in the African Sahel. All this female sexual freedom occurs in tandem with, or in spite of, an otherwise patriarchal Muslim culture in which women's political position is relatively low.

34. Ibid., 134.
35. Ibid.

There are other cases of role reversal in North Africa. The Bedouin tribes-men of the Sahara are known to use makeup and to paint the whites of their eyes a bluish tinge with kohl or antimony so as to be "more love-looking in the eyes of the women."[36] The Tuareg, a group of Berber-speaking tribes of the central Sahara, are famous for their preening males. Like the Wodaabe, they believe that men are more beautiful, more sexually appealing than women. Indeed, so powerful is this belief that the Tuareg men feel they must hide their physical charms from female prying eyes. Thus the Tuareg men are among the few males in the world who veil themselves. The men say that the veil is pretty and becoming and that they feel more attractive when veiled, especially during courtship, when a Tuareg swain takes "great care in the perfection of his dress, particularly the veil.[37] The men also lavish great care on their luxurious hair, and a man's braids are the "pride of his youth.[38]" All men carry around pocket mirrors all day to fuss over their precious coiffures, veil, and dress.

The Pokot tribe are another case in point. Sometimes referred to as the Suk, the Pokot are a Nandi- or Kalenjin-speaking people who occupy a remote area of western Kenya and eastern Uganda. They are farmers and herders living patrilineally and polygamously in dispersed homesteads. Among the Pokot, female appreciation of male beauty is lyrical and rapturous. In interviews with anthropologist Robert B. Edgerton, Pokot women were shown pictures of tall and well-muscled men from their own and neighboring tribes. The women "squealed with pleasure and unfailingly commented upon the beauty and virility of the men in the slides."[39] The women were ecstatic in their enthusi-asm. One said, "I would do anything to sleep with such a man. How beautiful! How wonderful! How can I get such a man to sleep with me!" Another said, "Oh, oh! What a handsome man. He is more than I can look at. He makes me feel weak. I should have married this man. I would like to have such a man in my bed." Other women spoke of how they "forced" their husbands or lovers to make love ten times a night, because women are more sexually voracious than men. One Pokot wife said of her exhausted husband, "He works very hard to make me happy. I must have it ten times—or more" each night.[40] So much for the Western image of the sexually passive female!

36. Liggett, *Human Face*, 48.
37. Susan Rasmussen, "Veiled Self, Transparent Meanings: Tuareg Headdresses as Social Expression," *Ethnology* 30 (1991): 106.
38. Ibid.
39. Robert B. Edgerton, *The Individual in Cultural Adaptation* (Berkeley: University of California Press, 1971), 140.
40. Ibid., 118.

Although the peacock complex reaches its apex in Saharan Africa, it occurs elsewhere as well, and I suspect is much more widespread than reported.[41] In the Pacific, men are as concerned about their appearance as women, sometimes more so. Among the Siuai people of the Solomon Islands, the men are fanatic about their hair, diligently combing and dressing it. These men also bleach and dye their hair for maximum affect.[42] The Fijian men, not otherwise noted for effeminacy, often have their own hairdressers.[43] The peoples of Highland New Guinea are equally concerned about male appearance. Among the Sambia of the central Highlands, a short, plain, or ugly man is an outcast. The Sambia call an ugly or puny man a "misfit"; his unhappy fate is to be rejected by women, scorned by men. The women stigmatize the homely man as a "rubbish man" not worthy of their attention. He is shunned and humiliated daily because of his unimpressive physique.[44] Among the neighboring Sepik groups of Highland New Guinea, we find that men are passionate about their body decorations. The males of the Wogeo tribe, for example, are avid cosmetic artists. When they first encountered mirrors, at the time of Western contact, they used them at every opportunity to adjust their gorgeous hairdos of cordyline leaves and cockatoo feathers as well as to admire their liberally applied face paint.[45]

In southern Africa, among the Bushmen of the Kalahari, women and girls are very concerned about their lovers' appearance. They express admiration for even teeth, a wide smile, straight, slender legs. A man must be muscular and wiry in physique. "They hate a big black belly" and will reject as a suitor any man who does not measure up in this regard.[46] Among the Yoruba peoples of Nigeria, standards of male beauty are "at least as rigorous as those for women."[47] Turning to North America, the Comanche males of the Great Plains also were known to dress and pomade their hair with unguents in order to cut a

41. David D. Gilmore, *Manhood in the Making* (New Haven: Yale University Press, 1990). Another good example of the African peacock complex occurs among the Samburu, a warlike and pastoral people of East Africa, distantly related to the Maasai. Samburu attitudes toward manly beauty and toward masculinity are explored in my book on the cultural meanings of manhood.

42. Douglas L. Oliver, *A Solomon Island Society* (Cambridge, Mass.: Harvard University Press, 1955).

43. Frayser, *Varieties of Sexual Experience*, 174.

44. Gilbert Herdt and Robert J. Stoller, *Intimate Communications: Erotics and the Study of Culture* (New York: Columbia University Press, 1990), 281.

45. Ian Hogbin, "Puberty to Marriage: A Study of the Sexual Life of the Natives of Wogeo, New Guinea," *Oceania* 16 (1946): 185–209.

46. Laura Marshall, "Marriage among the !Kung Bushmen," *Africa* 29 (1959): 335–64.

47. Anderson, *Art in Small-Scale Societies*.

dashing figure before the women.[48] These data just scratch the surface of male vanity around the world.

In aboriginal South America, male appearance also counts in some cases as much as female. This is true of the Mehinaku people, a group of slash-and-burn cultivators inhabiting the riverine banks of the Xingu River in Central Brazil. The ideal Mehinaku man, Thomas Gregor notes, is physically impressive, big and tall, and moves with grace and commanding confidence. He radiates self-assurance. As measured in material pursuits, tall men are indeed more success-ful than short men, as Gregor's field notes show. "On the average," he writes, "tall men are more likely than short men to sponsor rituals, be wealthy, have many girlfriends, and become village chiefs."[49] After having quantified the issue by a village survey, Gregor points out that the three tallest men in his village had nearly twice as many mistresses as the three shortest men, even though their average age was greater.[50] In contrast, the puny and ugly uncoordinated man is scorned as worthless and sexually undesirable and has much less chance to realize his manhood.[51] The small man is called *peritsi*, an abusive term connot-ing ugliness that is seldom uttered without a sneer or laugh. Scorned by women and rejected by prospective parents-in-law, the puny *peritsi* is a feeble excuse for manhood. Gregor gives an example of such a contemptible figure named Ahiri:

> Ahiri is . . . considered a *peritsi*. The shortest man in the village, less than five feet tall and shorter than many of the women, he is . . . abused behind his back. Many of the men conduct affairs with his wife and show contemptuously little concern about hiding their indiscretions. They not only make passes at her when her husband is nearby but flirt with her in his presence. To them a very short man does not merit respect. His size is a justification for taking advantage of him; not only is it safe to abuse him and to have relations with his wife, it is also what he deserves.[52]

The frequent humiliations suffered by the *peritsi* remind Gregor again of his own North American culture, where small or physically unprepossessing men

48. Ernest Wallace and E. Adamson Hoebel, *The Comanches: Lords of the South Plains* (Nor-man: University of Oklahoma Press, 1951), 83, 144.

49. Thomas Gregor, *Anxious Pleasures: The Sexual Life of an Amazonian People* (Chicago: University of Chicago Press, 1985), 36.

50. Thomas Gregor, *Mehinaku* (Chicago: University of Chicago Press, 1977), 198.

51. Gregor, *Anxious Pleasures*, 144.

52. Gregor, *Mehinaku*, 198.

face similar handicaps and ill treatment. That musculature and "manly" appearance should be the measure of a man should come as no surprise to Westerners, particularly Americans. Gregor is undoubtedly right to say, "Our own prejudice against short men is built into courtship, the chances of finding a good job, and even language, where a rich vocabulary of abuse impugns the short man."[53] As we shall see, others have argued the case on the basis of statistical research. The sociologist Saul Feldman, who expressly studied the issue in the United States, has argued that "heightism" affects our social relations, sexual patterns, employment opportunities, political success, and even our earning power.[54] What are height and musculature, after all, but male equivalents of voluptuousness in females?[55]

Western Parallels

Most feminist writers on beauty, especially those who call beauty a "trap" or "myth,"[56] rarely stop to consider the phenomenon of male looks and sexual appeal as aspects of the male life experience. Yet we know that throughout Western history, both men and women have made impassioned pronouncements on this subject. Women have written extensively on masculine magnetism, expressing in memoir and in fantasy their erotic excitement over the romantic-looking male. Many best-selling women's novels have conjured charismatic male archetypes, like Heathcliff in Wuthering Heights, that have set women's hearts aflutter.

We know also of the mesmerizing impact of such handsome specimens as

53. Gregor, Anxious Pleasures, 36.

54. Saul D. Feldman, "The Presentation of Shortness in Everyday Life—Height and Heightism in American Society, in Life Styles: Diversity in American Society, 2d ed., ed. Saul D. Feldman and Gerald W. Thielbar (Boston: Little Brown, 1975), 437–42.

55. Gilmore, Manhood in the Making, 110; Hatfield and Sprecher, Mirror, Mirror, 10–11; Thomas Laqueur, Making Sex: Body and Gender from the Greeks to Freud (Cambridge, Mass.: Harvard University Press, 1990), 31. Large size is prized in males throughout the world for much the same reasons: bigness is symbolically equated with power, strength, and forcefulness. "Bigness" may be measured in terms of morphology, but it may also be quantified in terms of objects, money, or accomplishments (Gilmore). Yet, bigness is also sexually exciting for females in ways that are often less symbolic of social than of purely erotic prowess. After all, Mae West said of her men, "Give me muscles," not "Give me millionaires." Penis size is of course relevant here as a kind of male "beefcake" (Hatfield and Sprecher). Yet interestingly, the ancient Greeks devalued penis size, and their idea of male anatomical perfection included a small penis, large ones being considered crass: "the preferred size was small and delicate" (Laqueur).

56. Nancy C. Baker, The Beauty Trap (New York: Franklin Watts, 1984); Brownmiller, Femininity; Wolf, Beauty Myth.

Lord Byron and Richard Francis Burton upon women of their day. Their very presence caused a virtual epidemic of mid-Victorian fainting. More recently, we are acquainted with the effect of good-looking public figures like Jack Kennedy. Handsome entertainers, like Elvis Presley in America and George Best and Paul McCartney in Britain, have caused near riots among female fans. Many television addicts remember the electricity caused by the appearance of strikingly handsome newsman Arthur Kent on CNN during the Gulf War. Intuitively understanding this, George Bush chose the good-looking, but possibly unqualified, Dan Quayle as his running mate in 1988, hoping to attract women voters and arousing the ire of many feminists. It is clear that, no matter what feminists or Victorians may say, male appearance is of critical importance to both men and women in Western culture. This concern has been elided in popular culture and sociological research for reasons of cultural bias: woman's culturally induced inhibition about expressing her sexual desires openly and man's equally culture-bound anxiety about appearing "vain" (that is, effeminate) by addressing the inner demons of bodily self-image.

Concern for male beauty is nothing new, not a product of recent feminist advances. It certainly predates Betty Friedan, Hollywood, and America, for that matter. Ancient Greek and Roman sculpture celebrates the male form more than the female. Indeed, male statues were more often nude than were female figures in classical antiquity. Properly proportioned musculature, not necessarily bulging muscles, was considered more stunning than female curvaceousness; hence the preponderance of Greek male nudes. Homer sings the praises of the winsome warrior, whose glistening, oiled body represents the Greek ideal of human sensuality. Vase painting depicts young men and boys in various seductive poses; the entire culture of ancient Greece worships the purely male sexual magnetism of the classically proportioned Adonis.[57] Not even Socrates was immune. There is, for example, the story of Critas and Charmides, in which Socrates discusses his intense feelings at the sight of a particularly gorgeous youth. And of course there are Greek and Roman myths of beautiful, godlike men who inspire passionate longings in girls and women, both mortal and divine.

A good example of the obscured power of male looks is found in the myth of Narcissus and Echo. Narcissus is the archetypical pretty boy, who, vain and

---

57. Thorkil Vanggaard, *Phallos* (New York: International Universities Press, 1972); Josine Blok and Peter Mason, *Sexual Asymmetry: Studies in Ancient Society* (Amsterdam: J. C. Gieben, 1987).

self-involved, ignores the allurements of swooning women, breaking countless hearts. In the myth, the object of sexual desire is the man, not the woman. The self-absorbed Narcissus excites so much female frustration that the angry gods drown him as punishment. Curiously, the very word used most often to disparage beautiful women, "narcissistic," derives thus from a male, not a female, model! The active-passive roles are reversed in this revealing myth.

In the Middle Ages, many romances and legends speak of the glories of masculine beauty. Walter Curry's book on medieval romances published in 1916[58] shows that Christian heroes were always depicted as physically gorgeous specimens: tall, muscular, robust, and winsome in physiognomy. English aristocrats in the early modern period were as concerned with masculine appearance as the ancients. Handsome men had a much better chance both of professional success and of marrying well did than their homely rivals. The spectacular rise of John Churchill, the Duke of Marlborough, for example, was said to be facilitated by his extraordinary physical beauty rather than by his mediocre intellectual capabilities.[59] The poets Byron and Shelley achieved fame and fortune both for their written work and for their delicate, yet romantically manly, appearance.

Male vanity did not start in the 1950s with Kooky and his comb, or in the 1970s with John Travolta and his precious hairdo. In fact, throughout history, men in Western societies have been aware of the power of their appearance both in winning women *and* in gaining advancement in the wider society. In Elizabethan England, men were notably vain about their looks. There are countless examples of male avatars and foppery in preindustrial Western culture: Shakespeare's "man of parts" and "man of wax" from *Romeo and Juliet*, and the pretty leg and "excellent head of hair" pridefully displayed by Sir Andrew Aguecheek in *Twelfth Night*. In Elizabethan England, men showed off their shapely legs in form-fitting tights and framed their genitals in bulging, bejeweled codpieces. English aristocrats, like the ancient Greeks, were very concerned about male beauty, and male elegance was a definite asset for social and political advancement in Britain, although perhaps less important than class. Like the Duke of Marlborough, the handsome Ramsey Macdonald owed part of his success to his physical appearance.[60] In the United States, studies of men at Princeton and Yale in the 1920s show that good looks were part of a

---

58. Curry cited in Marwick, *Beauty in History*, 67.
59. Ibid., 109–11.
60. Ibid., 309, 308.

positive evaluation of their peers and that men were as concerned about their beauty as college women were about theirs.[61]

In Italy, what Camille Paglia calls the "beautiful boy" syndrome marks all the Renaissance plastic arts.[62] A good example is Michelangelo's magnificent "David," which is always surrounded by admiring bevies of both gay men and women tourists. Perhaps this points to male archetypes of a purely physical elegance that can only be called beauty. It seems that men have always been evaluated as sex objects on the basis of appearance. Why have so many feminists ignored these facts?

Interestingly, when women have gained political power, they have responded powerfully to these male looks, rather as men do in response to voluptuous women. Freed from economic worries, Queen Elizabeth I flirted shamelessly with Raleigh, whose looks brought him temporarily to the pinnacle of royal favor. In Russia, Catherine the Great took a long list of comely, but otherwise ordinary, lovers—much to the dismay of her ministers. Today, many observers call the Russian Empress a nymphomaniac because of this wayward sexuality. Perhaps Catherine's behavior suggests how women would act if the double standard were eliminated by women's acquisition of political power. The point is that male beauty has always been recognized and esteemed. Moreover, it remains an underestimated aspect of human social relations and politics.

Belying conventional wisdom, sociological and psychological studies have shown that men in America today are almost as obsessed with their appearance as women are. Recent research summarized by Elaine Hatfield and Susan Sprecher shows that while 55 percent of women are dissatisfied with their appearance, the figure for men is 45 percent. Gay men are much more concerned about their looks than heterosexual women.[63] Other studies, based on extensive interviewing, have concluded that male self-esteem is as loaded toward physical appearance as female.[64] In fact, one may conclude that American men today are openly—as opposed to secretly—"beginning to define themselves in terms of outward appearance."[65] One sure sign of this is that

61. Paula Fass, The Damned and the Beautiful: American Youth in the 1920s (New York: Oxford University Press, 1977).

62. Paglia, Sexual Personae, 178.

63. Hatfield and Sprecher, Mirror, Mirror, 28–31.

64. Linda A. Jackson, Physical Appearance and Gender: Sociobiological and Sociocultural Perspectives (Albany: State University of New York Press, 1992), 186.

65. Robin T. Lakoff and Raquel L. Scherr, Face Value: The Politics of Beauty (Boston: Routledge & Kegan Paul, 1984), 235.

cosmetic surgery, once confined almost entirely to women, is now quite common among men. A recent article in the *San Francisco Chronicle* (2 June 1982) noted that cosmetic surgery for men is no longer a Hollywood phenomenon: at least 20 percent of the average cosmetic surgeon's practice is men. A sizable group of these men are eager for liposuction for flabby chest development or other body remodeling that they feel will bring them closer to the rigid cultural standards of masculinity. In America, male concerns seem to focus on two main issues: height and hair. As recent research has corroborated, most men are well aware that women want a man at least six inches taller than themselves.[66] Such an appreciation of the role of height for males goes back in sociological study at least to Pitirim Sorokin's 1927 correlation of stature with social mobility.[67] All Western men want to appear "tall in the saddle" or "tall, dark, and handsome," our culture's ideal for manliness.[68]

In America, as in most of the West, height in males is equivalent to voluptuousness in females and is equally salient in psychology and social relations. For men, "American society is a society with a heightist premise: to be tall is to be good and to be short is to be stigmatized."[69] Scientific research shows that the height of males correlates with the corresponding physical attractiveness of female partners in courtship.[70] A study of personal ads in periodicals found not only that 80 percent of women asked for a male at least six inches taller than themselves but that *all* females wanted a man at least four inches taller. For men, this feature in the partner was much less important, in fact almost irrelevant.[71] In his book on power, Michael Korda noted that "height means something to people, and it's wise not to forget it."[72] A man's height is critical when it comes to a political career. It has often been remarked that from 1900 to 1968, the taller of the two candidates for U.S. president was always the one elected. Richard Nixon was the first twentieth-century president to be elected over a taller opponent (George McGovern). This fact has not been lost on recent presidential candidates. For example, in the Bush-Dukakis debates of 1988, George Bush had the critical height advantage. Dukakis's

66. Hatfield and Sprecher, Mirror, Mirror, 203.

67. Pitirim Sorokin, *Social and Cultural Mobility* (Glencoe, Ill.: Free Press, 1927), 222–23.

68. Gordon L. Patzer, *The Physical Attractiveness Phenomenon* (New York: Plenum, 1985), 164–65.

69. Feldman, "Presentation of Shortness in Everyday Life," 1.

70. Patzer, *Physical Attractiveness Phenomenon*, 166.

71. Jackson, *Physical Appearance and Gender*, 173–74.

72. Michael Korda, *Power: How to Get It, How to Fight It* (New York: Random House, 1975), 51.

handlers spent weeks trying to neutralize this advantage with raised podiums and the like. Meanwhile Bush had to fight the "wimp" factor, not only because of his behavior, but also because of his effete, patrician looks. Jimmy Carter spent an inordinate amount of time disguising his stature, which, compared to Ford's and Reagan's, was rather diminutive (although he did have the hair advantage over Ford!). Keyes writes:

> The climax of Carter's efforts to keep us from realizing his height occurred during the first debate with Gerald Ford. Carter's camp was jittery at the thought of their candidate standing right next to the 6'1" Republican President for all the world to see who was bigger. For this reason they initially demanded that both debates be seated. Losing in this point, the Democrat's negotiators finally settled for the candidates' lecterns being placed far enough apart that the two men's height differences would not be so apparent. (In return the Democrats agreed to a background pale enough to camouflage Ford's paucity of hair).
>
> When the opponents finally faced off on national television, Jimmy Carter made their moment of physical proximity as short-lived as possible—by sticking his arm out stiffly to hold the President at bay as they briefly shook hands, then scurrying back to the safety of his lectern.[73]

Some commentators have suggested that John Kennedy beat out Hubert Humphrey in the 1960 primaries and Nixon in the presidential contest, because of his charismatic good looks. Other male politicians, like John Lindsay and Ronald Reagan, owed much of their success to their height and masculine elegance. A *Life* magazine profile in 1965 described Lindsay as an up-and-coming politician partly because of his "tall and handsome" appearance. Some American politicians have even resorted to cosmetic surgery to enhance their appeal to women voters. Scoop Jackson and David Duke both had surgery to remedy drooping eyelids. Such efforts are not confined to America. New Zealand's overweight Prime Minister David Lange underwent a dangerous stomach bypass operation in order to improve his appearance.[74]

Statistical research shows also that handsome men are more successful in their careers than are plain or puny ones. Taller men earn on the average

73. Ralph Keyes, *The Height of Your Life* (New York: Warner Books, 1980), 200.
74. Marwick, *Beauty in History*, 393, 13.

considerably more than short men in business and the professions.[75] A similar situation holds in professional sports. Handsome ball players may see their careers advanced by their looks rather than by talent. A good example is baseball's darkly handsome Lee Mazzilli, formerly of the New York Mets. A mediocre hitter and poor fielder, Mazzilli was rehired by the Mets in 1987, after an unsuccessful tryout. According to later management admissions, this was done to attract female fans to Shea Stadium. Certainly Frank Gifford's career, both in football and later in broadcasting, was enhanced by his square-jawed model's physiognomy.

Hair, as well as height and musculature, is important to a man's self-image. Many men interviewed by social psychologists expressed an obsessive fear of hair loss. Baldness is the great male fear, corresponding to a woman's fear of aging, for our culture has stressed, "To be sexy a man must have hair."[76]

My own interviews with men aged 30 to 50 have shown a similar vanity. Virtually every man I spoke to expressed deep-seated concerns about his outward appearance, many in terms that rival or surpass feminine self-involvement as reported in recent books on the "beauty trap." Men seem worried not only about their physical attractiveness in relation to sexual life but also about their masculinity as expressed in our culture's morphological imagery—a continual complaint. For men, bodily anxiety involves this secondary axis: a man is always worried about appearing unmasculine or feminine. This obsession especially attaches to body hair, chest development, waist, and hips. One man told of his anxieties about his chest, which he considered "breast-like, feminine." He finally underwent painful liposuction surgery to reduce the size of his chest—not an unusual extreme for men today. Another man spoke of his obsessive embarrassment about his lack of body hair, which he felt made him effeminate and "hideous." On the beach, he adopted a curious "penguin-like" walk (as he called it), keeping his arms at his sides, and declined to participate in games because of his fear of revealing his hairless armpits. Every man in the sample expressed similar fears about the inadequacy of his body shape or hair, musculature, height, neck size, weight, or hip size. These passionate worries struck me as no less poignant than those expressed by women on the same subject in feminist work on female victimization. Our culture, while stressing female bodily beauty as more critical, lays considerable stress on a manly physique and a stereotypical masculinity as attributes defining a man's worth.

75. Jackson, *Physical Appearance and Gender*, 174–75.
76. Lakoff and Scherr, *Face Value*, 231.

Thus, it appears that the ugly but beautiful bear in the Spanish proverb may be somewhat more ambiguous than it appears—at least in a large number of cultures, both preliterate and industrial.

The Good Male Body: Aesthetics and Ethics

We have seen that the male body is evaluated by various criteria in different cultures. In some of these, the male body becomes a passive sex object replacing the female; in others, as in classical antiquity, males are admired for their aggressive force and the nobility of their manly musculature. A few cultures, like the Mende (and Victorian England) regard male beauty as a metaphor for moral qualities of character. Interestingly, there appears to be no obvious correlation between the degree of power enjoyed by one sex and the degree of aesthetic or sexual objectification. While women's political position is higher among the Mende, female sexual freedom reaches an apex among the nearby Wodaabe, where women's political-economic position is relatively low.

We can draw a few conclusions from these data. For one thing, we see that males are almost as involved with their bodies as females are, although the angle of interest varies, involving more concepts of function. Female voluptuousness, on the other hand, is only indirectly related to fertility and child-rearing—women's ideal roles in virtually all cultures. Thus we see in many cultures that males' anxieties about their bodies relate as often to fears of appearing effeminate as to narcissistic fears of being ugly. These fears about masculinity run very deep, and it seems evident that such apprehensions cause psychic damage as profound as female concerns about appearance. My own interviews have shown that males' distorted body imagery is as profound and as obsessive as that of females—although, again, much of this worry has to do with apprehension at appearing "unmasculine."

Aside from the reversals of sexual roles we see in the Sahel and in areas of New Guinea, we also detect an interesting conflation of male physical ideals with ethical and ethnonational ideals. The Platonic association of the "beautiful" with the "good," the belief that physical beauty is a sign of interior or spiritual beauty, originates with the Greeks and runs as a thread throughout Western Christian civilization.[77] Yet such beliefs are not confined to the West and in fact are common throughout the world. For example, like classical

77. Umberto Eco, *Art and Beauty in the Middle Ages* (New Haven: Yale University Press, 1986).

Greek, many African languages, Navaho, and countless other non-Western tongues use the same term to mean both virtuous and beautiful.[78] Concepts of beauty virtually always represent visual metaphors for what Hatcher calls a culture's "normative postulates."[79] As Leach puts it, "Everywhere there is some intimate relationship between ethics and aesthetics."[80] This merging of aesthetics and ethics, pulchritude and probity, is, incidentally, a theme that remains strong—if unconscious—in our own culture's attitude toward human physical beauty, male and female. Psychological research shows that Americans perceive beautiful people (both sexes) as being not only happier, but morally better: "more intelligent, sensitive, kind, interesting, sociable";[81] in other words pretty people reflect those character virtues cherished by our own particular culture.[82]

The conflation of moral and visual properties leads to some curious associations when it comes to the physical attributes of the male. Frequently in patriarchal societies, and especially where warfare is practiced or where the group is threatened from without, masculine force and power are associated with group survival, so that qualities signifying masculinity are tied to the group's continued existence and prosperity, just as femininity is tied to its reproductive success. In these cases, male physique takes on a mystical or emblematic status reifying group self-image as a superior human "type" with military or chauvinistic overtones. This is true among the African and Melanesian peoples we have looked at, where all young men are warriors and their virile robustness is associated with an energetic defense of the group and its core values. For women of a group with this formal "type" of idealization, masculinity becomes both morally admirable and "sexy."

78. Gary Witherspoon, *Language and Art in the Navajo Universe* (Ann Arbor: University of Michigan Press, 1977), 151; Hatcher, *Art as Culture*, 129; John C. Messenger, "The Role of the Carver in Anang Society,"in *The Traditional Artist in African Societies*, ed. Warren d'Azevedo (Bloomington: Indiana University Press, 1973), 121; Susan Vogel, *Beauty in the Eyes of the Baule* (Philadelphia: ISHI, 1980); James Fernandez, "The Exploitation and Imposition of Order: Artistic Expression in Fang Culture," in *The Traditional Artist in African Societies*, ed. Warren d'Azevedo (Bloomington: Indiana University Press, 1973), 201–20. Among Ibo speakers in Nigeria, the same word *mfon* means both "beautiful" and "good," and in the Anang language, *idiok* means both "ugly" and "evil" (Messenger). Among the Baule of the Ivory Coast, all aesthetic terminology has also a moral sense: good/beautiful and bad/ugly are "inseparable pairs" (Vogel). Similarly the Fang people of Western Equatorial Africa conflate moral and aesthetic terms (Fernandez); Anderson, *Calliope's Sisters*, 131.

79. Hatcher, *Art as Culture*, 129.

80. Leach, "Aesthetics," 38.

81. Patzer, *Physical Attractiveness Phenomena*, 8.

82. Karen K. Dion, Ellen Berscheid, and Elaine Walster, "What Is Beautiful Is Good," *Journal of Personality and Social Psychology* 24 (1972): 285–90.

A good Western example of this tendency appears among the ancient Greeks, who regarded male physical beauty as morally superior to female. This moral primacy of male beauty, this "exaltation of maleness," consists of "the complete organization of the body as the supreme instrument of vital energy," in accordance with ethnocentric Greek ideals of nobility and chauvinistic self-imagery.[83] The cultural equation underlying this reification may be rendered as: "We as a people *are* what we *do*. Since men *do* and women *are*, male traits are a superior reflection of group spirit. Male beauty most fully represents us." We are reminded of the emphasis among the Wodaabe on the large nose as the essence of tribal self-identity.[84]

The exaltation of maleness as both heroic and beautiful leads to a dualism in male consciousness of the male body. Like women, men are concerned about their appearance in a social-sexual sense, much more so than previous observers have admitted. Yet a powerful secondary residual stress is placed upon physiologically "male" traits, such as robustness, height, body mass, and powerful musculature, which are "beautiful" in so far as these traits symbolize normative postulates apotheosizing and glorifying ethnic identity. Thus males are confronted with dangers of narcissistic injury from two sides: they fear ostracism and sexual rejection as ugly, puny, "rubbish man," and so forth. They also, however, experience the deeper psychic terror of failing literally to embody national ideals, not to mention anxieties they suffer about their carefully defended self-presentation as "masculine." What we can learn from the anthropological material presented here, then, is that the male body and consequently the male psyche, like the female, is a punishing crucible in which the ego is painfully subjected to the tyranny of the Ideal. One hopes that such observation will lead to a more productive dialogue between male and female writers on this subject.

83. Paglia, *Sexual Personae*, 159.

84. Sander Gilman, *The Jew's Body* (New York: Routledge, 1991). This use of positive physical stereotypes for political and chauvinistic ends is common in nationalist ideologies as a means of raising ethnic pride, as for example in the "Black is Beautiful" movement in the United States, or even—for more nefarious ends—the iconography of the "Great Blond Beast" in Nazi Germany, which was contrasted to "ugly" and "deformed" Jewish body stereotypes. Virtually all societies maintain human morphological ideals and self-images that symbolize and reinforce group identity, exclusiveness, or domination. Although normally a salutary stimulus to ethnic pride, under stress, such iconography can stir powerful and dangerous emotions. "We are better" also means, to many, "We are more beautiful."

12

Model Women

Mary G. Winkler

It is as if Venus looked in her mirror

and saw the face of Medusa

—D. M. Thomas, *The White Hotel*

On my television screen one morning, between news of atrocities in Bosnia and a story about breast cancer, a young, very svelte woman rose from a very blue swimming pool, looked deeply into the camera and announced in reassuring tones, "Nobody is perfect." Was she a contemporary avatar of the foamborn goddess come to relieve the anxiety created by the day's news? Indeed, the news often seems to warrant some reassurance about our collective or individual failures at love or the inexorable fact of our mortal condition: *nobody* is perfect. But this secular Aphrodite was on no such merciful or portentous mission. Rather, she was selling the services of a group of cosmetic surgeons. No *body* is perfect. More explicitly, no *female body is perfect*.

Now, this message comes as no great revelation to most American women. The concept so permeates our culture that it borders on cliché. The idea that the female body requires camouflage, alteration, or re-creation is promulgated regularly in the media. For example, a recent issue of *Woman's Day* (17 November 1990) blazons this question on its cover: "Hate Your Body? Clothes to Hide Every Bulge." In the same month *Vanity Fair* quoted David Geffen, a producer friend of Cher's, "Cher truly is a figment of her own imagination."[1] This article listed rumors of the star's numerous cosmetic surgeries, noted that she is "both sculptor and sculpture," and quoted her revelation that she herself is unsure whether her resculpting is the result of self-love or self-hate.[2]

If the message is that no body is perfect, its corollary is that each individual should strive to rise above this universal, but pathetic, condition and do her utmost to approximate an ideal as rigid as the canons of proportion set forth in classical antiquity and reworked in the Renaissance. Unlike these canons, the contemporary canon is not esoteric knowledge. Without pausing to reflect, the average American woman can call its particulars to mind. She knows that they are exemplified in the body of the high-fashion model: tall beyond the average (at least five feet, ten inches), "with a long, slender neck like the stem of a flower; a small head; long arms and legs; large hands and feet; small breasts; no thighs."[3] The canon also stipulates youth and something magazine copy consistently refers to as a "toned" body. There is one more important feature. The ideal female body has an extremely flat abdomen.

When an ordinary individual deviates from the canonical ideal, she frequently castigates herself mercilessly. Even if she does not have an eating disorder, she has learned to speak of a restaurant meal or an office treat as representative of the rankest, most swinish gluttony. Young women ritually address each other in front of department store mirrors. "I'm so fat." "Look how it pouches in front." "Thunder thighs!" Acting as the chorus to the tragedienne of bodily imperfection are the agents of popular culture and, often, the medical community.

The story of talk-show host Oprah Winfrey is a case in point. Winfrey, who has lost and gained weight in the past several years, is again slender. In January 1991, however, *People* magazine devoted several pages to Winfrey's weight regain after a widely publicized 1988 diet. What is noteworthy about the article (besides the fact that it was written at all) is the tone, which is censorious and even gloating. The author tells Winfrey's story in these terms: she "dropped out" of her diet group, "kissed off" maintenance programs—and opened a

1. Kevin Sessums, "Cher Starred and Feathered," *Vanity Fair* (November 1990), 168.
2. Ibid., 228, 232.
3. Holly Brubach, "In Fashion," *New Yorker* (June 10, 1991), 84.

restaurant! The conclusion: "Her own actions made piling the pounds on inevitable."[4] Lest the reader fail to grasp the significance of Winfrey's failure, a medical opinion is introduced. Dr. Theodore B. Van Itallie, professor emeritus of medicine at Columbia University in New York, draws the lesson from Winfrey's experience: "If patients simply lose weight and then *don't make permanent changes* in eating and exercising, regain is inevitable."[5]

What Dr. Van Itallie seems to suggest is a change as complete and fundamental as the change of heart Christian theology requires for salvation. Holly Brubach, whose words earlier delineated the model's ideal form, describes how we connect the beautiful and the good. In America, she writes, there is a "longstanding faith that the practice of virtue produces beauty in those who weren't born with it."[6] When we speak of faith and virtue in the context of physical improvement, we have entered a thought world where the subject is thoroughly secular but the language is that of morality and theology. Words like *despair*, coupled with *self-loathing* or *self-hatred*, seem to echo the language of Puritan theology. But the Puritan "abject sinner" despairs for her soul, not a protruding belly or "thunder thighs." Words like "make permanent changes" or "ideal" resonate eerily when heard in the context of the culturally prescribed tension between each individual's very particular body and the, by definition, unattainable ideal of physical perfection.

Vogue magazine's tribute to the New York City Ballet's Darci Kistler uses the ballerina to describe by implication the dilemma for all women seeking physical perfection: "Ballerina is a title of respect: it connotes achievement as well as the cruelly undemocratic process of natural selection that determines who can even aspire to be one. A women must work to become a ballerina, yet no amount of work will guarantee that she will."[7] This sounds strangely like a commingling of evolutionary theory and predestination theology. Work hard, but work is no guarantee. "Natural selection" may prevent your even "aspiring." You have to have the right stuff, good genes, or divine grace.

Most people have at least some understanding of the work a woman must do to become a ballerina. She must begin young, as a child. She must devote herself to an exacting life of rigorous, even tortuous, physical self-discipline so that she may eventually learn to use her very material, gravity-drawn body to create the illusion of immateriality and even transcendence of the body's

4. *People Weekly* (January 14, 1991), 84.
5. Ibid. My italics.
6. Brubach, "In Fashion," 95.
7. *Vogue* (February 1991), 224.

natural laws. Lincoln Kirstein celebrated the ballet and its dancers in these terms: "The essence of ballet . . . is order. What one sees in Balanchine's ballets are structures of naked order, executed by celebrants who have no other aim than to show an aspect of order in their own persons, testifying to an impersonal purity and a personal interest." Kirstein identifies the work of the ballerina with a search for "unfamiliar access to an absolute." The ballet is a rite in which the audience feels "corroborated in the hope that, despite the world and its horrors, here somehow is a paradigm of perfection."[8]

This is indeed a high calling. What Kirstein suggests when he writes of order and "impersonal purity" is that the rigors of the dancer's life are about something beyond the self and that, because the dancer subdues her body to deprivation and pain, she may experience the joy of creating order, which she in turn offers to her audience. What Kirstein describes is an asceticism akin to that of the medieval women ascetics whose lives Carolyn Bynum has studied with such sensitivity: "These women . . . afflicted their bodies in world-denial and sought, in considerable frenzy, the ecstasy of mystical union. But they all served their neighbors quite actively. . . . Ascetic suffering is both union-ecstatic, glorious, pleasurable union—with the suffering Christ and . . . service of one's fellows."[9]

In the case of the ballerina, at least while she is offering her art, beauty and virtue may unite. But what of the myriad women who fast, binge/purge, sweat, strain, pluck, prune (often with medical assistance), shop and suffer in their own pursuit of a paradigm of perfection"? What of the woman who works toward the ideal our culture places before her, knowing that "no amount of work can guarantee" that her efforts will transform her into Linda Evangelista? What is the absolute they seek, and why in spite of all the striving and dedication are they rewarded with self-loathing and unending dissatisfaction? Recent scholarship, especially feminist scholarship, offers sophisticated analyses of self-image and body politics. Investigations into perception, the use of images, and the psychology of the "gaze" have deepened understanding of the multidimensional relationship between object and viewer. A review of some of this scholarship serves as a guide in understanding the tensions and contradictions inherent in our construction of the ideal "good body."

In an important article, "Reading the Slender Body," Susan Bordo asserts

8. Lincoln Kirstein, "Maker and Teacher," *New York Book Review of Books*, 30, no. 4 (March 17, 1983), 8.

9. Carolyn Walker Bynum, *Fragmentation and Redemption: Essays on Gender and the Human Body in Medieval Religion* (New York: Zone Books, 1991), 69.

that preoccupation with fat, diet, and exercise may "function as one of the most powerful normalizing strategies of our century." She observes that this strategy of self-discipline may result in the very slender, toned body beloved of fashion designers and their prophets, but also produces "docile bodies habituated to self-discipline and self-improvement." She posits that the current cultural ideal of beauty appeals because it offers freedom from "the encumbrance of domestic, reproductive femininity" while simultaneously suggesting fragility and lack of power over social space. She concludes that the ideal thus reveals contradictions in the "social body" having to do with "cultural management of female desire and female flight from a purely reproductive destiny.[10]

John Fiske perceives even deeper implications for self-discipline (or lack of it) according to cultural norms. He argues that as the body is "where the power-bearing definitions of social and sexual normality are, literally, embodied," the meanings of beauty and health are emphatically sociopolitical. Thus, acceptance or refusal of the cultural ideal can be a powerful political utterance—even if only dimly understood by those making the statement. Fiske notes that corpulence, once a visible sign of what used to be called "substance," may now be a sign of resistance or subversion. Thus, the imperfect body may operate as a sign of working-class rebellion or as feminist self-assertion, refusing "the incarnation of patriarchy on the female body."[11] I am reminded here of Carolyn Heilbrun's observation that it requires courage for a middle-aged woman to gain weight,[12] or of this statement from Vogue: "There are . . . two kinds of fat girls: good fat girls who want to be thin; and bad fat girls who are in your face like militant blacks and homosexuals."[13]

Already, I think we can see where the tensions and contradictions lie. The slender body (when it is achieved against nature) resists patriarchy by renouncing a "purely reproductive destiny." The fat body resists patriarchy, or the values of the culture, by refusing the self-discipline required to achieve the ideal; in common parlance, it is a body that has "let itself go." The slender, consciously formed body signifies self-control (the opposite of "letting go") in a society dazzling with the sensual attraction of consumer goods as well as obedience to the norms. We mortify the flesh to atone for greed and to declare

10. Susan Bordo, "Reading the Slender Body," in Body/Politics, Women and the Discourses of Science, ed. Mary Jacobus, Evelyn Fox Keller, Sally Shuttleworth (New York and London: Routledge, 1990), 85, 88.

11. John Fiske, Understanding Popular Culture (Boston: Unwin Hyman, 1989), 90, 93.

12. Carolyn G. Heilbrun, Writing a Woman's Life (New York and London: W. W. Norton, 1988), 54.

13. Tracy Young, "Television," Vogue (March 1991), 286.

to our fellows that we are engaged in attending to our selves and are therefore no threat to the status quo in the body politic. To sum up, the ideal female body may signal refusal of a "purely reproductive destiny" while simultaneously displaying obedience to the ideals delineated by medical and consumer culture. Surely, this is a hard act to perfect: like the ballerina, the ideal woman must work hard, with no guarantee that her work will ever produce its desired end.

Finally, the ideal woman must willingly present herself for inspection. She must constantly monitor her own appearance for "flaws" or "blemishes" or "bulges," and she must consent to become the object of the observation of others. At least that is what advertising copy seems to suggest. As Carole Spitzack observed, the striving for beauty contains a paradox. In order to achieve the individuality that attends beauty, one must become very self-focused. In order to fit the cultural expectations of beauty—which will in turn mark one as individual—one must obtain an objective vantage point. In other words, one must become one's own mirror, submitting oneself continually to one's own scrutiny, as if one's own eye were the critical eye of the culture. Drawing on the work of John Berger and Michel Foucault, Spitzack notes that women become "at once the surveyor and the surveyed," learning to internalize the gaze of others in order to police their own visual image.[14]

I am convinced that these arguments greatly advance our understanding of the problem of self-loathing, but I want to speak of some of my own insights based on a study of photographs of models in some popular women's magazines. The magazines selected are Glamour, Mademoiselle, Mirabella, Elle, Vogue, and Allure. The implied reader of these magazines is a young urban career woman with an interest in fashion. Although the focus is emphatically on clothing, hairstyles, and makeup, there are also numerous articles and photographic essays on what might loosely be called "life-style." There are book and movie reviews and regular columns on medicine and health, food, and sexual and business etiquette. Frequently, these magazines run glossy articles about celebrities. Blander than Cosmopolitan, and less conservative than Good Housekeeping, they are mildly "politically correct" (that is, they are collectively against date rape and child abuse, for safe sex, tentatively pro-choice, and tolerant of sexual diversity) while maintaining the hip, aggressively urban stance required of arbiters of fashion.

There are two more points to be made. First, the magazines' editorial

14. Carole Spitzack, Confessing Excess: Women and the Politics of Body Reduction (Albany: State University of New York Press, 1990), 49, 34.

voices frequently affect an uncomfortable mixture of chumminess and cen-
sure. Questions of appearance are handled with the grave and admonitory
tone appropriate to the most pressing social concerns, and the reader is led via
text and pictures to a faith in the vision of the fashion industry, one true ideal of
the beautiful and the good. Second—and this is crucial—the pictorial layouts
are exceedingly pleasing to look at. The advertisements for cosmetics and
clothing are luscious and elegant, the fashion photography is artful, even
artistic. Thus, the reader is being schooled, guided, and admonished even as
she is being dazzled and seduced with creamy light, glowing color, and elegant
composition. She is offered a visual feast. And the centerpiece of the feast is the
model—the model of fashion and the model woman. This woman is the end
to which all articles on grooming, diet, business savvy, gynecological tips, and
political issues are directed. The makeup and health tips, "issue" articles, and
clothing all unite around the model to form one image (or set of related
images): that of the ideal woman. What kind of woman is she?

In exploring the meaning of the images and of the ideal they represent, I
begin with the thesis that the women who buy the magazines identify with the
images in some way. I posit that the viewer (with a greater or lesser degree of
perspective and skepticism) enters into a tacit relationship with the image that
may be reciprocal or even symbiotic. In other words, I explicitly do not argue
that the images are imposed on the women who adore them; I believe the
relationship between viewer and model woman is much more subtle and
complex. It might be illuminating in this regard to consider the use of printed
images in the history of European culture. David Freedberg, writing on religious images in western Christian culture, has much to say about the relationship between image and viewer that is pertinent to our discussion. In *The Power
of Images*, Freedberg argues that "for hundreds and hundreds of years [people]
used . . . images for directly affective purposes." He proposes that in our history
there is a long tradition of using "real" images to lead a worshiper by means of
empathic meditation to some absent entity, either "historical or spiritual."[15] In
other words, a worshiper forms an affective link, allowing the image to lead
him or her beyond the instance of the individual statue or picture to the ideal it
represents.

Freedberg's work on medieval religious icons is suggestive in the context
of advertising art. From the beginning, champions of images understood that

15. David Freedberg, *The Power of Images* (Chicago and London: University of Chicago
Press, 1989), 161.

they could school the "promiscuous and labile imagination"[16] toward an orthodox conception of the holy. If one imagines the models of advertising art as icons of our own culture, one may see how they define and shape individual women's self-image. These images are secularized remnants of a very ancient practice: the use of images as the foundation for self-reformation through empathy and emulation.

In studying the images in fashion magazines, I found four distinct types of poses. There are certainly others, but the four under discussion recur again and again. I have, somewhat fancifully, named these "mirror image," "woman as column," "splayed woman," and "woman with accessory man."

The "mirror image" woman is by far the most common and familiar type. Her number is legion. In these images the woman looks at the camera lens as if in a loving trance. The lens acts like a mirror, first reflecting the gaze of the "real" model, then offering her image to the magazine reviewer to mirror for her her fantasy self as the ideal woman. The models themselves are aware of this aspect of their work. On the 29 October 1991 *Today Show*, Christy Turlington observed, "Because we don't talk, people can imagine anything they want to about us."

The "column woman" conforms most closely to the type discussed by feminist scholars. This type seems most apt for the accusation leveled at the cultural ideal of the super-slender body. Typically the woman is whippet thin and posed so as to seem to have no anatomical features but legs. A recent Krizia ad, for example, poses a model in a short sheath dress against a plain backdrop. Her face is obscured by the brim of her hat, and her thin body makes a dark exclamation point on the white page. She is an abstraction of elegance, not an individual woman at all. In a Ralph Lauren ad for "footwear-hosiery," a model descends a staircase accompanied by her own shadow. The camera has cut off her head, so she also lacks personal identity. Moreover, one arm has been "amputated" by the airbrush, so as not to detract from the smooth line of her slender silhouette. She is indeed a shadow of herself. The columnar woman is often photographed alone, centered on the bare page so as to focus the eye on the isolated, tubular form—no hated "bulges" are allowed to mar the elegant geometry of these Galateas.

The "splayed woman" seems to me to be the most peculiar and provocative of all. This type appears in a variety of guises, some quasi-playful, others aggressively erotic, but all characterized by a bold, yet awkward, straddling

16. Ibid., 169.

stance. I want to begin by describing two Bettina Riedel advertisements which appeared in several fashion magazines in 1990–91. In each ad the photograph of a young woman is superimposed on a photograph of the New York skyline. The woman is gigantic, dominating the foreground with her size and with her pose: legs spread, arms akimbo. Her height corresponds to the length of the page, and her body is abstracted into a great inverted Y or a triangle. The pose is curious, simultaneously contrived and natural, carefree but uncomfortable. The message: young, carefree, modern (or postmodern), the model dominates her environment.

An even more provocative example is a Bergdorf Goodman ad for the work of designer Issey Miyake. The photograph is quite handsome and intriguing; the woman it shows has, however, become even more abstracted than her sisters, a pattern of angles and shadows, her face obscured. The whole composition is a pattern of inverted V. Where the other women retained a semblance of individual personality, this woman has become a robot-like object. The paramilitary stance of the other women is here transformed into an abstract form suggesting a witty threat. It is witty because the slight figure splayed across the visual space is not a weighty enough presence to carry out the threat implied in the bellicose stance.

The splayed stance appears, but further undermined, in a fashion layout from *Vogue*. The woman in these photographs is very young and playful—her girlish face, cropped hair, and self-deprecating laugh transform the splayed stance into a charmingly gawky ballet. Like her sisters, she fully dominates (in double) her pictorial space, but she wears a dress that is scarcely more than a chemise. She is like a little girl dressing up in a grown-up pose, but the grown-ups she is emulating seem like confused refugees from *Star Wars*.

Four more examples I find even more unnerving. In the first, a very long-legged model straddles the page in what looks like a Mondrian bathing suit (red and white sections banded with black). As in the pinup genre, she wears nothing else but earrings and stiletto-heeled, ankle-strap shoes. What is this picture about? This is a sophisticated woman, no recent college graduate eager to climb the corporate ladder, no coltish coquette. She has a hauteur that I find in uncomfortable disjunction with what appears to be the stop-frame of an awkwardly performed striptease. In another image, this from *Mirabella* (March 1991) the model's splayed pose transforms into a feral slouch; in the third, a Gianni Versace layout for *Vogue*, the model strikes a pose laden with sadomasochistic connotations to display the rich embroidery of a very expensive bathing suit.

Last, there is a layout from the initial issue of *Allure* in which the model is displayed like a frog on a dissecting table (Figure 1). In all cases, it is important to note the camera angle. All shots are from below, and all focus on an inverted V of the woman's spread legs. Of course, this serves the function of making the models' long, slender legs seem even longer than they really are. But the angle also makes the camera into a voyeur—in one instance the camera actually looks up the young model's dress. In each instance the visual focus of the picture is the woman's genital area. The images under discussion are only a sampling of a very large number of images. The splayed-leg pose, however, occurs so often that it is truly a type. The erotic message is seldom delivered undiluted. Usually there is ambiguity evoking ideas of action, freedom, and authority, while simultaneously suggesting a double-faced threat and a peculiar eroticized disequilibrium. The models are alone, they are women free of conventional strictures. They are slim, "toned," sexual, and very much on display.

Finally, there is the "woman with accessory man." This type is a double portrait, woman and man, and the relationship between them deserves attention. I will describe three that I find typical. The first example contains the salient features of the type. A beautiful, somewhat petulant young woman stands in the foreground. Her long hair is wind-blown or artfully tousled. She is wearing a tight, white-ribbed sweater (Ralph Lauren, $220), a black bathing-suit bottom, and a wide black patent-leather belt. She stands, gazing slightly upward out of the picture and past the camera, her back arched slightly in a way that accentuates her breasts, her lips slightly parted. No question that she is meant to be read as an object of erotic desire. Moreover, she is not alone. Behind her, but not touching her, is a young man in every way as physically polished as she is. He does not, however, seem to take notice of her existence but rather serves as a backdrop and foil (he, too, wears black and white) for her seductive beauty.

In another quite witty photograph the same noninteraction occurs. Here the female model strikes an athletic pose on a beach, while behind her Mikhail Baryshnikov (!) nonchalantly protects her from the sun with a large striped parasol. He—very certainly a sex symbol as well as a figure admired for his trained, disciplined body—is as indifferent to the model as is the man in the other photograph. Nevertheless, the star of ballet and film allows himself to appear as servant and accessory to the anonymous model.

Finally, there is a recent ad campaign for Guess? in which the young German model Claudia Schiffer cavorts on a Greek island: "A Holiday for

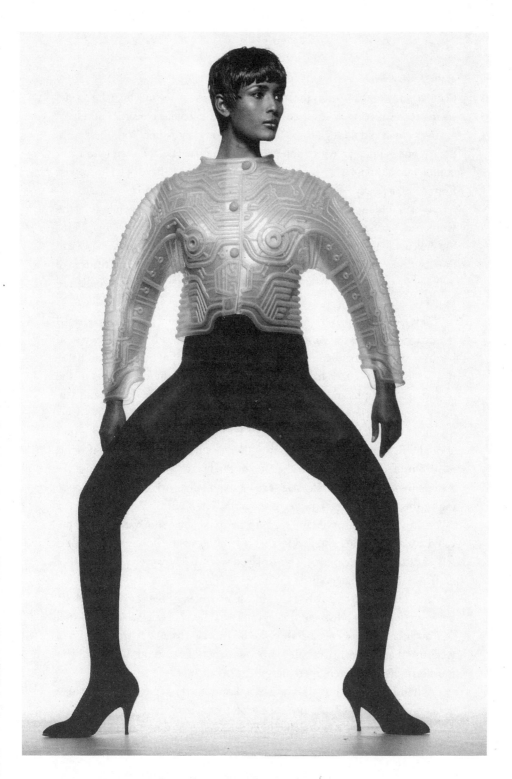

Photograph © Patrik Andersson.

Claudia in Mykonos." Surely the most startling scene is one in which the model seems to be playing waitress in a cafe whose clientele consists entirely of "native" males old enough to be her father—or grandfather. With the exception of one gentleman with a splendid white moustache, the men ignore her completely, although she wears a costume that seems to have been borrowed from *Never on Sunday*—tight dark skirt, tight striped knit sweater.

What I find most striking about these photographs is that, while all of the women are eroticized, while they strut and preen, they seem to be invisible to the men in their company. This undercutting of expectations is most marked in the Claudia Schiffer advertisements, where the reader's awareness of the role of women in traditional Mediterranean culture makes the scene even more piquant.

This extended analysis of several typical poses should offer some sense of the images presented to American fashion magazine readers. The discussion began with talk of perfection, tension and contradiction, theology and ballerinas. It is now my task to clarify the relationship of these concepts to the fashion photographs and to attempt some explanation of the despair and self-loathing many women confess.

In D. M. Thomas's novel *The White Hotel*, the fictionalized Freud writes about his fictional patient. Reflecting on her case he observes, "It is as if Venus looked in her mirror and saw the face of Medusa."[17] Venus and Medusa are ancient personifications of female sexuality, and I believe I see them reappearing in the advertisements under discussion. The "Mirror Woman" and the "Woman with Accessory Man" seem to be quite straightforward, uncomplicated avatars of Venus, the goddess who symbolizes the power of the erotic, whose attribute is the mirror. The "splayed woman," however, is rather more elusive—and more suggestive.

The French psychoanalyst Gérard Miller writes of the "sexual standoff" between (female) models and (male) photographers: *La beauté absolut et l'horreur de la castration!* He observes that there is "no more horrifying representation of woman" than these inaccessible embodiments of "absolute beauty" "who transform these impotent men into pillars of salt."[18]

When I was preparing this article, I discussed the types of stance with a colleague, saying that I was not sure what to make of the splayed pose. He suggested that I review my mental catalogue of art-historical images and ask myself what they reminded me of. Instantly, without thought, I called to mind

17. D. M. Thomas, *The White Hotel* (New York: Viking Press, 1981), 8.
18. Quoted by Brubach, "In Fashion," 87, from an article in French *Vogue*, March 1991.

the image of the Medusa. In the myth, Medusa is one of the three monstrous Gorgons. Serpent-haired, she destroys all who look at her until the hero, Perseus, beheads her by means of a strategem (he holds up a mirror and does not look at her directly). She has an important afterlife, however, in art and in early psychoanalytic interpretation.

Erich Neumann connects her immediately with the image of the destructive female: "The Gorgons, metallic-winged, serpent haired and serpent engirdled . . . with protruding tongues are urobic symbols of what we might justly call the 'Infernal Feminine.' Their sisters are the Graeae whose name means Fear and Dread. Among the symbols of the devouring chasm we must count the womb in its frightening aspect, the numinous heads of the Gorgon and the Medusa."[19]

In "The Medusas's Head," Sigmund Freud offered his interpretation of the relationship between the Medusa's head and what Erich Neumann called the "devouring chasm." Noting that the mythic figure appears in the stories of at least twenty-five peoples, Michael Grant picked up Freud's idea that the head wreathed in snakes represents female genitalia and used it in his discussion of the Perseus myth. The meaning of the figure, Freud asserted is fear of castration.[20] Finally, J. E. Cirlot defines the Gorgon as the "symbol of fusion of opposites: mobility and immobility, beauty and horror."[21]

Certainly, one can see the fusion of mobility and immobility in the photographs of the "splayed woman" and, in the fusion of opposites, a way of illuminating the tensions and contradictions that so many critics of contemporary society perceive.

Applying the Freudian theories of film critics, Laura Mulvey and Gaylyn Studlar open the subject to even deeper interpretation. In an important article, "Visual Pleasure and Narrative Cinema," first published in 1975, Mulvey set out to study film as a reflection of "straight, socially established interpretation of sexual difference . . . which controls images, erotic ways of looking, and spectacle." Applying Freudian theory, she concluded that in cinema the representation of the female body "speaks castration and nothing else." She concluded that in film woman stands "as a signifier for the male other . . . tied to her

19. Sigmund Freud, "The Medusa's Head," *Imago* 25 (1940): 105. The manuscript is dated May 14, 1922, and was published posthumously: Erich Neumann, *The Origins and History of Consciousness* (Princeton, N.J.: Princeton University Press, 1970), 214; Michael Grant, *Myths of the Greeks and Romans* (New York: New American Library, 1962). 347–48.

20. Freud, "The Medusa's Head," 87.

21. J. E. Cirlot, *A Dictionary of Symbols*, trans. Jack Sage (New York: Philosophical Library, Inc., 1962), 115.

place as a bearer of meaning, not a maker of meaning. Her meaning is sexual difference, clearly demonstrable by her lack of a penis. Hence, she connotes the threat of castration and provokes male anxiety. The disavowal of this anxiety, said Mulvey, leads to a fetishistic fascination with some object or body part to replace the missing penis.[22]

Studlar built on Mulvey's thesis to discuss the function of costume, which she claimed functions to disguise the woman's castration. She argued that the whole woman can be fetishized by means of lighting, costume, and so forth. Thus, film can offer woman "as a comforting phallicized totality," sometimes with her body encased in a "phallic dress" of the type worn by Mae West (and, I add, later by Marilyn Monroe).[23] In the representations Studlar discusses, the women *become* phallic substitutes.

I found the work of Mulvey and Studlar very suggestive in terms of understanding my "model women," especially the "column woman" (type 2). But nothing is simple. Having found the *Dictionary of Symbols* so satisfying in its definition of the Gorgon, I decided to look up "column." I was not surprised to discover that this symbol has more meanings than the most obvious. Of course, Cirlot says, "there is a phallic implication," but the column also implies, "an upward impulse of self-affirmation." He further connects its meaning with the spinal column with its implications of autonomy, of "stiffening your spine" and "standing up for yourself."[24]

So, as with the "splayed woman," there is tension and contradiction. We return to the images with new eyes. Are they images of autonomy, freedom, and wholesome self-assertion; or are they about fetishized bodies costumed, posed, and displayed for an imagined—and eternally anxious—male gaze? Are they images of healthy, liberated female sexuality, or are they hypereroticized monsters? (A "monster" is by definition on display.) Are the women in the images pictures of health or obsessive body shapes? Are they models of self-control, or themselves controlled by a society that reads "bulges" as symptoms of lethargy, greed, hostility, and bad citizenship? Do they represent beautiful ideals or narcissistic reveries?

22. Laura Mulvey, "Visual Pleasure and Narrative Cinema," in *Issues in Feminist Film Criticism*, ed. Patricia Eterns (Bloomington and Indianapolis: Indiana University Press, 1990), 28, 29, 35.

23. Gaylyn Studlar, "Masochism, Masquerade and the Erotic," in *Fabrications: Costume and the Female Body*, ed. Jane Gaines and Charlotte Herzog (New York and London: Routledge, 1990), 231.

24. Cirlot, *Dictionary of Symbols*, 57, 58.

Poor Ophelia in her madness said, "Lord, we know what we are, but know not what we may be." Many women viewing the models may know neither who the models are nor who they themselves may be. Yet the whole society knows how to achieve the ideal good body: Self-denial and self-control are always tempered with the bittersweet recognition that the goal remains slightly beyond reach. A model woman (and this includes all women who work or dream toward the high-fashion ideal) must work hard with no guarantee that she will succeed. No body is perfect.

The layouts in the magazine photographs make implicit promises. Susan Bordo argues that one promise of the model body is an escape from the onerous implications of female physiology:in other words, pregnancy, child-birth, motherhood. Indeed, it is not difficult to imagine why a woman might today be deeply ambivalent about her reproductive function. The whole society has become increasingly anxious about women's bodies and mother-hood. Centuries-old expectations about reproduction and maternity have been altered beyond recognition in many segments of society. The ideal of western theological and legal teaching is no longer a clear and unquestioned imperative.

The legal right to abortion is one of the most passionately argued issues of our day. As new reproductive technologies have placed in human hands what was once the sole prerogative of God or of nature, ancient mythologies about mother and child, about the childbearing function of a woman's body, fade in the light of effective birth control and the medical knowledge to prevent the high rate of infant mortality that menaced parents for millennia. At the same time, social reformers view the increase in teenage pregnancy with alarm, and young professional women weigh the disabilities of the "mommy track" against the desire for a baby. Emily Martin, with wisdom and insight, observes that the lack of institutional support for mother and child care in a major industrial nation like the United States makes it truly difficult for a woman to be both "productive and reproductive" at the same time. In fact, she notes, "the only way to be realistic in the world of work is to be a man." Further, she describes two models that are incompatible: "pro-production" and "pro-reproduction."[25]

The images in the glossy fashion magazines may seem to offer a way out of the dilemma. The viewer may read the model body as a liberated body—a

25. Emily Martin, The Woman in the Body: A Cultural Analysis of Reproduction (Boston: Beacon Press, 1987), 100, 105.

body that is erotic without suggesting maternity. I agree with Bordo's reading of the slender body in this regard. But the eroticized body presented on MTV and in fashion layouts is not necessarily an easy body to acquire or to wear. When the body is displayed as aggressively eroticized, either as hostile Medusa or as object of a fetishistic gaze, the cultural lies about embodiment and sexuality are revealed. The eroticized body is presented as a body simultaneously free from the imperatives of gender (many aspects of the new canonical ideal are suggestive of a young boy's body) and free to use the body to display goods. As Mike Featherstone asserts, "The basic freedom in [our] culture is the freedom to consume."[26] The consumption, of course, has nothing to do with food. On the contrary, the more readily the body consumes goods to make it appear younger and more sexually available, the less it may welcome food. The more a lonely and trivial sexuality is offered as an ideal, the less is the awesome power of the erotic acknowledged.

Among the model women in the fashion magazines we find no image of an integrated, fully adult, sexual woman. Instead, the female viewer is offered the sight of other young women fetishized. Louise Kaplan poignantly asserts that women who pose in "suggestive or explicit postures" do so to reassure themselves that they will not be abandoned or annihilated. She is writing specifically here of stripteasers and pornography stars, but her insight may shed light on the type of ideal many of the fashion photographs promulgate. Kaplan notes that by displaying jewelry and frills, a woman may be indulging an unconscious fantasy that instead of her own "inadequate" body, she displays that of a phallic woman.[27] The images of women in fashion culture may seem to offer freedom from gender stereotyping, but in fact they evoke an erotic nightmare. The photographs offer the viewer images of danger, aggression, or uncertainty, which surely reflect our society's ambivalence about and fear of "liberated" women, women who don't "know their place" or function, "wild women." There is nowhere to go with these images, no road to development, only a choice between mirror-gazing Venus and destroying Medusa. (In the images of women with men, the men are no more than indicators of the models' erotic power.) There is no vision that incorporates all ideas of womanhood or femaleness. There is no vision of a love that is not self-love, focused

26. Mike Featherstone, "The Body in Consumer Culture," in *The Body: Social Process and Cultural Theory*, ed. Mike Featherstone, Mike Hepworth, and Bryan S. Turner (London: Sage Publications, 1991), 176.

27. Louise J. Kaplan, *Female Perversions: The Temptations of Emma Bovary* (New York: Doubleday, 1991), 257.

and self-absorbed; no vision of giving, nurturing, working, maturing, "letting oneself go." Carole Spitzack notes that we admire middle-aged women like Jane Fonda, who retain the bodies of adolescents; she continues, "The liberation promised by a reconstruction of youth, in effect, demands of all women confinement in a permanent state of adolescence."[28]

It is, therefore, small wonder that women like Cher do not know whether the continued making, unmaking, and remaking of themselves is motivated by self-love or self-hate. If the hated "bulges" only signify, in Spitzack's words, "women's sexual function [that] predisposes them to the illness of obesity and moral jeopardy,"[29] if the choices seem to be a mindless maternity, perpetual adolescence, or an incipient destructive power, is it any wonder that young (and not so young) women feel that they must strive eternally and with great effort to control themselves through ascetic exercises worthy of a medieval mystic?

In an ideal vision, biology is neither destiny nor the cause of damnation, but the ideal vision of the fashion world is of eroticism without connection, domination over nothing, little to do but engage in endless, worried contemplation of an imperfect self. George Orwell's admonition against an unbalanced striving for perfection seems poignantly applicable here:

> The essence of being human is that one does not seek perfection, that one is sometimes willing to commit sins for the sake of loyalty, that one does not push asceticism to the point where it makes friendly intercourse impossible, and that one is prepared in the end to be defeated and broken up by life, which is the inevitable price of fastening one's love upon other human individuals.[30]

Perfect means complete, lacking nothing essential to the whole. The images fashion culture offers women are incomplete, and therefore the ideal is forever unattainable. If the only ideal images are of dolls, Medusas, and phallic women, if the search for perfection must supersede love and self-transcendence, it is small wonder that women feel a need to atone for their female flesh by a ceaseless, untiring, and joyless asceticism. But it is the image that is imperfect, not the body.

28. Spitzack, *Confessing Excess*, 39–40.

39. Ibid., 11.

30. George Orwell, "Reflections on Gandhi," in *The Orwell Reader: Fiction, Essays and Reportage*, intro. Richard H. Rovere (New York and London: Harcourt Brace Jovanovich, 1956), 332.

Afterword

Mary G. Winkler

This book embodies the concerted work of a group of scholars representing disciplines that do not customarily speak to each other. We approached the body as both a cultural construction and a biological and social entity. Our immediate task was to examine the resurgence of asceticism in contemporary culture. As we came together from different backgrounds and disciplines to add our tesserae to the mosaic of body studies, we discovered that contemporary asceticism—perhaps all asceticism—has many faces.

The germ of the conference, and of the book, was the shared recognition that the current epidemic of eating disorders is only a symptom of a larger problem involving the interaction between embodied individual lives and societal norms. As Susan Bordo asserts, "The body—what we eat, how we dress, the daily rituals through which we attend the body—is a medium of culture. . . . Our conscious politics, social commitments, strivings for change, may be undermined and betrayed by the life of our bodies—not the craving, instinctual body imagined by Plato, Augustine and Freud but the docile, regulated body practiced at and habituated to the rules of cultural life."[1] It is exactly this "docile, regulated body"—the body in society—that is the focus of this book.

On two consecutive days, the morning talk-show host Sally Jessy Raphael offered what must together be seen as a postmodern bricolage commentary on American body culture. The first day Cher regaled the audience with routines from her exercise video, after chiding her sister for a slothful reluctance to join her in a daily workout. "You just have to make the commitment," she said sternly. The next day, talk-show host Sally Jessy Raphael presided over a beauty contest for obese women. The atmosphere was tense with pious "support" as a group of very heavy women carried out a parody of the Miss America pageant: swimsuit competition, talent competition, evening gown competition. On both programs women testified, perhaps a shade too intensely, that they felt good about themselves and their bodies. In the first case, the satisfaction derived from a body disciplined and formed into a multimillion-dollar commodity and a paragon of late twentieth-century female beauty. The women interviewed on the second day declared their triumph over cultural prejudices and expectations to achieve a sense of self-esteem and well-being *against* the American grain.

The audience gave equal applause to Cher's puritanical admonitions and to the confessions of the obese women. Everyone recognized that, however one views it, the body—especially the female body—is a problem. It is not a simple matter to "feel good about yourself," even if you are indeed "worth it." Feeling good about oneself may be the goal, but there is confusion about how to achieve that desired end as feeling good is attributed to diet plans, cereals, makeup, running shoes, and hair dye. The distance between the feeling and the larger concept of the good widens. What good do we feel when we feel good about ourselves? What is the self seeking? And how does the search affect attitudes toward the body?

One theme recurs again and again in discussion of the self about which one may *feel* good: control—in particular, self-control, which leads to a feeling of well-being, even triumph. Contemporary medical problems may, more than we customarily acknowledge, be related to issues of self-control. Eating disor-

1. *Gender/Body/Knowledge: Feminist Reconstructions of Being and Knowing*, ed. Alison M. Jaggar and Susan R. Bordo (New Brunswick and London: Rutgers University Press, 1989), 3.

ders, addictions of all kinds, the tendency to label any number of practices as addicting, the recent exercise mania, food fads, cosmetic surgery—all merge into practices of, or obsessions with, self-control.

The older term for practices of self-control and self-denial is asceticism. The past decade has witnessed a resurgence of scholarship on asceticism, particularly on the history of Christian asceticism. I am thinking here particularly of the work of Margaret Miles, Elaine Pagels, Peter Brown, and Caroline Walker Bynum. Equally interesting to scholars is the issue of social control of the body, the "cultural construction" of the body. This interest is broad enough and popular enough to have elicited a feature article on body scholarship in the *Journal of Higher Education*. Very likely this scholarly interest reflects and responds to a resurgence of a secularized asceticism and passion for control in our own culture. True ascetics are always a minority in any given culture, but the focus on a minority suggests the presence of symptoms of the movement within the larger culture. The virtue of the new research is that it enables a more sympathetic, less judgmental assessment of the ascetic impulse. Perhaps there is even an implicit and empathic dialogue between contemporary anorectics and body builders and their counterparts in late antiquity and the Middle Ages. Perhaps without real, living ascetics and their less devoted followers and imitators, we would continue to be horrified by accounts of desert fathers and female mystics, seeing them solely in the light of psychopathology or as flat caricatures of body haters. Thanks to recent scholarship they may seem less bizarre and more (if dimly) recognizable. Fasting, body building, cosmetic surgery, liposuction, and the rage for self-control make historical ascetic practices seem less foreign and more explicable, but what do historians of asceticism offer to our understanding of body-control issues in our own society?

In a series of essays published in 1965, E. R. Dodds observed that the idea that matter is evil is very ancient, with roots in both Near Eastern and Greek thought. Moreover, incarnation, embodiment, was viewed as a punishment or humiliation. In a thought world where spirit and matter are split, "spiritual" individuals must perforce feel themselves alien. These ideas occur in the writings of pagans as well as early Christians. Marcus Aurelius, for example, saw human existence as "a warfare and sojourn in a strange land." Dodds uses the writings of the Stoic emperor to instantiate the deep malaise that permeated the culture of Late Antiquity. Marcus Aurelius describes a world in which life is fleeting, the times are out of joint, one has no control. We are, he wrote, "puppets jerking on a string." In a letter to his mentor, Fronto, written at the age of twenty-five, he wrote, "I do penance, I am cross with myself, I am sad and discontented, I feel starved." The sense of alienation from a world too large, mysterious, and ominous to understand led many sensitive souls to turn in on themselves, to strive for self-perfection through self-discipline without any expectation of success. Moreover, this retreat into the self had two important components: a lack of impetus to improve or explore the external world, and a division of self and body with the resentment of external conditions heaped on the body. Dodds argues that "contempt for the human condition and hatred of the body, was a disease endemic in the entire culture of the period." True to his psychological approach, he further asserts that this "disease" was "an endogenous neurosis, an index of intense and widespread guilt feelings."[2]

Dodds, writing almost thirty years ago, is not altogether sympathetic to ascetic practices, especially those of the early Christians. Scholars like Peter Brown, Margaret Miles, and Caroline Bynum offer more sympathetic insights on the phenomenon. Peter Brown, like Dodds, acknowledges a world, the world of Christian radicals, almost too big to be seen: "Its measureless demonic structures had engulfed the very stars. There was no outside viewing point from which to take the measure of its faceless immensity, and no hope of disengagement from its clutches other than through drastic rituals that promised total transfiguration."[3]

Professor Brown is writing here of the most extreme of ascetic practices, of the most radical of ascetic practitioners. He writes of men who fled their communities, "the World," for the harsh physical realities of the desert, each bringing with him "the fragile tokens of enduring humanity that he had to defend tenaciously if he was to survive at all and maintain his sanity." The aim was a transcendence of the greedy body, the body that longs for food, cool drink, warmth, the touch of another. Only after they had "faced out the terrible risks of remaining human in a non-human environment [were] the men of the desert . . . thought capable of recovering . . . a touch of the unimaginable glory of Adam's first state."[4]

These fierce men had no fear of death, for their acts of self-discipline and self-denial were only preparations for a radiant, purified body that lives in eternity. Only the perverted will, impelling passion and greed, stood between

2. E. R. Dodds, *Pagan and Christian in an Age of Anxiety* (Cambridge: Cambridge University Press, 1965), 20, 21, 8, 26–28, 35.

3. Peter Brown, *The Body and Society: Men, Women and Sexual Renunciation in Early Christianity* (New York: Columbia University Press, 1988), 216.

4. Ibid., 218, 220.

them and their transfigured bodies. These ascetics controlled and remade their bodies so that they could begin the long return of the human person, body and soul together, to an original, natural, uncorrupted state."[5]

Like their spiritual forefathers, the medieval female ascetics denied their bodies food. Caroline Bynum's important work explores the relation of food to female practices, noting its central role not only for female ascetics but for all women. Food, she observes, is "a woman-controlled resource"—it is the resource women control. As Brown is the eloquent spokesman for the desert ascetics, Bynum speaks with great sensitivity of the desires and motivations of medieval saints and fasting women. She disagrees with previous scholarship that finds their behavior dualistic and pathological, perceiving instead an attempt to find practices within the restrictions of their society that would give them power and their lives meaning.[6]

These contemporary scholars surveying the ascetic practices of early and medieval Christian ascetics thus see many of the same themes articulated in American popular culture: an attempt to find individual meaning in a large impersonal society, a flight from the pressures of "the world" (the job, freeway traffic, pollution, crime, cancer), a desire for self-control and goodness expressed through the body. The Christian ascetics fled the material world to regain a more perfect world, to transcend the very real constrictions and temptations of their communities. They used their mortal bodies to attain deathless bodies.

If we turn to our own society with empathic eyes, we may perceive an analogous struggle for transcendence. Contemporary scholarly commentary often tacitly acknowledges the link between the religious asceticism of hermits and mystics. In a review of a book on body building by Samuel Wilson Fussell, Justin Spring perceives that, for Fussell, body building offers a kind of psychic protection. His muscles are "physical palisades and escarpments [that] served as a rocky boundary [and] permitted no passage." The body builder cultivates "his aches and pains as a monk might cultivate roses." The body builder's body is like Baroque art: "a turgid form less expressive of a natural ideal than of the desire to transcend nature altogether—and so, through abstraction of the body, to give a representation of agony."[7] But the struggle, however we might

5. Ibid., 223.
6. Caroline Walker Bynum, *Holy Feast and Holy Fast: The Religious Significance of Food to Medieval Women* (Berkeley: University of California Press, 1987), 189, 208.
7. Justin Spring, "Head to Toe," *Art Forum* (February 1992), 20, 21.

sympathize with an individual martyr's desire for a perfect body, seems less magnificent and exalted than that of the religious ascetics. Indeed, there is a strain of depression that runs through the texts of fashion magazines and self-help literature. The exhortations to refashion and rejuvenate seem frequently to mask a deep despair. One wonders what would happen if people did not "make the right choice," "nutri-size their bodies," and take control of their lives. Rage? Collective suicide? Mass destruction? Failure to strive?

In *Facing West: The Metaphysics of Indian Hating and Empire Building*, Richard Drinnon connects the asceticism of the Puritan colonists, who "fled from their animal bodies," with the national saga of asceticism marching out into the modern world—building economies, founding national states—all the while corrupting the senses and fashioning an "iron cage" for humankind. Max Weber lamented in *The Protestant Ethic and the Spirit of Capitalism*: "For the last stage of this development . . . it might truly be said: 'Specialists without spirit, sensualists without heart; this nullity imagines that it has attained a level of civilization never before achieved.' "[8]

Indeed, we recognize a declining belief in progress. Peter and Jean Medawar acknowledge a darkening of mood in contemporary life:

> At no time since the early years of the seventeenth century have human thoughts been so darkened by an expectation of doom. In their apocalyptic moods people nowadays foresee a time when pressure of population will have become unsupportable, when greed and self-interest have so far despoiled the environment that the life of man will once again be solitary, poor, nasty, brutish and short.[9]

Is there not a connection among spiritless specialization, heartless sensuality, and the passion for self-control? It seems to me significant that *bulimia nervosa* was first described in the late 1970s just before a decade of cultural bulimia that was notoriously characterized by societal gluttony and a desire for luxe items. The media have paid a great deal of attention to the binges and purges of the 1980s finally announcing a leaner, more moderate decade to come, while fashion magazines give their blessings to a larger-breasted, more "nurturant" female body. Yet these cultural pundits do little to explicate con-

8. Richard Drinnon, *Facing West: The Metaphysics of Indian Hating and Empire Building* (New York: Schocken Books, 1990), xxi; Max Weber, *The Protestant Ethic and the Spirit of Capitalism*, trans. Talcott Parsons (New York: Scribner's, 1976).

9. Peter and Jean Medawar, *The Life Sciences* (New York: Harper & Row, 1977), 172.

temporary "body talk," in which the language of political expression becomes interchangeable with the description of self-concern. It passes unnoticed, for example, that Cher, on a television commercial, has adopted the language of the pro-choice movement to sell artificial sweetener. How are we to find our way out of the maze?

There is, I believe, a need to change the terms of our culture's conversation about the body. We have become accustomed to the ideal of a medicalized, eroticized body to ward off our loneliness and fear of death. Media culture substitutes eroticism for transcendence, making a shabby parody of the creative, life-giving power of the erotic, promising trivial substitutes for our dreams of immortality. We need to think about the self in a way that is not so intensely concentrated on self assessment; we need to find a way of thinking about our needs and desires that avoids the kind of medicalized neo-puritanism that demands conformity to a healthy straight-and-narrow "for your own good." In short, we need to formulate the concept of the body without focusing so single-mindedly on control. We need to review the tensions in our society between wholesome self-regard and selfishness, between the human need for love and approval and autonomy, between our enjoyment of life and our fear of death, between delight in the body and hatred of the flesh (particularly the flesh of other races and cultures). We need to understand more fully the relationships between the individual and the community, the triangular relationships of the "good body," good health, and good citizenship; we need to think deeply and critically about what kind of body our scientific and social thinkers construct and idealize.

Contributors

Judith Andre, Ph. D., associate professor of philosophy, Center for Ethics and Humanities in the Life Sciences, Michigan State University, East Lansing, Michigan

Reina Attias, Ph.D., specialist in childhood trauma, Santa Fe, New Mexico

Estelle Cohen, Ph.D., scholar-in-residence, Francis C. Wood Institute, College of Physicians of Philadelphia, Philadelphia, Pennsylvania

Letha B. Cole, M.D., clinical assistant professor, Department of Psychiatry, Baylor College of Medicine, Houston, Texas

David D. Gilmore, Ph.D., professor of anthropology, Department of Anthropology, State University of New York at Stony Brook, Stony Brook, New York

Jean M. Goodwin, M.D., professor of psychiatry and behavioral sciences, Department of Psychiatry and Behavioral Sciences, University of Texas Medical Branch, Galveston, Texas

Janet de Groot, M.D., assistant professor of psychiatry, University of Toronto director, Out-Patient Psychiatry Department, The Toronto Hospital Western Division, Toronto, Ontario, Canada

Arthur P. Leccese, Ph.D., assistant professor of psychology, Department of Psychology, Kenyon College, Gambier, Ohio

Margaret R. Miles, Ph.D., Bussey Professor of Historical Theology, Harvard Divinity School, Cambridge, Massachusetts

Allison M. Moore, Ph.D., curate of Grace Episcopal Church, White Plains, New York; formerly director of the Sanctuary for Families, New York, New York

William F. Monroe, Ph.D., associate dean, Graduate Studies and Research, College of Humanities, Fine Arts and Communication, University of Houston, Houston, Texas

Mary Brown Parlee, Ph.D., visiting professor, women's studies, Massachusetts Institute of Technology, Cambridge, Massachusetts

Sara van den Berg, Ph.D., associate professor of English, University of Washington, Seattle, Washington

Mary G. Winkler, Ph.D., assistant professor, Institute for the Medical Humanities, University of Texas Medical Branch, Galveston, Texas

Index